The Other Hybrid Archipelago

After the Empire: The Francophone World and Postcolonial France

Series Editor
Valérie Orlando, University of Maryland

Advisory Board
Robert Bernasconi, Memphis University; Alec Hargreaves, Florida State University; Chima Korieh, Rowan University; Obioma Nnaemeka, Indiana University; Kamal Salhi, University of Leeds; Tracy D. Sharpley-Whiting, Vanderbilt University; Nwachukwu Frank Ukadike, Tulane University

See www.lexingtonbooks.com/series for the series description and a complete list of published titles.

Recent and Forthcoming Titles

Memory, Empire, and Postcolonialism: Legacies of French Colonialism, edited by Alec G. Hargreaves

Ouregano: A Novel, by Paule Constant, translated and annotated by Margot Miller, and introduced by Claudine Fisher

The Transparent Girl and Other Stories, by Corinna Bille, selected and translated by Monika Giacoppe and Christiane Makward

Time Signatures: Contextualizing Contemporary Francophone Autobiographical Writing from Maghreb, by Alison Rice

Breadfruit or Chestnut?: Gender Construction in the French Caribbean Novel, by Bonnie Thomas

History's Place: Nostalgia and the City in French Algerian Literature, by Seth Graebner

Collective Memory: France and the Algerian War (1954–1962), by Jo McCormack

The Other Hybrid Archipelago: Introduction to the Literatures and Cultures of the Francophone Indian Ocean, by Peter Hawkins

The Other Hybrid Archipelago

Introduction to the Literatures and Cultures of the Francophone Indian Ocean

Peter Hawkins

LEXINGTON BOOKS

A division of
ROWMAN & LITTLEFIELD PUBLISHERS, INC.
Lanham • Boulder • New York • Toronto • Plymouth, UK

LEXINGTON BOOKS

A division of Rowman & Littlefield Publishers, Inc.
A wholly owned subsidiary of The Rowman & Littlefield Publishing Group, Inc.
4501 Forbes Boulevard, Suite 200
Lanham, MD 20706

Estover Road
Plymouth PL6 7PY
United Kingdom

Copyright © 2007 by Lexington Books

All rights reserved. No part of this publication may be reproduced,
stored in a retrieval system, or transmitted in any form or by any
means, electronic, mechanical, photocopying, recording, or otherwise,
without the prior permission of the publisher.

British Library Cataloguing in Publication Information Available

Library of Congress Cataloging-in-Publication Data

Hawkins, Peter, 1942–
 The other hybrid archipelago : introduction to the literatures and cultures of the francophone Indian Ocean / Peter Hawkins.
   p. cm. — (After the empire)
 Includes bibliographical references and index.
 ISBN-13: 978-0-7391-1676-0 (cloth : alk. paper)
 ISBN-10: 0-7391-1676-2 (cloth : alk. paper)
 1. French literature—Indian Ocean Region—History and criticism. 2. Indian Ocean Region—Intellectual life. I. Title.
PQ3897.H39 2007
840.9'9182409045—dc22   2007028342

Printed in the United States of America

♾™ The paper used in this publication meets the minimum requirements of American National Standard for Information Sciences—Permanence of Paper for Printed Library Materials, ANSI/NISO Z39.48–1992.

Contents

Foreword		vii
Introduction		ix
Chapter 1	The Francophone Indian Ocean	1
Chapter 2	Postcolonial Perspectives	27
Chapter 3	Critical Strategies	47
Chapter 4	Madagascar	65
Chapter 5	Mauritius	93
Chapter 6	La Réunion	119
Chapter 7	The Comoros, the Seychelles	145
Chapter 8	Trouble in Paradise	163
Bibliography		179
Discography		193
Index		195
About the author		207

Foreword

In the preparation of this book I have benefited from help and support from many quarters. My colleagues in the Department of French and the University of Bristol have generously shouldered a large part of the burden of my teaching and administration work during my period of research leave in 2005-2006. The Arts and Humanities Research Council of the UK provided me with the resources for an extended period of leave without which the wide coverage and the detailed drafting of this book would not have been conceivable. My colleagues in the Université de la Réunion and the CNRS research unit LCF (Linguistique et Littératures créolophones et francophones) have been helpful and supportive, as have my friends Claude Clergue and Anna Asperti, who have separately provided me with a warm and welcoming home from home in Reunion in which to work. I should not have been able to develop my knowledge of the region without several visits to the Université de la Réunion funded by the European Socrates exchange scheme, in which I was involved as an organiser and participant in student and staff exchanges. I am grateful for the advice of my colleagues Nikki Cooper and Jae Maingard on the final draft of the typescript, and for the efficiency of the editorial staff at Lexington Books. Finally, I have enjoyed the constant love and moral support of my wife Margot during the long absences and the periods of absent-minded hibernation that have accompanied this enterprise.

There are relatively few quotations in this work, but I must gratefully acknowledge the permission given by the copyright holders to reproduce short extracts from the following books:

Malcolm de Chazal, *Petrusmok*. Curepipe, Mauritius: Editions de la Table Ovale, 1951.
Edouard Maunick, *Les Manèges de la mer*. Paris: Présence africaine, 1964; and *Fusillez-moi*. Paris: Présence africaine, 1970.
Esther Nirina, *Rien que lune*. Saint-Denis de la Réunion: Grand Océan, 1998.

Peter Hawkins
Bristol, May 2007

Introduction

The main purpose of this volume is to fill a gap in the coverage of the literatures and cultures of the Francophone world outside metropolitan France. Although scholars have published articles on individual texts, there has so far been no general study published in English of the literatures of the region of the Francophone Indian Ocean. Other areas, such as the Maghreb, Sub-Saharan Africa, and even Indo-China are becoming familiar territories for researchers, but apart from articles, chapters and analyses on specific authors, there has been no systematic coverage of this one. The region has found a place even so in broad surveys such as Belinda Jack's *Francophone Literatures*;[1] but here it seems rather like an afterthought, with Mauritius and Reunion tacked on to the coverage of the Francophone Caribbean in a section called "Creole Islands"; Madagascar is similarly appended to the section on "Sub-Saharan Africa." The Seychelles are only referred to twice and the Comoros are not even dignified with a mention. One of the secondary aims of this study is to establish the region as an area with its own cultural specificity, its own shared characteristics and particular preoccupations, which are reflected in a rich and abundant literary output.

At the time of writing the body of theorizing which has emanated from the predominantly Anglophone school of Postcolonial Studies is only now beginning to be applied to the literatures and cultures of the present and former colonies of France. It seemed appropriate to attempt to make use of these general reflections on the conditions of literary production in the former colonies of the British Empire, which have been predominantly their focus of attention, as a tool with which to analyse the writing of a hitherto little-studied area. It is in a way encouraging that the most influential Francophone writers in the area of Postcolonial Theory originate predominantly from the French Caribbean: Aimé Césaire,[2] Frantz Fanon[3] and Edouard Glissant.[4] There are many points of comparison to be explored between the cultures of the Francophone islands of the Caribbean and those of the Indian Ocean. The latter are not merely lesser examples of the same themes, however, as seems to be suggested by Belinda Jack's categorisation. This literature is older, in fact, and arguably more substantial, but in reviewing it I shall necessarily be led to make comparisons with the Caribbean. This body of writing has its own identity, I shall argue, and it is also too extensive to be properly covered in one volume, with major texts going back as far as the eighteenth century. This is another reason for the choice of a postcolonial approach: this will limit the range in both a practical and a theoretical way, focusing attention on the period since the Second World War, when, over a period of some thirty years, all the islands ceased to be colonies, even if it was, in the case of Reunion in 1946, to become a *Département d'Outre-Mer* within the French Republic, like Guadeloupe and Martinique in the Caribbean. This will not preclude us from taking into consideration some texts from earlier periods, highlighted precisely because they appear as postcolonial in the discursive rather than the temporal sense.[5]

It has to be admitted that, even in mainland France, the literary production of the Indian Ocean area has not attracted much critical attention. Most of the academic studies devoted to it emanate from universities in the region itself, and have often been published locally, in Madagascar, Mauritius or Reunion. This has not always helped to give the region's literary output a higher profile in metropolitan France, or in the wider world. Even when these studies were in fact published in Paris, all too often it was with an eye to the Indian Ocean market rather than the metropolitan French one, with surveys and anthologies designed for the burgeoning educational sector in the islands themselves, rather than for wider use. The result is that this material remains little known outside the region, and suffers to some extent from the cultural introversion which is all too often typical of island cultures and communities. This present volume is also intended to address this issue by aiming for the broader and more international market of Postcolonial and Francophone Studies in the English-speaking world. A major French precursor to this study is Jean-Louis Joubert's *Littératures de l'Océan Indien*,[6] which is admirable in its detailed coverage of the whole region's literatures from their origins to the end of the 1980s. A lot has happened since then, however, and most notably the emergence of postcolonial theory in the Anglophone world. This study is amongst other things a modest attempt to build a bridge between these two major enterprises, whilst at the same time bringing the survey up to date.

Quite apart from their relatively neglected literatures and cultures, knowledge of the political and social characteristics of the Indian Ocean islands is not well developed, particularly in the Anglophone world. This is probably because they are regarded, not without some justification, as a French sphere of influence, even if two of the island states, Mauritius and the Seychelles, are also members of the Commonwealth. They tend to be grouped, as we have seen, along with the many and varied centres of Francophone culture outside of mainland France, so that their specificity is subsumed, not to say obscured, by this broader picture of *La Francophonie*. It has been necessary to provide a brief contextual picture of each island and of the whole region, so as better to situate the literary and cultural production in relation to the society that has generated it. As argued in chapter 3, this seems an indispensable element in any attempt to characterise a literature as postcolonial, however summary the formulation of the relationship between the two. This work is not intended as a socio-political study as such, but some knowledge of this aspect of the islands' recent history seems essential so as better to appreciate the significance of their literatures and cultures. The sources of this information have been difficult to identify, since they cannot rely simply on traditional historical writing which is usually too old to be useful. I have had to resort to less reliable sources at times, such as websites and guidebooks, which are in most cases regularly updated. Whenever possible, I have checked the information gleaned in this way across several identifiable sources, so as to confirm its accuracy.

The study opens, therefore, in chapter 1 with a broad contemporary survey of the "Francophone Indian Ocean" and an attempt to define its particular characteristics. Since, in order to identify a culture as postcolonial and despite the earlier assertion of the a-temporal character of the term, it is also necessary to give some notion of what kind of colonial past the literatures are responding to, chapter 2 outlines the main features of this under the heading of "Postcolonial perspectives." Chapter 3, as already suggested, will outline some of the "Critical Strategies" which might be deployed in the survey of the literatures to be recognised as postcolonial, briefly identifying some of the key concepts which may serve as markers in this process, but also reviewing some of the alternative ways of reading the literatures that have already been explored by earlier critics, mostly emanating from universities in the region itself. For all their many shared features, the islands are sufficiently differentiated for it to be necessary to treat each of them as a separate literary and cultural field, and to situate that field in some detail in relation to its own particular social and political context. Chapters 4 to 7 each open with a sketch of these socio-political characteristics, inasmuch as they are relevant to an understanding of the cultural output in question, which will then be analysed in the latter part of the chapter. The islands are dealt with in descending order of size and importance, which by a happy coincidence appears also to be very close to an alphabetical sequence—the exception being the Comoros, grouped together with the Seychelles in chapter 7. The final chapter, playfully labelled "Trouble in Paradise," will attempt to draw some general conclusions and to re-situate the islands' cultures in a broader international and global context.

Some may be tempted to find the inclusion of a review of the World Music production of the islands an unnecessary distraction from the main purpose of this study. I would defend its relevance on two grounds. The first is that in several cases there has been a clear interaction between the literary field proper and that of local popular musical forms: Reunion is the most salient example, with the rediscovery and promotion of the traditional musical form of the *maloya* as a vehicle for the expression of Creole language and culture. The second is that, even where this kind of connection is not so obvious, as in Madagascar, the island's musical output has probably reached a much larger audience worldwide than its literature. Several of its best-known artists are now internationally-known stars, such as Justin Vali,[7] Rossy[8] and the group Tarika,[9] and are able to represent the culture of Madagascar much more effectively than the literature, which has remained somewhat confidential in its diffusion. Even so, the musical resources of the region are only patchily known in World Music circles, as evidenced by their uneven coverage in volume 1 of the *Rough Guide to World Music*.[10]

Another area that could not be covered in full at least deserves a mention: it is the region's output of cartoons and graphic novels. It was difficult to obtain comprehensive information on this, apart from some fragmentary and particular examples. The output of the Reunionese novelist Daniel Vaxelaire as a scenario-writer for *bande dessinée* is one of these.[11] Another is the thriving cartoon culture of the Reunionese publishing house named, with delicious irony, Le Centre du Monde, and who publish, amongst others, the cartoonist Tehem[12] and the magazine *Le Margouillat*. A further example is the inclusion of an article on cartoons in Madagascar in the special issue of the Francophone journal *Notre Librairie*, entitled "Les Gasy font des bulles."[13] Not enough to provide a comprehensive picture, however, so discretion has regrettably remained the better part of valour in this area. It is perhaps worth mentioning that there is also a thriving culture of the visual arts, painting and sculpture in most of the islands, but particularly in the better-endowed ones such as Reunion. This has to remain beyond the scope of this study, as a field with very different parameters from the broadly literary and para-literary culture I shall be attempting to analyse here.

An area which has been included, on the other hand, and which has obvious links with literature, is that of the popular theater of the islands, a thriving feature of their cultural life. This form of cultural creativity has been responsible for some major international successes, such as the Reunionese groups Théâtre Vollard[14] and Théâtre Talipot,[15] and some remarkably prolific writers, such as the Mauritian Creole dramatist Dev Virahsawmy.[16]

This is after all an introductory study and is also intended as a guide to further reading. Each chapter will carry an appendix of bibliographical "Notes." In general these endnotes will be kept to a minimum, and will mostly be used to provide references and cross-references for sources of information. Within each chapter bibliographical references will be given in full the first time they are used, so that the notes at the end of each chapter can also serve as a select bibliography for the area covered, retro-actively annotated by the text of the chapter itself. This resource will be backed up by a General Bibliography and Discography which can be referenced alphabetically, in the time-honoured way, by author's or artist's name and date of publication, or by the title of the website. This is intended to facilitate further research and exploration, since this study, within its limited dimensions, can only aspire to be a broad survey and an interpretative essay for what is, even within the restricted parameters already indicated, a vast area of knowledge. It has not been possible to cover all the works and all the critical writing, and so it has been necessary to make a choice of what appear to be the principal figures and the major landmarks of critical comment.

Even so, this is more than a purely academic exercise. The personal motivation for this study arises mainly from the stimulation of confronting a rich body of literary and artistic creation arising out of a most unpromising situation: several of the major ethnic groups of the planet thrown together on a group of isolated island territories with a history of slavery and violent colonial exploitation. It may be as a result of the beauty of these island settings, but there is a flavour of redemption in this literary culture. Out of this cruel and violent history has emerged a tolerant and multi-ethnic culture where religious acceptance is the rule, where distinctive cultures are on the whole respected while at the same time racial mixing is commonplace and most often welcomed. This miracle is reflected in the literature of the region, and it represents a challenge to the residual racism of the cultures of the former colonial powers, Britain and France. Yet the same divide exists between the rich and the poor of the region, as between the extravagant comfort of the technological West and the most deprived of Third World nations, a gap that seems to be getting ever wider. Studying this literature is potentially a rewarding and life-affirming experience even so; and it carries within it some possible lessons for the future of our beleaguered planet.

Notes

1. Belinda Jack, *Francophone literatures: an introductory survey* (Oxford: Oxford University Press, 1996). A very recent book also uses Indian Ocean texts as a basis for a discussion of hybridity, but does not attempt a comprehensive survey of the region: see Anjali Prabhu, *Hybridity: Limits, Transformations, Prospects* (Albany, NY: State University of New York Press, 2007).

2. See, for instance, extensive references to Césaire in Charles Forsdick and David Murphy, eds., *Francophone postcolonial studies: a critical introduction* (London: Arnold, 2003); and in Neil Lazarus, ed., The Cambridge companion to postcolonial literary studies (Cambridge: Cambridge University Press, 2004).

3. See, for instance, the section on Fanon in Homi K. Bhabha, *The location of culture* (London and New York: Routledge, 1994), 40-65.

4. See Peter Hallward, *Absolutely postcolonial* (Manchester and New York: Manchester University Press 2001), 66-125.

5. See chapter 3, "A-temporal postcoloniality," for a brief review of this issue, first raised in the seminal volume Bill Ashcroft, Gareth Griffiths and Helen Tiffin, *The Empire writes back* (London and New York: Routledge, 1989), 1-2.

6. Jean-Louis Joubert, *Littératures de l'Océan indien* (Vanves, France: EDICEF, 1991). A similarly useful, but shorter and less comprehensive survey is provided by Martine Mathieu in a joint volume with Michel Hausser: Martine Mathieu, "Océan indien" Pp.152-255 in Michel Hausser and Martine Mathieu. *Littératures francophones. III. Afrique noire, Océan indien.* Paris: Belin, 1998.

7. Justin Vali, *The truth* (Box, UK: Real World, 1995), CD No. CDRW 51.

8. Rossy, *One eye on the future, one eye on the past* (USA: Shanachie records, 1993), CD No. 64046.

9. Tarika, *Soul Makassar* (London: Sakay, 2001), CD No. SAKD7037.

10. Simon Broughton, Mark Ellingham and Richard Trillo, eds., *World Music, Volume I: Africa, Europe and the Middle East* (London: The Rough Guides, 1999).

11. For instance, Michel Faure and Daniel Vaxelaire, *La Buse* (Reunion: Editions AGM, 1978-9).

12. Téhem, *Tiburce: Ilet Titby* (Reunion: Centre du Monde / Association Band' décidée, 1996), cartoons.

13. Nestor Rabéarizafy, "Les Gasy font des bulles," in Siméon Rajaona, ed., "Madagascar. 2. La littérature d'expression française" in *Notre Librairie*, 110 (1992), 83-92.

14. See chapter 6, "Postcolonial theater, neo-colonial subsidies" and Emmanuel Genvrin, *Votez Ubu colonial* (Saint-Denis: Grand Océan, 1994), etc.

15. See chapter 6, "Postcolonial theater, neo-colonial subsidies" and Philippe Pelen, *Mâ* (Saint-Denis: Grand Océan, 1996).

16. See Dev Virahsawmy, *Toufann* (Port Louis, Mauritius: La Sentinelle, 1991), etc.

Chapter 1

The Francophone Indian Ocean

The islands of the Francophone Indian Ocean have often been regarded as a peripheral zone of the African continent. There are many reasons why this viewpoint is unsatisfactory: in the first place, the smaller islands such as Mauritius, Reunion and the Seychelles are geographically a long way from the African coastline. The history of their population is very different from that of the supposed ancestral home of the human race: they have only been inhabited since the seventeenth century. There is perhaps more justification for regarding Madagascar as part of Africa; but here again the history of its population, not to mention its very distinctive ecology and wildlife, suggests that it belongs in a different category: a large proportion of its inhabitants originated from south-east Asia rather than Africa. This is perhaps one of the reasons why Léopold Sedar Senghor, when publishing his celebrated *Anthologie de la nouvelle poésie nègre et malgache* in 1948,[1] to mark the centenary of the abolition of slavery in France, chose to distinguish between the Africans and their diaspora and their Malagasy neighbors, even though a proportion of the latter were probably of African descent. What then would be the logic of this regional grouping of islands? All of them are home to a population of mixed ethnic and geographical origins. All of them have at some time been colonised by France, and in all of them French is used as an official language, even if not exclusively so. There the geographical and historical similarities end, however: the islands stand in contrast with each other in most other respects, even if there are also many particular points of comparison. In many ways their cultures resemble those of the Caribbean islands, with which they are often confused, rather than those of Francophone Africa; and this is a comparison which will be developed further in this and subsequent chapters. The islands provide ample material for a complex analytical discussion, which will here be undertaken in relation to their literary and analogous cultures, principally but not exclusively expressed in the French language. The islands provide us with a body of literary and cultural production through which we can examine the cultural effects of colonization, not only by the French, but also by the British, who were the colonial rulers of Mauritius and the Seychelles for over one hundred and fifty years, and who also intervened decisively in the development of Madagascar during the nineteenth century, prior to its annexation by France in 1896.

This analysis will focus on the broad period since independence rather than the colonial experience itself. The purpose of this is to examine what have been the fruits of that experience, in terms of the present-day cultures of the region. The length of the period since the end of colonial rule varies in each case. Even if it has not achieved independent status, since 1946 Reunion is no longer strictly speaking a colony, but a *Département d'Outre-Mer* and as such an integral part of the French Republic. Madagascar was granted independence in 1960 as part of the wave of decolonization initiated by General de Gaulle, in the wake of a bloodily repressed anti-colonial uprising in 1947. Mauritius achieved a negotiated independence in 1968, remaining nominally under the supervision of the British crown until 1992, when it became a republic. The Comoros were granted independence in 1975, except for the island of Mayotte, which chose to remain a French territory. The Seychelles became an independent republic in 1976. These dates are clearly landmarks, but we shall not be limited too strictly by them, since the vagaries of cultural output rarely correspond exactly to such precise periodizations.

In order to understand better their contemporary situation it is necessary to bear in mind the particularities of each of the islands in terms of their political status, their geography and their recent history, inasmuch as these bear directly on our reading of their contemporary cultural output. What follows is a brief sketch of the terrain, the social, economic and political development of each island, so as better to situate some of the themes of their present-day cultures.

Madagascar

Often called the "Grande Ile," the landmass of Madagascar is impressively large: at 597,041 square kilometers,[2] it is greater than metropolitan France, and exhibits considerable variations of terrain and climate. The coastal regions are tropical, whereas the mountainous central highlands are temperate; the north is heavily forested whereas the south is semi-desert. It is home to nearly 16.5 million inhabitants, which makes it by far the largest geographical unit in our study. Its population, very mixed, includes peoples of African descent, mostly inhabiting the coastal regions, and peoples of southeast Asian origin, who settled in the central highlands in about the sixth century AD, or possibly earlier.[3] There are small minority populations of Arab, Indo-Pakistani and Chinese origin. In the seventeenth century the French *Compagnie des Indes Orientales* established a short-lived trading post in the south east of the island, still often called Fort Dauphin despite its modern Malagasy name of Toalagnara. The French later claimed sovereignty over the offshore islands of Nosy Boraha (Ile Sainte-Marie) in 1750 and Nosy Be in 1841. Until the late eighteenth century the country was divided into separate tribal fiefdoms, but at this time these were conquered and unified under a central monarchy by the Merina peoples of the central highlands. In the early nineteenth century this monarchy, under King Radama I, was courted by the British, who signed treaties, supplied arms and were accompanied by the Protestant missionaries of the London Missionary Society. The latter were responsible for the transcription into the Roman alphabet of the Malagasy language, related to the Malayo-Polynesian languages of South-East Asia and the Pacific, which has today become the effective *lingua franca* of the island. Catholic missionaries and French entrepreneurs such as Jean Laborde were also active in the island in the mid-nineteenth century and after several dramatic changes of regime and alliance on the part of the monarchy, the French army under Gallieni annexed the island as a French colony in 1896. After several decades of French colonial rule under the Third Republic, during the Second

World War the French colonial regime at first remained loyal to Vichy and the island was attacked and invaded by Allied forces in 1942; it was subsequently handed over to the Free French. After the Liberation of France and the establishment of the French Fourth Republic, a revolt by the Malagasy population in 1947 was brutally suppressed and Malagasy *députés,* such as the poet Jacques Rabémananjara, were imprisoned.[4] Eventually, after the return to power of General de Gaulle in 1958, Madagascar was granted independence in 1960. The first Malagasy Republic was overthrown in 1972 by a military *coup d'état* that eventually brought to power Admiral Didier Ratsiraka, with left-wing socialist and nationalist policies such as the nationalization of the banks and the "malgachization" of the education system.[5] Despite the support of Communist China and North Korea, the Malagasy economy stagnated, until in 1991 Ratsiraka was overthrown by a popular uprising and a new democratic republic established. French was reinstated as the official language of the education system. Ratsiraka managed even so to get reelected to power in 1997, but after accusations of vote-rigging was ousted in 2002 by Marc Ravalomanana; but not before an armed challenge to the result of the election which brought the country to the brink of civil war in 2001-2002.[6] This turbulent history of political instability since independence has left the country seriously impoverished and underdeveloped, and its population among the poorest on the planet,[7] which has meant that its cultural influence in the region has not been proportional to its size and population.

Mauritius

Mauritius is a small, fertile island of volcanic origin, of some 2040 square kilometers, which remained uninhabited until the seventeenth century. The Dutch were the first to occupy it in 1638, naming it after Crown Prince Maurice of Nassau. They did not sustain their presence there, however, and eventually in 1715 the island was claimed by the French, who occupied it in 1722 and developed it during the eighteenth century as a base for slave trading and as a source of tropical agricultural products such as spices, coffee, tea and later sugar cane. The island was renamed Ile de France and became a plantation economy, importing slave labor from Africa and Madagascar.[8] The British invaded the island in 1810, during the Napoleonic wars, and, despite the small but dominant French landowning class, maintained their control of the island until independence in 1968. Slavery was abolished on the island in 1835 and a massive importation of indentured labor from India was organized, so that today the population of the island is predominantly of Indian descent, and 52 per cent practice Hindu beliefs. The value of the island's sugar cane has declined, so the sugar estates have diversified their activity to include textile manufacturing and microelectronics. Mauritius has also established itself as an offshore banking center. One of its principal sources of income is its highly developed tourist industry, providing high-quality and attractive hotel accommodation and exploiting the resources of its beautiful coastline and lagoons. Mauritius has achieved an impressive standard of living for most of its 1,160,000 inhabitants, thanks to astute management of its very limited economic resources.[9] Its population is educated to a high standard and most Mauritians speak some French and English as well as the unofficial *lingua franca* of Creole. Its parliamentary political institutions seem stable and effectively democratic, although from time to time community rivalry boils over into public disorder, as in the riots of 1999, when the minority Creole population protested about the death in custody of one of their cultural hero figures, the reggae singer Kaya. In general the ethnic and cultural communities maintain their particular and separate identities in the island, such as the 3 per cent of Chinese origin, or the 16 per cent of Muslims.

Reunion

Reunion island, like Mauritius, is a territory of volcanic origin, of some 2,500 square kilometers. It is extremely mountainous, at its highest point over 3,000 meters high, with an active volcano, the Piton de la Fournaise. It is less densely populated than Mauritius, with some 700,000 inhabitants, but much of the island's rugged terrain is unsuited to agricultural use and the population is concentrated around the coast. Like Mauritius, its economy has for a long time relied on sugar-cane, but much less successfully than its sister island: Reunion remains heavily dependent on metropolitan France to maintain its generally high standard of living. It is an integral part of the French Republic and consequently of the European Union.[10] The official language is French, although most native Reunionese also speak Creole, which has only since the beginning of the present century been officially recognized as a regional language. To all intents and purposes the island has always been French, apart from a brief inter-regnum when the British occupied it from 1810-1815, during the Napoleonic wars. It was originally an uninhabited island until the French *Compagnie des Indes orientales* deposited some mutineers there in 1646, as a punishment, from their trading post at Fort Dauphin in Madagascar.[11] The mutineers prospered, which led to the colonization of the island in 1665 and its subsequent development as a plantation economy growing first coffee and subsequently sugar cane, and using imported slave labor.[12] Slavery was finally abolished in France in 1848, and as in Mauritius an indentured labor force was brought to Reunion from India, China and elsewhere. The Hindu population today is not numerically dominant, however, but no statistics of the ethnic composition of the island's population are available, as stipulated by French republican law. To all intents and purposes the island is governed and administered as a part of France, but the level of unemployment remains as high as one third of the workforce, and this can lead to some social tensions.[13] In recent years, large numbers of metropolitan French have settled on the island, and there is a considerable Reunionese diaspora in mainland France. Most Reunionese are Catholics, but there are substantial minorities of Hindus, Muslims, Buddhists, mostly of Chinese origin, and Protestants, often of Malagasy background.

The Comoros

The Comoros, an archipelago situated in the Mozambique channel between Madagascar and mainland Africa, for many centuries underwent the influence of the Arab and Persian traders who plied along the east coast of Africa, bringing with them their Islamic culture. The influence of the rival Islamic sultanates they established in the islands was eventually supplanted by the French in the mid-nineteenth century, and the Comoros became a colony of France. French is still the official language of the archipelago, although in practice the inhabitants speak a variety of local languages including Malagasy, Arabic and Swahili. In 1975 independence was negotiated, and three islands, Grande Comore (or Ngazidja), Anjouan and

Moheli, formed the Federal Islamic Republic of the Comoros. The fourth island, Mayotte, chose to remain French, and is currently negotiating to obtain the same status as Reunion as a *Département d'Outre-Mer*. It is already a *collectivité départementale*, effectively a part of the European Union, and its 128,000 inhabitants enjoy a comparable standard of living.[14] Since independence the Republic of the Comoros has undergone a period of chronically unstable political regimes, interspersed with *coups d'état* undertaken by mercenaries in the pay of right-wing forces in France or the former apartheid regime in South Africa.[15] A constitutional crisis was provoked in 1997 when Anjouan declared its intention to secede from the federation and appealed to the French government for support. A new, more decentralized federal structure, the *Union des Comores*, was negotiated in 2001, but this seems fragile.[16] In the meantime the independent Comoros islands are heavily over-populated, with some 590,000 inhabitants sharing 2, 230 square kilometers of mountainous, volcanic terrain, and remain among the poorest countries in the world, relying heavily on the economic assistance of their expatriate population.[17] Not surprisingly, there is a steady stream of illegal immigration from the other Comorian islands to Mayotte.

The Seychelles

The Seychelles are a confetti of 32 granite islands and 83 coral atolls, some 450 square kilometers of terrain, originally uninhabited, set in 800,000 square kilometers of territorial waters in the middle of the Indian Ocean.[18] The principal islands of Mahé and Praslin were originally colonized by French settlers in the latter half of the eighteenth century, and as on Mauritius, they established a plantation economy by bringing in slaves from Africa and Madagascar, farming spices, timber and coconut products. The islands were named after a finance minister at the court of Louis XV, the Vicomte de Séchelles.[19] The islands were originally governed from Mauritius, then called Ile de France, and after some uncertainty fell into British hands after the conquest of Mauritius in 1810.[20] Eventually, in 1903, the Seychelles were given the status of a separate colony[21] and in 1976 were granted independence as the Republic of the Seychelles.[22] A year later, in 1977, a *coup d'état* by the then Prime Minister France-Albert René made the Seychelles a one-party state.[23]

The socialist-style government practiced a policy of restricted luxury tourist development of the islands, protection of its fragile ecology and commercial exploitation of the islands' massive fishing reserves. Multi-party democracy was subsequently re-established in 1991.[24] The relatively small population of some 83,680 inhabitants enjoys a good standard of living, but the economy remains heavily dependent on the fluctuations of the international tourist market and the country is currently experiencing a chronic shortage of foreign currency.[25] The population of the Seychelles is extremely mixed, coming from European, African and Asian origins; most are Catholic with a small minority presence of Protestants and Muslims.[26] The Seychelles are the only state in the world where Creole is an official language, alongside English and French, and most Seychellois have some knowledge of all three, although Creole dominates in day-to-day exchanges.[27]

A common heritage of French colonialism, and British rivalry

What is clear from these preliminary sketches is that all the cultures we shall be examining have been profoundly marked by the French colonial enterprise. In the case of three, Mauritius, Reunion and the Seychelles, the beginnings of human habitation of the islands are directly attributable to the colonial designs of the French *Compagnie des Indes orientales* and subsequently, the French monarchy, after the company collapsed in 1769. The first long-term settlements on these islands were established by French colonists, and even when these islands subsequently came under the control of the British, as in the case of Mauritius and the Seychelles, the strong French influence remained and is obvious even today. In Mauritius, the economic control of the island is still to a large extent in the hands of the small Franco-Mauritian community, who remain the principal landowners. French is the dominant language of the Mauritian press and the majority of the literary output of Mauritius is published in French. In the Seychelles, French is still widely taught in the school system, and the French international TV channel TV5 is one of two terrestrial channels available on the islands. In the case of Reunion, the long, almost unbroken association with France over three centuries is what justifies the absorption of the island into the French republican state, and its institutions reflect this. The French colonial system of the *ancien régime* was also responsible for bringing a large population of African and Malagasy slaves to the islands as part of the development of a plantation economy. The attempts of the French Revolutionary Convention to abolish slavery in 1792 were effectively ignored and by-passed in the islands by the French landowners who had a vested interest in its maintenance.[28]

British colonial rivalry in the region altered the course of history in Mauritius and the Seychelles by imposing in the early nineteenth century a British stewardship on an already well-established French slave-owning plantation culture. The relationship between the British authorities and the local French "plantocracy" was never an easy one, but relied to a large extent on a "laissez-faire" approach by the British. Slavery was progressively abolished even so in 1835, but this led in its turn to the massive recruitment of an indentured labor force in India, by then under the control of the British. This strategy has led to the effective dominance of an Indian and Hindu majority in present-day Mauritian politics. British influence is mostly visible in the political and social institutions of the two states: both were fairly autonomous crown colonies as early as the beginning of the twentieth century, and later elected their own local parliaments. The parliamentary tradition has subsisted in Mauritius even after the relatively late conversion to republican status in 1992. The education system in Mauritius bears the recognizable marks of British influence: a strong "eleven-plus" examination at the end of the primary cycle, highly competitive and hierarchized secondary schools and drastically selective university entrance, as well as the integration of confessional schools into the state education system.

British influence in Madagascar was effectively limited to attempts to establish a protectorate-style alliance with the nascent Malagasy monarchy during the early years of the nineteenth century. Apart from the strategic sale of armaments, this centered on the influence of the protestant missionaries of the London Missionary Society, who were largely responsible for the initiating the strong tradition of Protestant churches in the island which survives to this day. Unexpectedly, this quite strongly Francophone island still boasts a well-established network of Anglican churches. British Protestant missionaries were also responsible for the transcription of the Malagasy language into Roman characters—it had previously been written in Arabic script—which no doubt helped it to become the working language of the modern independent Malagasy state, alongside French. British influence in the Comoros has been negligible, mostly restricted to the activities of individual adventurers, except perhaps in encouraging the French to compete in the "scramble for Africa" of the late nineteenth century by annexing the islands one by one, so as better to assert their influence in Madagascar by military conquest.

Widely differing political status

The political regimes currently operating in the islands show a marked differentiation, probably attributable to the vagaries of their colonial and postcolonial histories. Reunion became a full *Département d'Outre-Mer* in 1946, along with the Caribbean islands of Guadeloupe and Martinique, and the French South American territory of Guyane. The 1946 law was largely the fruit of the collaboration between the Martinican politician and poet Aimé Césaire, his colleague Gaston Monnerville and the Reunionese *députés* Raymond Vergès and Léon de Lapervanche.[29] It has to be seen in the context of the re-establishment of the French claim to their former colonies after the disgrace of German Occupation and the Vichy régime. The new Fourth Republic in France incorporated the project of a greater fusion with its former colonial territories in the assimilationist and probably utopian project of the "Union française": as we have already seen this was immediately rejected by the Malagasy people in the uprising of 1947, and similar nationalist-inspired revolts were brutally suppressed in Algeria and Vietnam at around the same time. The explanation for the acceptance by left-wing politicians such as Césaire and Vergès of this assimilationist strategy probably lies in their awareness of the inevitable economic dependency of their islands on metropolitan France, and the not unjustified expectation of a vastly improved standard of living for their electorate. The island has benefited considerably in recent years from its membership of the European Union, in particular in improvements to its infrastructure. Autonomist movements and politicians are active in Reunion even so, as in the Caribbean, but with the moves towards decentralization and regionalization in France the locally elected political bodies such as the Conseil Régional are able to show considerable initiative in their relations with their independent neighbors. This model is in the process of being adapted for the Comorian island of Mayotte, but for a population much less Gallicized than that of Reunion.[30]

The alternative solution of complete political independence has not always brought the anticipated stability and prosperity to the other former colonies of France. The Comoros islands have suffered from a chronic political instability since independence in 1975, of which the crisis of the attempted secession of Anjouan in 1997 is only the most recent example. The uneasy federal compromises and the sudden shifts from the extreme radical socialism of Ali Soilih (1975-1977) to the Islamic republic of Ahmed Abdallah (1978-1989) have not helped the economic development of the islands, not to mention the foreign-backed armed interventions of Bob Denard and his mercenaries.[31] The current federal Union des Comores, designed to reconcile the three quarrelling islands by giving them more autonomy, seems doomed to suffer the same fate as its predecessors.[32]

Madagascar has also suffered in recent years from political instability and abrupt changes of political direction, but not to the same extent as the Comoros.[33] The country's democratic and republican institutions, originally modeled on those of France, have functioned effectively, but have also been vulnerable to corruption and autocratic abuse, as the recent crisis of 2001-2002 when the outgoing president Didier Ratsiraka could claim to have obtained enough votes for a second round run-off in the face of overwhelming evidence to the contrary. The dispute with his challenger Marc Ravelomanana led to a yearlong paralysis of the country and a breakdown of the rule of law that verged on a civil war. The country could ill afford such a crisis, coming as it did after the onslaught of devastating tropical storms that had laid waste to large areas of the east of the country. Both events showed the limitations of democratic institutions in the face of poor communications, a drastic lack of resources and an under-educated electorate.

In 1976, the first President of the newly independent Republic of the Seychelles, James Mancham, lasted less than a year before being overthrown in a *coup d'état* by his Prime Minister, France-Albert René, who declared the country to be a one-party state under his party the Seychelles People's Progressive Front.[34] This regime continued until the restoration of multi-party elections in 1991, but it has at least ensured stability and continuity: it has since survived several elections until the retirement of René in 2003, and his replacement as President by the former Prime Minister James Michel.[35] There has been a notable absence of power sharing, however, which has led to accusations of abuse and corruption.

Mauritius in this context appears as a model pupil of British-style parliamentary democracy, ensuring a smooth transition in 1992 from a constitutional monarchy to a republican regime in which the first President, Cassam Uteem, played the role of neutral figurehead, leaving executive power in the hands of Prime Minister Navinchandra Ramgoolam. The new institutions have since then survived a change of government, albeit with a less impartial President in Anerood Jugnauth, closely allied with Prime Minister Paul Bérenger. In a recent election Ramgoolam was returned to power, confirming the alternation of political regimes, even under a less neutral presidency.

Contrasting cultural heritages

One of the most fascinating aspects of the Indian Ocean islands remains their mixture of diverse cultures emanating from different parts of the globe. The predominant influence is undoubtedly European, however, transmitted through the lasting influence of the two rival colonial systems of the French and the British, and which is clearly reflected in the political institutions of the islands, but also, as we shall see, in their education systems. Notwithstanding our differentiation of the region from the African continent, African traits are often recognizable in its populations. This is most obvious in the territories closest to the continent, Madagascar and the Comoros: African-style village communities and subsistence farming are still the rule in the rural areas of these islands. The most widespread influence of Africa is perceptible in the popular music of the islands: the predominance of rhythm and percussion instruments and the importance of dance all betray the African strain in the region's culture. The *sega*, a musical and dance form developed in Mauritius, the Seychelles and Reunion is traceable back to the improvised music of the slaves brought in to work on the islands' plantations. In

Reunion, a variation of the original form called the *maloya*, associated with the animist rituals and beliefs of Malagasy ancestor worship, and probably influenced by Tamil religious drumming, was for many years repressed and was only rediscovered in the late 1960s, becoming a popular dance music.[36] The frenetic rhythms of the varied dance-music styles of Madagascar, such as the *salegy* are also recognizably African in style, resembling closely the styles emanating from central and southern Africa, such as the *soukous*.[37]

Indian culture is very visible in Reunion and Mauritius, where it is common to see women and men dressed in traditional Indian-style dress. The Indian cultural influence centers on Hindu religious festivals such as Divali that may be celebrated by the whole population, regardless of their religious affiliations. Indian films, emanating from Bollywood, are often programmed on Mauritian television, but are less popular in the other islands; a similar pattern applies to Indian music and dance, which are most widely practised in Mauritius and to a lesser extent in Reunion.

The influence of south east Asia is obliquely present in the distinctive culture of the Merina peoples of the central highlands of Madagascar. This centers on rice growing and cattle herding, and the very strong presence of traditional animist beliefs such as ancestor-worship. These practices are recognizably different from the more African cultures of the coastal areas of Madagascar, although in many regions there is no clear separation of the two influences.

Other recognizable presences include the Chinese community in Mauritius, Reunion and Madagascar, originally recruited as indentured laborers, but more recently involved in the retail and trading sectors, and increasingly in professional sectors such as medicine.[38] Another distinctive group is that of the Islamic traders originating from Northern India and what is today Pakistan, who make up the bulk of the Islamic minority in the islands. They are identifiable by their traditional Islamic dress and dominate much of the commercial and retail distribution sectors in the Comoros, Reunion, Mauritius and Madagascar.

Rival linguistic traditions

As we have already suggested, French is the dominant language of the region, but it is by no means the only one; it maintains its presence in a situation of linguistic competition. In practice, vehicular languages such as Malagasy or Creole are probably more widely used in their particular zones of influence. Malagasy dominates everyday exchanges in Madagascar, of course, but also in some parts of the Comoros islands. Malagasy is widely used in its written form by the administration of the Republic of Madagascar, and there is also a substantial literature written and published in Malagasy.

The various regional varieties of Creole are predominant within their particular zones: they are similar, to some extent mutually comprehensible, but not the same in vocabulary and syntax. All of them originated in similar circumstances: the slaves brought to work on the island plantations usually did not possess a common language. They were overseen by French slave masters, who often spoke in a regional French dialect, so that Creole developed as a working language, as an Africanized version of French. It shares a lot of vocabulary with French, but its syntax is often markedly different. Since the launch of *Lekritir 1977* by an international committee for the use of Creole, it is usually written phonetically.

Mauritian Creole is spoken by virtually all the communities in Mauritius, and yet, paradoxically, has no official status and is not taught nor widely studied. Yet there is a growing literature written in Creole, notably by the dramatist Dev Virahsawmy. The Mauritian government has recently appointed a commission to establish norms and standards for written Creole.[39] In the Seychelles, on the other hand, it has been an official language since 1977, alongside English and French, as well as being widely used by the local population. The Seychelles government maintains a Creole Institute, *Lenstiti kreol*, which publishes a burgeoning popular literature in Creole; yet in practice the language is little used in public notices and official communications. In Reunion Creole was for many years repressed, unacceptable in the French administrative and legal system, and its use forbidden and punished in schools. According to clause 4 of the French constitution, the language of the Republic is French. Under the European Charter for Minority Languages, however, the regional languages of France were at last given official recognition in the first months of the 21st century, although the issue was referred by President Chirac to the French Constitutional Commission. In Reunion, Creole is now studied at the university, and is an optional part of local teacher training. There has been a growing body of locally published literature in Creole since the 1950s.

English, in spite of its currency as a worldwide vehicular language, remains a minority tongue in the region. It is an official language of the administration in Mauritius and the Seychelles, alongside French, but it is not widely spoken by the populace. It is also the principal teaching language of the education system in both island states, although Creole is predominantly used in the primary sector in the Seychelles. There is a limited but significant literary output in English in both islands, but it is marginal compared with literature written in French.

Other languages are also taught from primary school onwards in Mauritius, on an optional basis, as part of the heritage of the island's diverse communities: Hindi, Mandarin Chinese or Urdu. In the rural regions of Mauritius, a creolized Indian language called Bhojpuri is also commonly spoken.

Contrasting education systems

The educational institutions of the islands not surprisingly reflect the influence of their former colonial rulers, who were largely responsible for establishing them. The French influence is most obvious in Reunion and Mayotte, where the practices, standards and qualifications of the French educational system are essentially the same as in metropolitan France. The two islands possess a considerable network of free state nursery schools, compulsory primary education where the teaching is conducted in French, universal free secondary education in colleges and *lycées*. There is a small parallel network of private confessional schools, mostly Catholic, and extensively integrated into the national system of qualifications. Reunion also possesses a well-endowed university and an advanced technical institute that serve students from the whole region.

Not surprisingly, the Malagasy education system is modeled on the French one, but suffers from a chronic shortage of resources. During the 1980s "malgachization" was imposed but inadequately funded, with disastrous results. With the reintroduction of French as the principal teaching language in the early nineties, the French government is widely involved in co-operation schemes to redevelop the country's educational structures. The country's universities, established in all the regional centers, benefit from extensive assistance from their French counterparts, notably the Université de la Réunion. The weakest parts of the Malagasy system lie at the primary level in the rural areas, where the local community is expected to fund the salary of the primary school teacher. There is in any case a chronic shortage of qualified staff, so that in many areas the state provision is non-existent. In the cities this gap in provision is filled by private sector schools, but in the rural areas it often falls to mission schools, usually Catholic or Protestant, to fulfill the basic need for primary education. Not surprisingly the levels of illiteracy in the rural areas of Madagascar are alarming.[40]

The picture in the independent Comoros islands is even more disturbing and the illiteracy rates even higher. In many areas the only form of education is the Koranic school, where students learn to recite the Koran by heart. The Comoros have no higher education institutions, and rely on sending their best qualified students to Reunion, France or South Africa. Mayotte on the other hand has a French-style education system that is comparable in most respects to that of Reunion.

Mauritius possesses a highly developed and very competitive education system, which is recognizably modeled on the British one. The teaching language is English, and other languages such as French are taught in primary school, along with the other optional languages mentioned earlier: Hindi, Mandarin Chinese and Urdu. The Certificate of Primary Education, a competitive "eleven-plus" style of examination, allocates pupils to a hierarchy of more or less prestigious secondary schools, some of which are confessional but essentially funded by the state, such as the Catholic Loreto College or the Hindu Mahatma Gandhi Institute. Entrance to university is highly selective, so that although the island possesses two universities, many students are obliged to go abroad to study, most often in Commonwealth countries such as the United Kingdom, Australia, Singapore, India, but also to Reunion and metropolitan France. The standards of the island's education system are in most respects comparable to those of Europe, and the island's pupils sometimes suffer from an excessive culture of educational achievement comparable to Singapore or Japan. Private tutoring is very common from the secondary school level onwards, complementing the deficiencies of the state schools and the low salaries of their teachers.

A similar pattern operates in the Seychelles, except that the system is somewhat less competitive and less dependent on private tutoring. The islands possess no university, but a tertiary-level Polytechnic teaches applied disciplines, however, and prepares students for study in overseas universities.

A variety of religions

The majority of the inhabitants of the Indian Ocean islands practice Catholicism, as one would expect given the predominant French influence. The principal exception to this general rule is Mauritius, where Hinduism is dominant. Hindu temples are a prominent feature of Reunion as well as Mauritius. Protestantism is the principal alternative to Catholicism in Madagascar, as we have previously noted: it is subdivided into several different churches, from Anglican and Lutheran to the evangelical groups also found in the United States and South Africa. Most of the islands feature a substantial Islamic minority, usually composed of the trading communities originating from northern India: the exception here is the Comorian archipelago, which is overwhelmingly Muslim, including the French-administered territory of Mayotte. The Chinese immigrants who came to the islands for the most part at the end of the nineteenth century and the early twentieth often brought their Buddhist faith with them. The final element, variable but present in all on the islands, is made up of the often clandestine practice of African religious beliefs, such as animism, ancestor-worship and sorcery. This is most evident in Madagascar, where animism and ancestor worship are widely practiced, even among Christians, and a complex system of taboos often influences everyday life.

In general, religious conflicts are rare in the region, and religious tolerance is the general rule. Conflicts between the different communities in the islands, even when they affect a particular religious group, are usually centered on social and economic issues rather than religious ones. In most of the islands, the spiritual leaders of the diverse religious groups maintain a cordial relationship with each other and may even, as in Reunion, sit together on consultative committees concerning religious matters. It is interesting to speculate on the reasons for this tolerance, which unfortunately does not always extend to social and political differences.

An ethnic melting-pot?

The degree of inter-marriage and fusion among the various ethnic groups present in the islands varies considerably from one island to another. Although the ethnic communities still form recognizable groupings in Reunionese society, the degree of intermarriage is considerable and the community is very racially mixed. Even the original French settlers coming from Madagascar often brought Malagasy companions with them: so even the oldest land-owning families are not of purely French origin. Family names of French, Indian, Malagasy or Chinese origin often provide no reliable guide to the ethnic type of their owners.

The same is less true of the population of Mauritius: in general the ethnic groups that make up Mauritian society tend to remain separate, and marry among themselves. It is interesting to speculate why this should be so, since the ethnic and cultural origins of the population of the two islands are broadly similar. There are certainly marked differences in the political dispensations of the two islands in respect of their populations: the French constitution of Reunion emphasizes egalitarian citizenship, whereas the British-inspired system of political representation in Mauritius guarantees parliamentary representation to minority ethnic and religious groups, thus enshrining their difference at a constitutional level. Whether this is a cause of the separation or simply a symptom of the undercurrent of ethnic rivalry prevalent in the society remains an open question.

The population of the Seychelles on the other hand appears to be a well-integrated mix of peoples from widely differing backgrounds: mostly African and French, with smaller numbers of Indian and Chinese extraction. These groups scarcely maintain a separate identity, so that the society, although small, appears as the best example of fusion of ethnic groups in the region.

In Madagascar there does not appear to be a clear dividing line between the communities of Asian and African descent. The population is nevertheless divided into recognizable ethnic groups who inhabit particular regions: the Merina around the capital Antananarivo, the Sakalava in the north west, around Mahajanga, the Antandroy in the far south, etc.⁴¹ The vestiges of the Merina aristocracy seem to constitute a recognizably "noble" caste and their attachment to the memory of the centralized Malagasy monarchy is very noticeable, for instance in the public emotional response to the fire that destroyed the Queen's Palace in Antananarivo in 1996. According to a commonly held belief, Malagasy society is haunted by a rivalry between the peoples of the central highlands and those of the coast, a division well illustrated by the recent conflict between the two presidential candidates, Ratsiraka (from the coastal town of Toamasina) and Ravelomanana (from the capital, Antananarivo, in the highlands).⁴² Malagasy society has also occasionally erupted into violent xenophobia, as in the massacre of the Comorian population of the west coast in 1977,⁴³ and the riots directed at the group of Islamic traders, the "Karana," in 1987.⁴⁴

The Comoros islands, including Mayotte, appear to be home to a population of predominantly African origin, with some presence of Arabs, Indians, Chinese and Malays, as well as Europeans (particularly in Mayotte). These groups seem to mix freely and there is little sense of rival ethnic groups, although the French community, mostly made up of expatriates who do not settle permanently in the islands, appear to form a separate social group. This sense of difference is no doubt exacerbated by the religious and cultural distinction between the overwhelmingly Islamic majority and the small Catholic minority.

Caribbean comparisons

One of the most interesting points of comparison with the Francophone Caribbean is that of the size of the population. The Francophone Indian Ocean islands have a population well over twice as large as that of the Francophone territories of the Caribbean, even including French Guyana. The former group currently totals some 17,116,002 inhabitants, as against 8,629,140 for the latter.⁴⁵ One might argue that these figures are distorted by the 14 million inhabitants of Madagascar, who are not all genuinely Francophone; the same could no doubt be said, however, of the 7 million inhabitants of Haïti. What is striking about this comparison is the lack of attention paid generally to the Indian Ocean islands, as against those of the Caribbean, which seem to wield an influence and notoriety out of proportion to their actual size. One of the reasons for this is no doubt that the Francophone sector of the Caribbean is only a small component of a much larger zone including the Anglophone, Hispanic and Dutch Caribbean. Yet even if, for the sake of comparing like with like, one includes the Anglophone Caribbean with the Francophone one, the total population is still only 13,805,239. One possible explanation for the higher profile traditionally accorded to the Caribbean is its proximity to the United States, and the influence the world's superpower wields in the region, in such heavily-populated countries as Puerto Rico and Haïti.

There are of course many factors in common between the two regions. Reunion shares the paradoxical status of *Département d'Outre-Mer* with Guadeloupe, Martinique and French Guyana, as well as an improbable membership of the European Union and a chronic economic dependency on metropolitan France. The Francophone Caribbean has also developed the Creole language in much the same way and for similar reasons as Mauritius, Reunion and the Seychelles. A French-based Creole is also spoken in the neighboring Anglophone islands of Dominica, St. Lucia and the Grenadines.

The comparisons with the Anglophone Caribbean are also interesting: Trinidad, for instance, has a large Indian population, initially brought there for the same reasons as the Indian population in Mauritius and Reunion, to replace the African slaves in the sugar-cane industry, after the abolition of slavery. There are also smaller populations of Indian extraction in Guadeloupe and Martinique. The Caribbean islands thus can also claim to be a "melting-pot" culture in which different ethnic traditions are blended: this is the basis of the claims made by the Caribbean theoreticians of cultural creolization, such as Edward Kamau Brathwaite, Edouard Glissant and the Martinican authors of the *Eloge de la Créolité* of 1989, Bernabé, Chamoiseau and Confiant.[46] The latter seem particularly concerned to incorporate the cultures of the Indian Ocean islands under their banner of *créolité*:[47] while this is a superficially seductive idea, it ignores the fact that Reunionese writers such as Axel Gauvin and Jean-François Sam-Long were championing the cause of Creole culture some ten years earlier, in Gauvin's pamphlet of 1977 *Du Créole opprimé au Créole libéré*,[48] for instance. It also leaves out of account the strongly nationalist literature of Madagascar, which uses the

Malagasy language as well as French, but not Creole, which has no significant presence in Madagascar.[49]

These issues will be explored further in subsequent chapters, in the light of theories of hybridity developed by theorists such as Homi K. Bhabha.[50] For the time being it will be enough to observe that many points of comparison suggest themselves and that their development is a potentially fruitful area of reflection.

A happy fusion?

It seems a reasonable proposition to suppose that, with the increase of mobility of the world's population, migration will become more and more common and most formerly national societies will become more and more multi-ethnic and multi-cultural. The process is clearly already under way, and the predictable reactions of xenophobia clearly visible, not least in the formerly colonialist societies of Britain and France. The notion of an ethnically based nationality is being seriously challenged, and even more abstract notions of national citizenship seem to be under threat from the increased ability of whole communities to transplant themselves from one nation state to another.

In this broader context, what can we learn from the societies of the Indian Ocean? To what extent do they provide a model for what is likely to be a multi-cultural, multi-ethnic future? Certainly in societies such as Reunion religious tolerance seems to be securely established, and there the intermingling of ethnic groups is probably the furthest advanced of all the societies we are considering here. The same could be said for the Seychelles, except that the range of different ethnicities and cultures is less wide. As we have observed, there is a blurring of the ethnic divisions in Madagascar, but the regional tribal groups still maintain a sense of their ethnic identity, and an undercurrent of rivalry and hostility survives between Malagasy groups of Asian and African descent. Violent xenophobic reactions to groups perceived as external to Malagasy society are not unknown.[51] On the other hand there seems to be little tension between religious groups, admittedly predominantly Christian, and the strong presence of traditional ancestor-worship does not seem to present a problem either.[52] In Mauritius religious tolerance seems to be broadly accepted, although particular cultural groups occasionally vociferously demand public respect for their specific identity. The inter-mingling of ethnic groups, on the other hand, seems less well advanced than elsewhere in the region, although it is by no means unknown. As we have already observed, tension between the ethnic groups on the island has sometimes given rise to violent confrontation, but in general the social fabric of the island's society appears stable and based on mutual acceptance.

This is not to say, however, that conflict is absent from these islands often compared to the mythical Garden of Eden. In most cases where violent conflict has erupted, it is usually attributable to glaring economic inequality. The riots of 1991 in Reunion may have taken the form of a nationalistic revolt against a heavy-handed French central administration, but the underlying cause, as is very often the case in the island's social conflicts, remains the difference in living standards between the long-term unemployed and the privileged élite of well-paid metropolitan French civil servants.[53] A similar interpretation can be advanced for the attacks in 1987 on the "Karana" group of Islamic traders in Madagascar, originating from what is today Pakistan, who were seen as profiteering from the most impoverished groups in Malagasy society.[54]

It remains to be seen whether the flagrant inequalities between the various societies of the region are likely to give rise to social tensions between them. Already there is a noticeable tendency of the inhabitants of the most impoverished societies in the region, Madagascar and the Comoros, to migrate in ever larger numbers towards the more prosperous zones, such as Reunion and Mayotte. This has led to the imposition by the French government of visas for non-French visitors to their territories and the banning of informal sea crossings between Mayotte and the other islands of the Comorian archipelago. These economic migrants have not yet been the subject of a xenophobic reaction on that part of the general population, except perhaps in Mayotte, where the large group of illegal immigrants from the neighboring island of Anjouan are regularly blamed for petty criminality and insecurity in the island.[55] It is foreseeable, however, that this situation may well develop into a problem of regional importance, further complicated by the fact that Reunion and Mayotte are also the distant frontier posts of the European Union.

The older colonialist societies of Britain and France, still clinging to their sense of ethnic and cultural homogeneity and the belief in their inherent superiority, can learn something from the religious tolerance and the well-advanced ethnic integration of these peripheral outposts of their former empires. All is not perfect in these islands, nor are they the best of all possible worlds, but in terms of their open-ness and multi-cultural tolerance they can serve as an image of what the societies of old Europe might aspire to in the not too distant future.

Notes

1. Léopold Sedar Senghor, ed., *Anthologie de la nouvelle poésie nègre et malgache* (Paris: Presses Universitaires de France, 1948).

2. See Bertrand Clare, ed., *Atlaséco 2005: Atlas économique et politique mondial* (Paris: MédiaObs/Le Nouvel Observateur, 2005), 133.

3. For this and further general information, see Hilary Bradt, ed. *Guide to Madagascar,* fifth edition (Chalfont St. Peter, UK / Old Saybrook, CO: Bradt, 1997), 3-70; and Deanna Swaney and Robert Willox, *Madagascar and Comoros,* second edition (Hawthorn, Australia: Lonely Planet, 1994), 46-86.

4. See Jean-Louis Joubert, *Littératures de l'Océan indien* (Vanves, France: EDICEF, 1991), 73.

5. See Bradt, *Guide to Madagascar*, 13.

6. See Bradt, Hilary ed., *Guide to Madagascar*, eighth edition (Chalfont St. Peter, UK / Old Saybrook, CO: Bradt, 2005), 10-12.

7. See Clare, *Atlaséco*, 133. Madagascar's per capita gross national product is ranked 210th out of the 227 nations of the world.

8. See Joubert, *Littératures de l'Océan indien*, 97-98.

9. See Clare, *Atlaséco*, 141-42.

10. See Clare, *Atlaséco*, 178-89.

11. See Sonia Chane-Kune, *Aux Origines de l'identité réunionnaise* (Paris: L'Harmattan, 1993), 17-20.

12. For a detailed history of the early years of Reunion as a colony, see Yvan Combeau, Prosper Eve, Sudel Fuma and Edmond Maestri, *Histoire de La Réunion. De la colonie à la région* (Paris and Reunion: SEDES / Université de la Réunion, 2001), 12-13, 14-48; also Chane-Kune, *Aux Origines de l'identité réunionnaise,* 15-151.

13. See Clare, *Atlaséco*, 179.

14. See Clare, *Atlaséco*, 143.

15. See Swaney and Willox, *Madagascar and Comoros*, 296-99.; and Dominique Auzias and Jean-Paul Labourdette, *Mayotte Comores* (Paris: Nouvelles Editions de l'Université, "Petit Futé" guide series, 2004), 33-59.

16. See Auzias and Labourdette, *Mayotte Comores*, 60-64.

17. See Clare, *Atlaséco*, 56

18. See Clare, *Atlaséco*, 195.

19. See Deryck Scarr, *Seychelles since 1770: history of a slave and post-slavery society* (London: Hurst, 2000), 4-14.

20. See Scarr, *Seychelles since 1770*, 17-38.

21. See Scarr, *Seychelles since 1770*, 89.

22. See Scarr, *Seychelles since 1770*, 192.

23. See Scarr, *Seychelles since 1770*, 193-98.

24. See Judith and Adrian Skerrett, *Seychelles* (London and Singapore: Insight Pocket Guides / APA publications, 2004), 14-15; and Jan Dodd, *Mauritius, Réunion and Seychelles*, 5th edition, (Footscray, Australia: Lonely Planet, 2004), 274.

25. See Clare, *Atlaséco*, 195.

26. See Skerrett, *Seychelles*, 15-16; and Dodd, *Réunion and Seychelles*, 243.

27. See Skerrett, *Seychelles*, 15-16; and Dodd, *Réunion and Seychelles*, 243-4.

28. See Joubert, *Littératures de l'Océan Indien*, 98-99.

29. See Combeau et al. *Histoire de La Réunion*, 147-49.

30. See Auzias and Labourdette, *Mayotte Comores*, 55-56, 108-9.

31. See Auzias and Labourdette, *Mayotte Comores*, 47-59.

32. See Auzias and Labourdette, *Mayotte Comores*, 60-64.

33. For an overview of the period 1972-1991, see Charlotte-Arrisoa Rafenomanjato, *La Marche de la Liberté* (Paris and Saint-Denis: L'Harmattan / Azalées, 1992).

34. See Scarr, *Seychelles since 1770*, 192-98.

35. See Skerrett, *Seychelles*, 14-15; Dodd, *Réunion and Seychelles*, 242.

36. See Simon Broughton, Mark Ellingham and Richard Trillo, eds., *The Rough Guide to world music*, vol. 1, (London: Rough Guides, 1999), 506-7.

37. See Broughton, Ellingham, Trillo, *Rough Guide to world music*, 526.

38. Chane-Kune, *Aux Origines de l'identité réunionnaise*, 134, notes the recruitment of a thousand Chinese indentured laborers for Reunion as early as 1843.

39. See Arnaud Carpooran, *L'Ile Maurice: des langues et des lois* (Paris: L'Harmattan / Agence intergouvernementale de la Francophonie, 2003).
40. See Bradt, *Guide to Madagascar* (1997), 9.
41. See Swaney and Willox, *Madagascar and Comoros*, 73-75.
42. See Bradt, *Guide to Madagascar*, (2005), 10-12.
43. See Auzias and Labourdette, *Mayotte Comores*, 53, for a brief account of the massacre of Comorians in Madagascar in 1976.
44. See Swaney and Willox, *Madagascar and Comoros*, 72.
45. Total arrived at from the population statistics provided for each territory by Clare, *Atlaséco*.
46. Jean Bernabé, Patrick Chamoiseau and Raphaël Confiant, *Eloge de la créolité* (Paris: Gallimard, 1989).
47. See Bernabé et al., *Eloge de la créolité*, 31-33.
48. Gauvin, Axel, *Du créole opprimé au créole libéré* (Paris: L'Harmattan, 1977).
49. See Joubert, *Littératures de l'Océan Indien*, 9-10.
50. See chapter 2, "*Métissage* and hybridity" and chapter 3, "Hybridity and cultural difference."
51. See Auzias and Labourdette, *Mayotte Comores*, 53.
52. See Bradt, *Guide to Madagascar* (1997), 8-9, 17-23; and Swaney and Willox, *Madagascar and Comoros*, 83.
53. See Dodd, *Réunion and Seychelles*, 150.
54. See Swaney and Willox, *Madagascar and Comoros*, 72.
55. For a detailed account of this issue, see Auzias and Labourdette *Mayotte Comores*, 56-59.

Chapter 2

Postcolonial Perspectives

Following on from an introductory survey of the defining characteristics of the Francophone Indian Ocean, we shall now examine in more detail some of the ways in which the heritage of colonialism has conditioned the contemporary situation of the islands and marked their distinctive cultures.

Colonial trade rivalries

The competition between the European maritime powers in the seventeenth century for the lucrative spice trade in the Far East was probably the major reason for their interest in the islands of the Indian Ocean, and consequently for their colonization. Their presence in the region was preceded, however, by that of the Arab and Persian traders who developed commercial links along the east coast of Africa and as far south as Madagascar, from as early as the seventh century AD. This led to the establishment of Islamic sultanates in the coastal islands, most famously in Zanzibar, but also, from the fifteenth century onwards, in the Comoros islands.[1] The Islamic culture of the Comoros is an ancient and well-established one, predating by many centuries the influence of the European colonisers and their missionaries. Thus the earliest known transcriptions of the Malagasy language are in Arabic script.[2] It is likely that these Arab trading routes were also involved initially in the slave trade, although this was predominantly a European activity in relation to the slave populations brought to the Mascarene islands of Mauritius and

Reunion, as well as to the Seychelles, sometimes benefiting from active collaboration with Malagasy tribal rulers.[3]

The Dutch East India Company dominated trade along the lucrative "Spice Route" to Indonesia in the seventeenth and eighteenth centuries: this is the probable reason for their initial colonisation of Mauritius from 1638 onwards, as a staging post for their fleet.[4] With their colony established at the Cape in 1652 they lost interest in Mauritius, and left it to be taken over by their rivals, the French, keen to get a share in the lucrative spice trade. The French experimented with using Mauritius, renamed the Ile de France in 1722, as a naval and slave-trading base and Reunion, then called Bourbon, as a place to cultivate tropical products such as coffee and spices.[5] In the Ile de France and the Seychelles, Pierre Poivre, the botanist and chief administrator of Mauritius, pioneered the implantation of spices in the late eighteenth century, but in the end coffee, tea and sugar cane proved the most profitable plantation crops. In the longer term coffee proved too vulnerable to the devastating effects of tropical storms, with the result that sugar cane became the dominant export crop in Mauritius and Reunion, and remains so to this day.[6] Commercial considerations were thus the principal incentive for the colonization of these previously uninhabited islands, and for the establishment of a slave-based plantation economy. As noted earlier, the decision to populate and develop them as colonies lay largely with the French *Compagnie des Indes orientales*.

Virgin territories and tropical paradises

Mauritius, Reunion and the Seychelles were all uninhabited islands until the seventeenth and eighteenth centuries. All of them possessed a specifically indigenous wildlife, of which the most famous example was the dodo, unprepared by evolution for the arrival of hungry seafarers in search of a convenient food supply.[7] The islands were regularly raided by passing ships in this way, but it took some time for the colonial trading companies to recognize the commercial potential of the islands. The first human inhabitants of Reunion were sent there in 1646 from the French trading post of Fort Dauphin on the south east coast of Madagascar, as a punishment after an attempted mutiny. They found the island a pleasant and fertile territory, rich in game and wildlife, with no venomous plants or insects, and they prospered in the two years that elapsed before they were relieved.[8] This encouraged the French authorities to develop the island's agriculture and after several unsuccessful attempts at colonization the first permanent French settlers arrived in 1665 from Madagascar, with their Malagasy slaves and partners.[9]

Although there is no evidence of human habitation on Mauritius before the early seventeenth century, Phoenicians probably visited the island about 2,000 years ago, and Malays and Arabs stopped on the island in subsequent centuries. The Portuguese charted the waters surrounding the island, which they called Ilha do Cirne (Island of the Swan), in the early sixteenth century. In 1638 the Dutch began colonizing the island, which they named after Maurice of Nassau, the *stadthouder* (head of state) of Holland.[10] The island's first governor, Cornelius Simonsz Gooyer, presided over a small population of Dutch convicts and slaves from Indonesia and Madagascar, who sought to export ambergris, ebony, and other resources. After twenty years, the colony failed, as did a second settlement established in 1664. Poor administration and harsh conditions forced the Dutch to withdraw permanently by 1710. In addition to presiding over the extinction of the dodo bird and leaving behind perhaps some runaway slaves, swarms of rats, and ravaged ebony forests, the Dutch introduced a plant that was to be prominent in the island's future—sugar cane.

French efforts to colonize the area were more successful. Around 1638 they had claimed the islands of Rodrigues and Reunion, and in 1715 an expedition of the French East India Company claimed Mauritius for France. The company established a settlement on the island, which they named Île de France, in 1722.

The Seychelles islands were regularly visited by passing ships, who used them to replenish their supplies of food and water. They were known to the early Portuguese explorers and probably to the Arabs. A British ship, the *Ascension* under Captain Robert Sharpeigh, recorded a visit there in 1609, and described the welcome supply of fresh water, coconuts and giant tortoises.[11] It wasn't until 1742, however, that Mahé de la Bourdonnais, the Governor of the already well-established French colony of Ile de France, sent an expedition to explore the islands and claim them for France.[12] Several similar exploratory expeditions followed, but it was only in 1770 that the first settlers arrived, to exploit the timber resources of Mahé island, and to create spice plantations, using seeds procured by the botanist Pierre Poivre.[13] The initial settlers consisted of 14 Frenchmen, 7 African slaves, 5 Indian laborers and 1 French woman. By 1786 a military base had been set up, on the principal island of Mahé, to protect it from British invasion, and it had a population of 24 military personnel, 4 civilians and 122 slaves. Its principal commercial activity was no longer agriculture, but supplying timber and turtle and tortoise meat to passing ships.[14]

The image of an unspoilt tropical paradise subsequently corrupted by human exploitation is a potent one for all the formerly uninhabited islands. The biblical myth of the Garden of Eden has often been applied to the destiny of the islands, most famously by General Gordon in the late nineteenth century, who was convinced, after a visit to the groves of suggestive *coco de mer* palms on the island of Praslin in the Seychelles, that he had discovered the site of the original garden.[15] The myth is perpetuated by endless tourist brochures for all the islands and even by taxi drivers who welcome newly-arrived visitors to Mauritius on their first visit to Paradise.

Trading posts, tribal conflicts, pirates and settlers.

Apart from the wave of immigration from south-east Asia, approximately dated to the fifth or sixth century AD, but according to some accounts much earlier, the first outsiders to establish contact with Madagascar were Arab sailors and merchants, who established trading posts at various places on the coast.[16] The first Europeans to visit Madagascar were some shipwrecked Portuguese sailors in 1504, who managed to settle in the south of the island for some 20 years before being ousted by hostile local tribes in 1527.[17] It was the French who then established a trading post in the south east of the island at Fort Dauphin, today called Taolagnaro, in 1642. The local tribes remained inhospitable, however, and Fort Dauphin was abandoned in 1674, and its surviving inhabitants fled to Reunion.[18]

In the early eighteenth century the island of Nosy Boraha on the east coast of Madagascar, under its French name of Ile Sainte-Marie, became a base for international pirate activity.[19] Later in the century a Frenchman called Jean-Onésime Filet, nicknamed "La Bigorne", fleeing from a jealous vendetta in Reunion and shipwrecked on the island, successfully courted a local princess and was given the island by her father, a local tribal ruler. The couple ceded it to France in 1750, and so the Ile Sainte Marie became the earliest French colony in Madagascar.[20] Similar apocryphal tales concern the establishment by reformed pirates Olivier Misson and Angelo Carraccioli of the utopian community of Libertalia in the north of Madagascar, at Antsiranana, often called Diego Suarez; this too, so the story goes, eventually fell victim to the hostility of local tribes.[21] These tales have drawn attention to the role of pirates and adventurers in the early development of the region, adding to the mythology of an area outside the boundaries of civilization and beyond the rule of law.[22] There are records of pirate activity in the Comoros archipelago[23] and in the Seychelles islands, whose isolation lent itself to such activities.[24] Not surprisingly, these stories have provided a rich vein of inspiration for the novelists of the region, and pirate mythology is a major element in the imaginative identity of the region.[25]

The baleful heritage of the slave trade

As we have already seen, the very earliest settlers on the uninhabited islands of the region arrived accompanied by slaves. The first economic exploitation of the islands' resources was usually through the establishment of plantations that relied heavily on slave labor. Within a few years of their initial colonization, the populations of slaves on the islands of Mauritius, Reunion and the Seychelles were more than double those of Europeans. This situation subsisted for at least a hundred years in the principal islands, until the mid-nineteenth century. It is very hard to determine what were the exact origins of the slave population: it was a common practice to mix together slaves of different backgrounds, so as better to "divide and rule". Many were taken from the African mainland, and not necessarily, as one might expect, from the nearby eastern seaboard of what are today Mozambique, Tanzania, Kenya and Somalia. Most were bought from the warring tribes of Madagascar, before the unification of the island under the Merina monarchy: typically slaves were prisoners of war taken in tribal conflicts and sold off by their captors.[26] Some of the tribal rulers of Madagascar raided the adjacent coasts and islands such as the Comoros and Mozambique, as slave hunters on behalf of the French, keen to acquire slaves for plantations in Bourbon and Ile de France.[27] Some slaves may even have come from as far away as West Africa, from well-known slave ports such as Gorée island off Senegal and Ouidah in present-day Benin.[28]

The first attempt at the abolition of slavery was undertaken by the French Revolutionary Convention in 1794, but the French-ruled islands of the Indian Ocean, Bourbon, Ile de France and Seychelles managed to avoid implementing the reform, under pressure from the plantation-owning élite.[29] The reform was in any case short-lived, as slavery was re-instated by Napoleon in 1802.[30] The British, having outlawed the slave trade in 1807, persuaded the enlightened monarch Radama I of Madagascar to discontinue the practice,[31] and after their conquest of Mauritius and the Seychelles during the Napoleonic campaigns of 1810-1815, the British eventually managed to impose the abolition of slavery on the Franco-Mauritian plantation-owners, from 1835 onwards.[32] It was not until 1848 that the French Second Republic successfully renewed the attempt to outlaw slavery, under the influence of the campaigner Victor Schoelcher, and the news was proclaimed to Reunion by the Commissar of the Republic Sarda Garriga on the 20th December of that year.[33] Since 1982 that date has been a public holiday in Reunion.

Thus the bulk of the early populations of Mauritius, Reunion and the Seychelles were slaves, mostly of African origin, and were brutally denied their own linguistic and cultural heritage. Traces of it survived even so, in the Creole language, which grew up on the plantations as a working language among slaves and their masters who otherwise had no common tongue. Creole was not written down until the early nineteenth century, and then usually transcribed as a type of *patois*, using the conventions of French.[34]

Another cultural heritage of the slave population that survives to this day is the dance form of the *sega*. This was originally the dance music of the slave population, initially frowned upon by the plantation owners, and consisting of improvised rhythmic percussion instruments accompanying a chant / response singing.[35] The style, with its typical ternary rhythm, was subsequently adopted by the white population who added the harmonic instrumentation of the European country dance band, such as the violin, the guitar and the banjo, and it became a local dance form practised alongside the traditional European dances such as the waltz and the quadrille.[36] It has now become the typical folk music of the islands, and is exploited as such in hotel spectacles for tourists.[37] The original form still survives, using the simple drum accompaniment of a "ravane," a kind of tambourine; in Mauritius it is called the *sega ravane* and in the Seychelles the *moutia*.

A more subversive form of slave music survived in Reunion as part of the clandestine practice of African ancestor-worship. The *maloya*, similar in musical form to the *sega*, was banned for many years by the French authorities as an incitation to public disorder. It was practised as part of the "servis kabare," probably of Malagasy origin, a nightlong festival in which the music induced a trance-like state favorable to the incarnation of the spirits of the ancestors. This was rediscovered and eventually legitimized in the 1970s and its most famous practitioners, Gramoune Lélé, Firmin Viry and Lo Rwa Kaf became popular local stars.[38]

Despite this tardy recognition of the African heritage of the islands' cultures, the slave origins of the Creole language and the musical forms of the *sega* and the *maloya* led to their marginalization, suffering the stigma of their supposedly uncivilised ancestry. To this day the Negro communities of the islands still make up the majority of the poorest sectors of the islands' populations,[39] although it is today far from easy to identify the ethnic origins of particular individuals, because of the degree of intermarriage among the various communities. In general, the present-day island inhabitants do not care to be reminded of their heritage of slavery: it remains a partially taboo subject, rarely openly acknowledged.

Plantations, abolition and indianization in the Mascarene islands

By the early nineteenth century the islands of Mauritius and Reunion, as well as the Mauritian dependency of Rodrigues, were well-established economies based on thriving plantations of sugar cane and dependent on slave labor. The principal islands of the Seychelles had developed similar social and economic structures, but on a smaller scale and not centered on sugar cane, but rather on timber, coprah and spices. The outlawing of the slave trade created labor shortages for the plantations well before the final abolition of slavery, and these were remedied by a variety of means: illegal importation of slaves, which continued long after the legal abolition of trading, but also the recruitment of indentured labor in southern India, Madagascar, east Africa and even as far away as China. The majority of these contractual laborers were Indian, however, and this has led to a numerical predominance of the Indian and Hindu population in present-day Mauritius. This process was accelerated after the abolition of slavery in Mauritius from 1835 onwards and in Reunion after 1848. In spite of attempts to retain the freed slaves on the plantations, their numbers rapidly declined and the sugar industry became much more heavily dependent on indentured labor. The conditions of work for these immigrants were only marginally better than those of the slaves, and in spite of the legal right to repatriation after the expiry of the contract, few were able or willing to take advantage of it. The different patterns of importation of indentured labour in the two islands are probably attributable to the different zones of influence of the ruling colonial authorities. The British not surprisingly relied more heavily on India, which they by then dominated, whereas the French were obliged to diversify their sources of recruitment, drawing more on Madagascar and the eastern coast of Africa, as well as China. The importation of indentured labour continued well into the early years of the twentieth century, although the British ceased to allow recruitment to Reunion from India in 1882. This phase of the colonial history of the islands is largely responsible for the extreme diversity of the ethnic mix of their population, as well as for the strong presence of the Hindu religion on both Mauritius and Reunion.[40]

Colonial and missionary rivalry in Madagascar

In the late eighteenth century, the ruler of the Merina people of the central highlands of Madagascar, King Andrianampoinimerina began a campaign to conquer the other tribal kingdoms of Madagascar and to unify the island under his rule. His project was completed by his son Radama I, who came to power in 1810. In 1817 and 1820 Radama I signed treaties with the British, who brought him firearms and military advisors to advance his campaign, but also Protestant missionaries from the London Missionary Society. The latter undertook to establish a written form of the Malagasy language using Roman script, and to translate the Bible into the vernacular by 1835.[41] The Protestant evangelization of the island was well under way by the time of the death of Radama I in 1828, and he was succeeded by his widow, Queen Ranavalona I. The new queen was much less tolerant of foreign intervention, however: she banished all missionaries and cruelly persecuted their followers. Later in the century her son Radama II reverted to Christian beliefs and by 1869, under the reign of Queen Ranavalona II, Protestantism had become the official religion of Madagascar. The Protestant churches and mission schools used the Malagasy language and it was in this context that a considerable body of devotional literature in the indigenous language was first developed. In the intervening years Catholic missions had grown in importance, in parallel with the influence of French entrepreneurs like Jean Laborde,[42] with the result that the country's Christian community is today more or less evenly divided between Catholic and Protestant churches. Despite this evangelization, traditional Malagasy ancestor worship is still very strong, accounting for the beliefs of about half the total population.[43]

Towards the end of the nineteenth century French claims to Madagascar became increasingly insistent, inspiring the Franco-Malagasy war of 1883-1885, with the support of the colonial élite in Reunion. The British did not intervene, however, and in 1890 signed an agreement with the French not to challenge their claim to Madagascar. The island was eventually annexed in 1896 by the French army under Gallieni, who sent the last queen, Ranavalona III, into exile, and became the first colonial governor of Madagascar.[44] Thus it was that the island became Francophone, but the Malagasy language remains the *lingua franca* of the country and maintains a strong tradition of written literature that had already been established prior to the French annexation.

French republican culture the dominant political model

Madagascar experienced some 65 years of French colonial rule, and at independence in 1960 adopted a constitution modeled on the French one, which lasted until 1972. After adopting for a period the socialist model of the People's Republic under President Didier Ratsiraka from 1975 to 1992, Madagascar reverted to a more conventional French-style republican constitution in 1992, which has lasted until today, although not without some tensions and instability.[45] Reunion, after 300 years as a far-flung colonial territory, often impoverished and neglected, finally acceded to the status of *Département d'Outre-Mer* (often abbreviated as DOM) in 1946, along with Guadeloupe, Martinique and Guyane in the Caribbean. As mentioned in the previous chapter, the inspiration for this assimilationist policy came from left-wing politicians such as Aimé Césaire of Martinique, and Raymond Vergès and Léon de Lapervanche from Reunion, all at that time members of the French Communist Party. Their belief was that the egalitarian principles of France's post-war Fourth Republic would help to raise the standard of living of the islands' populations.[46] Reunion is now a well-established integral part of the French republican state and enjoys all the privileges of that status, including membership of the European Union. Mayotte, in the Comoros archipelago, after well over a century as a French colony, now aspires to a similar status; its population are already citizens of the European Union. The other islands of the Comoros have not achieved the same stability and prosperity, however, having experienced a variety of regimes since choosing independence in 1975, from a Federal Islamic Republic to the current Union des Comores.[47]

After over 150 years as a British colony, and some 65 enjoying a relative autonomy, Mauritius retained the status of a nominal constitutional monarchy when it achieved independence in 1968, but more recently, in 1992, it adopted a republican constitution comparable to the French model of the Third and Fourth Republics, with an executive Prime Minister and a figurehead President. It has remained within the Commonwealth, but is also an active member of *La Francophonie*, the International Francophone Organisation. The Seychelles adopted a republican constitution in 1976, but after a *coup d'état* in 1977 became a one-party state. The country reverted to a multi-party regime in 1991, and since then has enjoyed a stable presidential-style government, while remaining in the Commonwealth as well as also belonging to the International Francophone Organisation.[48]

The common denominator of all the political regimes in the zone is clearly that of an adherence to the principles of French-style republicanism and participation in the International Francophone Organisation, *La Francophonie*. Given the long-standing association of all the cultures with France and its colonial history this is scarcely surprising, but it is interesting even so in the light of the strong influence of British colonialism on the institutions of Mauritius and the Seychelles and on the early development under the Malagasy monarchy of a politically and culturally unified Madagascar.

Cultures of complex and uncertain identification

The tangled threads of the islands' colonial history make the question of the ethnic and cultural identity of the islands populations an extremely complex one. It exercises the imagination of the inhabitants and regularly resurfaces at times of social and political crisis. Broadly speaking, there are several ways of situating the origin of a particular social group. One is by ethnic origin, if that can be determined: Indian, African, Malay, Chinese, European, etc. In the many cases where there has been racial mixing, it is far from clear. This is further complicated by regional and tribal identities, as in Madagascar: Merina, Sakalava, Betsimileo, Antandroy, etc; there is even some perpetuation of Indian caste divisions among the Hindu population of Mauritius. Another category of identification is by national citizenship: Malagasy, Mauritian, French, Seychellois, Comorian. This too can be problematic: "Reunionnais" and "Mahorais" are of course not national categories, but regional and geographical groupings within the French state. Yet another is by religious affiliation: Catholic, Protestant, Hindu, Muslim, Buddhist: yet these often overlap with various varieties of traditional beliefs. None of these categories are all-encompassing, however, but all are regularly used to situate the inhabitants of the islands in the context of their social fabric.

This complexity is one of the most interesting aspects of the islands' cultures. In microcosm, it foreshadows a situation that is likely to become increasingly common in the previously more ethnically unified societies of Europe and elsewhere as migration and social mobility increases. The hybridity of the islands' cultures is one of their strengths, and has not yet led to a major breakdown in the cohesion of their social structures. The issue of social status is a common preoccupation throughout the region, however, and this betrays a certain insecurity about cultural identity among the population of the islands.[49]

Métissage and hybridity

The French term "métissage" literally means inter-breeding, but it is often used figuratively to refer to "métissage culturel," without necessarily using the adjective "culturel." This usage is difficult to render into English, but has often been expressed as hybridity, in the works of postcolonial theorists such as Homi Bhabha.[50] "Métissage" was the term favoured by Léopold Sedar Senghor, the Senegalese poet-president, to describe his ideal of a culture that would fuse African and French values,[51] and it has often been used since in a similar way to describe situations of cultural fusion. The notion is extremely relevant, it goes without saying, to the islands of the Francophone Indian Ocean. Not only are they home to an extremely mixed-race population, but their cultures are similarly composed of a complex fusion of elements drawn from many different origins. The purpose of this book is, amongst other things, to determine the extent to which this mixture has given rise to a distinctive regional culture that has taken on an identity separate from that of its constituent parts.

The terms are not neutral and objective, however. After Senghor "métissage" usually carries a positive connotation in French, whereas "hybridity" is not necessarily regarded as favourable. The term "hybrid" is commonly used of plants and animals rather than human beings and their cultures, and can carry connotations of artificiality and genetic manipulation, as well as a pejorative association with impurity. In a situation of exacerbated nationalism, "hybrid" can carry negative associations comparable to the notion of "half-caste," with implications of duplicity and falsity. In the present intellectual climate it has largely lost these associations, however, and has taken on a more positive value for theoreticians such as Bhabha, who associate it with the notion of the "third space" which subverts the binary oppositions of racial and cultural difference. It is clearly in this light that the term is used here, to express the particular quality of the cultures of the Francophone Indian Ocean, and the value that they embody as an antidote to the binary oppositions of nationalist and colonialist cultures such as the French and the British. To what extent do the cultural productions of the region embody this notion of hybridity, and how do they contribute to the formulation of a "third space" not reducible to the cultural categories of the French or British colonial project? This will be a recurrent theme of the chapters that follow.

Linguistic competition in an increasingly Anglophone world

One of the most important colonial legacies of the region is undoubtedly the French language, and its use is institutionalized in the International Francophone Organisation. One of the principal aims of the association is of course the promotion of the use of French as an international language, and yet French is threatened by the international proliferation of English as a worldwide *lingua franca*. In the south west Indian Ocean area its status is secure, but that is not to say that it is the only language in use, or that its dominance is not challenged by other tongues.[52] The strongest linguistic rival on the world stage, English, is paradoxically less of a threat in the region, in spite of being an official language and the teaching language of educational institutions in the former British colonies of Mauritius and the Seychelles.[53] Even so French remains the dominant language of cultural expression, of the media and journalism in these two island states, although more so in Mauritius than the Seychelles. Both countries have produced a minority literary output in English —plays, novels, short stories, poetry—but French remains the privileged vehicle for such productions.

Creole is the effective *lingua franca* for all the populations of the Seychelles and Mauritius, and to a considerable extent among the native population of Reunion. There has been a considerable output of literary work in the Creole language, particularly since the adoption of the phonetic transcription of the language in 1977. It is predominantly an oral form of expression, however, and the literary works reflect this: most commonly plays and song lyrics. There have also been novels and poems published in all three islands, albeit for a limited readership. The official status of Creole is different in the three islands, however. In the Seychelles it is an official language, and the principal teaching language of the primary education sector. In Reunion, after many years when its use was officially discouraged, it has now been recognized as a regional language and can be studied and taught in schools and higher education: French remains even so the predominant partner in this situation of institutionalized diglossia. In Mauritius, Creole has only very recently been given a tentative official recognition, in spite of its predominant everyday use in oral communication, and does not yet figure in the primary and secondary education system. The Creoles of the islands are not the same, but are to some extent mutually comprehensible.

The other main rival to French in the region is the Malagasy language, which, as noted earlier, was first transcribed in the early nineteenth century and has developed a considerable literary culture since then. It is the effective *lingua franca* of by far the largest population group of the region, but the development of its written culture is hampered by the lack of resources of an impoverished economy and book publishing is rare, although the daily press makes considerable use of the language, and publishes poems and serialized fiction.[54] The Malagasy language was imposed as the teaching language of the education system during the revolutionary years of the mid 1970s and 1980s, but with inadequate resources, and education reverted to the use of French in the early 1990s with the change of political regime.[55]

In Mauritius there is also a substantial body of literary work written in Hindi, and published in India: the best-known name in this field is the novelist Abhimanyu Unnuth.[56] His work is increasingly being translated into French and this solution to the multilingual output of the region has been adopted elsewhere. Bilingual editions of texts in Creole or Malagasy, with translations into French, are becoming increasingly common, and represent a useful way of broadening the audience for writing in languages whose written forms are often limited in readership.[57]

French thus remains the dominant language of the region, but cannot be taken for granted as the only medium for cultural output, particularly for oral forms of expression such as theatre and popular music. The linguistic situation in these former French colonies is similar to that of other countries of the Francophone zone: French remains an official language and the dominant language for addressing an international audience, but local languages are also important vehicles of an alternative, regional identity.

A regional identity in a globalized world?

To what extent have the multifarious influences outlined here blended together into a recognisable regional culture? It is certainly the case that the islands each have very specific cultural characteristics and are clearly differentiated from each other, by their political regimes, by the particular ethnic and cultural mix of their populations, amongst many other factors. Yet these can be seen, with a degree of detachment, as different permutations of a certain number of shared elements, such as, for instance, the influence of the two former colonial powers in the domains of government, constitution and education; the proliferation of the Creole language; the variable presence of the major religious groupings; the importance of mission schools; the development of a literature in French; the evolution of distinctive styles of popular music and dance; of popular theatre in indigenous languages, etc. All these elements are shared by several of the island states, if not all of them.

There exist a certain number of embryonic regional institutions, such as the Conseil de l'Océan Indien and the Université de l'Océan Indien; they are useful liaison organisations, but seem to have little independent political and economic power in comparison to that of the national governments, and tend to be relegated to the role of talking shops. There is considerable mobility of the populations between the various island states, even when it is strictly controlled by the imposition of visas and residence permits: all the islands are host to considerable diasporic populations originating from the other islands, often living away from home on a permanent basis. There is also a certain undercurrent of xenophobia in relation to immigrants from other islands, often accompanied by popular stereotypes, such as the metropolitan (usually French) expatriate—*zorey, wazungu* or *vazaha*, depending on the local language (Creole, Mahorais, Malagasy, respectively)—or the "*Morisien*," the "*Malgas*," the "*Comorien*," exploited by Creole comedians and satirists for facile comic effect. Yet there are many instances of close co-operation between the islands, in the area of university collaboration, for instance, between the well-endowed Université de la Réunion and the struggling provincial universities of Madagascar, and in the area of medical services for disaster relief for the many cyclones that regularly devastate the region, between the Centre Hospitalier Universitaire of Saint-Denis and the Malagasy civil authorities. Air Mauritius and Air Seychelles have recently agreed to collaborate and code-share on their tourist flights to and from European destinations, and they both already work in close collaboration with the Reunion-based carrier Air Austral.

It is hard to guess what the future may bring for the region. Even though it is now ever more integrated into the global economy and participates increasingly in international cultural movements, thanks to the development of cheaper air travel, satellite telecommunications and the internet, it is still dependent on archaic economic factors such as the price it can obtain for its sugar and agricultural products such as vanilla, spices and perfume essences. The global village in any case doesn't often reach as far as the real village, especially when it is situated in the rural areas of Madagascar or the Comoros. The next few years may well be crucial for these fragile island economies, however buoyant some of them may seem at the moment, such as Mauritius and Reunion, and even more so for those which are struggling to service massive international debts, such as Madagascar, the Comoros and the Seychelles. The scarcity of energy resources and the effects of global warming could well have a drastic negative effect on the possibilities available to them for their future development.

Notes

1. See Auzias and Labourdette, *Mayotte Comores*, 38
2. See Joubert, *Littératures de l'Océan Indien*, 28.
3. See Auzias and Labourdette, *Mayotte Comores*, 39
4. See Dodd, *Réunion and Seychelles*, 46.
5. See Joubert, *Littératures de l'Océan* Indien, 98; Dodd, *Réunion and Seychelles*, 46.
6. See Dodd, *Réunion and Seychelles*, 24, 47, 150.
7. See Dodd, *Réunion and Seychelles*, 46.
8. See Dodd *Réunion and Seychelles*, 154; Chane-Kune, *Aux Origines de l'identité réunionnaise*, 18-19. For a fictional re-constitution of the experiences of some of the earliest inhabitants of Reunion, see Daniel Vaxelaire, *Vingt-et-un jours d'histoire. Ile de La Réunion* (Saint-Denis: Azalées, 1992), 29-34.
9. See Vaxelaire, *Vingt-et-un jours d'histoire*, 35-40; Chane-Kune, *Aux Origines de l'identité réunionnaise*, 20-21.

10. See Joubert, *Littératures de l'Océan Indien*, 97; Dodd (2004), 46.
11. See Lyn Mair and Lynnath Beckley, *Seychelles* (Chalfont St. Peter, UK: Bradt, 2001), 9-10.
12. See Scarr, *Seychelles since 1770*, 5.
13. See Scarr, *Seychelles since 1770*, 7-8.
14. See Mair and Beckley, *Seychelles*, 13.
15. See Mair and Beckley, *Seychelles*, 131; Scarr, *Seychelles since 1770*, 75, 83-84.
16. See Bradt, *Guide to Madagascar*, 10; Joubert, *Littératures de l'Océan Indien*, 15.
17. See Joubert, *Littératures de l'Océan Indien*, 15.
18. See Joubert, *Littératures de l'Océan Indien*, 16.
19. See Swaney and Willox *Madagascar and Comoros*, 50.
20. See Swaney and Willox *Madagascar and Comoros*, 50.
21 See the later chapters of Daniel Vaxelaire, *Les Mutins de la liberté* (Paris: Lieu Commun, 1986) and my own article: Peter Hawkins, "*Libertalia*: le métissage utopique de Daniel Vaxelaire" in *L'Océan Indien dans les littératures francophones*, ed. Kumari R. Issur, and Vinesh Y. Hookoomsing (Paris and Mauritius: Karthala / Presses de l'Université de Maurice, 2001), 455-462.
22. See Bradt, *Guide to Madagascar* (1997), 10 and Swaney and Willox, *Madagascar and Comoros*, 50.
23. See Swaney and Willox, *Madagascar and Comoros*, 294.
24. See Guy Lionnet, *Par les Chemins de la mer* (Saint-Denis: Université de la Réunion, 2000), 31-34.
25. See Vaxelaire *Les Mutins de la liberté*, *Vingt-et-un jours d'histoire*, 49-53 and *Supplique pour ne pas être pendu avec les autres pirates* (Saint-Denis de la Réunion: Orphie, 2003); and Bibique, *Sur la piste des frères de la côte* (Saint-Denis: Editions de La Réunion insolite, 1984).
26. See Swaney and Willox, *Madagascar and Comoros*, 47-50.
27. See Swaney and Willox, *Madagascar and Comoros*, 294.
28. See Vaxelaire, *Vingt-et-un jours d'histoire*, 74.
29. See Chane-Kune, *Aux Origines de l'identité réunionnaise*, 93-94.
30. See Chane-Kune, *Aux Origines de l'identité réunionnaise*, 96.
31. See Swaney and Willox, *Madagascar and Comoros*, 51.
32. See Dodd, *Réunion and Seychelles*, 47.
33. See Combeau et al. *Histoire de La Réunion*, 77-82.
34. See Joubert, *Littératures de l'Océan Indien*, 250-55.
35. See Chane-Kune, *Aux Origines de l'identité réunionnaise*, 118-21.

36. See Jean-Pierre La Selve, *Musiques traditionnelles de La Réunion*, second edition, (Saint-Denis: Azalées, 1995).
37. See Dodd, *Réunion and Seychelles*, 52.
38. See Dodd, *Réunion and Seychelles*, 152, 244.
39. See, for instance, Dodd, *Réunion and Seychelles*, 49-51.
40. See Chane-Kune, *Aux Origines de l'identité réunionnaise*, 163-74; Combeau et al., *Histoire de La Réunion*, 77-90; and Dodd, *Réunion and Seychelles*, 47.
41. See Swaney and Willox, *Madagascar and Comoros*, 51-52; Bradt, *Guide to Madagascar*, 10-11.
42. See Joubert, *Littératures de l'Océan Indien*, 18.
43. See Swaney and Willox, *Madagascar and Comoros*, 83.
44. See Swaney and Willox, *Madagascar and Comoros*, 53.
45. See Swaney and Willox, *Madagascar and Comoros*, 54-56.
46. See Combeau et al., *Histoire de La Réunion*, 147-9.
47. See Auzias and Labourdette, *Mayotte Comores*, 55-59.
48. See Mair and Beckley, *Seychelles*, 16; Dodd, *Réunion and Seychelles*, 241-42.
49. For similar observations, see Dodd, *Réunion and Seychelles*, 24-25.
50. See Homi K. Bhabha, *The location of culture* (London and New York: Routledge, 1994), further elucidated in chapter 3, "Hybridity and cultural difference," and illustrated in subsequent chapters.
51. See Léopold Sedar Senghor, "De la liberté de l'âme ou éloge du métissage," in *Liberté 1. Négritude et Humanisme* (Paris: Seuil, 1964), 102-3.
52. See Joubert, *Littératures de l'Océan Indien*, 9-10.
53. See Dodd, *Réunion and Seychelles*, 49, 242.
54. See Joubert, *Littératures de l'Océan Indien*, 28-32.
55. See Swaney and Willox, *Madagascar and Comoros*, 75. More recently, with the arrival in power of Marc Ravalomanana in 2002 and particularly since his re-election in 2007, English has grown in influence and is now an official language of the Malagasy Republic. It remains to be seen, however, what effect this may have on the education system of Madagascar.
56. See chapter 5, "The influence of Hindu culture" and General Bibliography.
57. See, for example Unnuth, *Les Empereurs de la nuit*, *Le Culte du sol* and *Sueurs de sang*; Bourgeacq and Ramarasoa, *Voices from Madagascar*; Nirina, *Mirolana an-tsoatra / Dire par écrit / Le dire par écrit* and Marimoutou, *Romans pou la tèr ek la mèr*. All these texts are either translations from Hindi into French, as in the novels of Unnuth, or

multi-lingual editions, as in *Voices from Madagascar*, in English, French and Malagasy, or Marimoutou's collection of poems in both Creole and French.

Chapter 3

Critical Strategies

The logic of the postcolonial turn

Following on from earlier introductory surveys of the characteristics of the Indian Ocean islands and the burden of their colonial past, the question arises as to the most appropriate tools for the analysis of their recent cultural production. The last decade has seen the proliferation of postcolonial theory, initially mostly concerned with the Anglophone cultures of the former British Empire and Commonwealth. Increasingly, this theorizing has incorporated Francophone writers such as Frantz Fanon[1] and Edouard Glissant[2] as well as recognizing a debt to the French post-structuralist thought of Derrida, Lacan, Foucault, Deleuze and Guattari, etc.[3] It is inevitable that this body of thought will have a direct and immediate relevance to our discussions, even if in French academic circles there has been a considerable resistance to its adoption.[4] Even so it is a daunting prospect, such is the complexity and diversity of the various positions and approaches so far developed, and the corresponding complexity and diversity of the subject matter to which they might be applied. It becomes necessary to outline a general strategy and to make some choices as to what might be most appropriate among the multifarious approaches on offer, so as best to illuminate the implications of a body of writing so far little explored. One of the commonest observations about the enterprise of postcolonial theory has been to highlight its reflexiveness, not to say its self-absorption[5]: some of its own practitioners have even taxed it with accusations of unavowed imperialist designs, emanating as it does from the bastions of the

Western academic establishment, and under suspicion of appropriating the right of non-Western peoples to their own voice and their own self-definition.[6] This study cannot be assumed to be exempt from such criticisms and must attempt to forestall them while at the same time drawing on the richness of insight potentially provided by such reflections. In general, it has to be said, the postcolonial critical enterprise has so far been more marked by its self-referentiality than by its fruitful application to the analysis of literary texts. This is perhaps an opportunity to redress that balance, since we are dealing here with a body of literary and analogous production which, to adopt an all too revealing metaphor, is almost a virgin territory for literary criticism. Precious little has so far been written, in effect, about the literary output of the Francophone Indian Ocean, even in French,[7] and even less in English.

This marginality itself illustrates a recurrent theme in postcolonial criticism: the binary opposition of centre and periphery, as illustrated by the title of one of the movement's pioneering texts, *The Empire writes back*.[8] We are dealing here with one of the peripheral zones of what was once the French colonial empire, and not one that has attracted a lot of critical attention. As mentioned earlier, the much smaller area of the Francophone Caribbean has received a much wider coverage. Why should this particular zone command a renewed interest? The principal reason lies in its remarkable ethnic and cultural diversity, proportionately much greater and arguably better integrated than that of its former colonial centre, mainland France, which has been experiencing some difficulties in accommodating the much lower level of disparity in the ethnicities and cultures of its population. Needless to say, it cannot be taken for granted that the secret of the region's relatively harmonious postcolonial development will be reflected in its literary output, but it does at least provide an incentive for a renewal of interest in relation to the former colonial centre, France and indeed, the much larger postcolonial axis of Britain and North America.

A further illustration of the appropriateness of the postcolonial approach lies in the obvious relevance of many of the recurrent themes of the movement. The importance attached to the conception of hybridity by writers such as Homi K. Bhabha[9] is clearly exemplified by all the societies of the region, and is a perennial element in their quest for a sense of cultural identity. Bhabha's analysis of cultural difference is also pertinent here, as is his foregrounding of the subversive effects of mimicry.[10] The notion of the subaltern, first developed by Indian social historians[11] and further elaborated by Gayatri Chakravorty Spivak,[12] is not surprisingly applicable to a region which has experienced slavery and a massive importation of indentured labour from the Indian sub-continent. Attendant themes such as the importance of diaspora and migration correspond to the foundational experiences of most of the islands, and form an essential element in their imaginative heritage. The analysis of discursive constructs of otherness, as elaborated by Edward Said,[13] are clearly relevant to the cultures of the region, as are the warnings of critics such as Robert Young[14] concerning the ownership and legitimacy of the discourse currently being formulated here. Finally, the idea of "Relation," of relatedness, as formulated by Edouard Glissant,[15] will briefly be situated in the Indian Ocean context, and in contrast with its Caribbean origins All these themes will now be addressed in more detail and will recur intermittently in subsequent chapters, according to their particular relevance.

Hybridity and cultural difference

The relevance of Homi Bhabha's notion of hybridity[16] has already been highlighted in the previous chapter. It is almost a commonplace to use it when describing the cultures of the Indian Ocean islands, particularly in its Francophone formulation as *métissage*. The population of islands such as Reunion or the Seychelles have been of mixed-race origins from their very beginnings, and the other islands also, but to a lesser degree and in less obvious ways. The metaphorical use of the term to refer to the textuality of literary discourse, as Bhabha does, is less easy to explain in the Indian Ocean context and needs to be situated in relation to its linguistic and philosophical context as a product of the notion of cultural difference. The notion of difference is one of the cornerstones of Saussure's linguistics and has been given a particular resonance by Derrida's critique in *De la Grammatologie*, which transposes the terms of the debate from the spoken language to the written one. It is this which no doubt inspired Bhabha's interpretation of the term when applied to postcolonial discursive formations which highlight the notion of cultural difference. The tension between different cultural formations gives rise to Bhabha's conception of hybridity as an indeterminate and deferred "third space" of unresolved contradiction. For Bhabha this hybrid effect of textual discourse is a defining feature of postcolonial writing, and it can be identified in many of the texts we shall be referring to. For Bhabha it is a positive feature of a cultural production which is able to go beyond the binary oppositions implicit in the colonial situation: master/slave; coloniser/colonised; dominant /subordinate; centre/periphery, etc. Much of the writing of the Indian Ocean region exhibits such a paradoxical notion of hybridity in one or more aspects of its formulation, and it can be a useful criterion for the identification of postcolonial writing as against the more manichean characteristics of colonial literature.

Subversive mimicry

In a similar way, Bhabha sees mimicry as a feature of colonial domination, as manifested in the imitation of aspects of the colonial culture by subject peoples.[17] This characteristic of the binary opposition between coloniser and colonised is similarly subverted by a process of cultural misappropriation on the part of the colonised. The process of imitation then becomes a discreet form of subversion of the cultural patterns of colonial authority, a space in which the colonised peoples can assert their right to self-determination. It is not difficult to illustrate this process through numerous examples: even the development of pidgin versions of colonial languages such as English and French can be seen as examples of the process, leading eventually to the creation of an alternative language such as Creole. A similar process can be seen at work in the adoption of literary forms that originated in the colonizer's culture and find themselves appropriated and adapted for other ends in the postcolonial sphere. The concept is thus a useful one to understand the complex interactions of the colonial culture and that of the colonised peoples, and has relevance to a number of specific examples drawn from the Indian Ocean region.

Subaltern status

The notion of the subaltern was originally adopted by the group of Indian historians calling themselves the Subaltern Studies Group, concentrating on the social history of the lower caste sectors of Indian society.[18] The notion was further refined and explored in the celebrated article by Gayatri Chakravorty Spivak entitled "Can the subaltern speak?"[19] The implications of this pointed question opened up a debate, again inspired by the theorizing of Jacques Derrida, about the access of disenfranchised groups to a discourse, whether colonial or anti-colonial, which systematically excludes them. Spivak's intervention also brought to prominence the sexual politics of the issue, which identified women as doubly disenfranchised by their class status and their gender. Her question called into doubt the very possibility of self-expression for groups colonized and exploited, not only because of their lowly social standing but also because of their sex. The notion of the subaltern, with all its postcolonial connotations, is a useful one in dealing with a literature which, as has been noted elsewhere, is that of an intellectual elite, and particularly when it attempts to give voice to the aspirations of the less privileged sectors of society. As we have observed in other contexts, this is a region where the inequalities of access to the conditions of self-expression are as dramatic as anywhere on the planet.

Otherness and the ownership of discourse

The notion of "otherness" or alterity is already built in to the title of this study, as is the notion of hybridity. This notion was central to one of the foundational texts of postcolonial criticism, Edward Said's *Orientalism*,[20] which set out to analyse the construction of the notion of the "Orient" as the "other" to Western civilisation and created as a concept through the Western artistic and intellectual discourse of orientalism. The idea of discursive "otherness" is one that we cannot afford to ignore, as it is a necessary feature of any study such as this which attempts to identify a body of knowledge hitherto unexplored and to analyse it from a Western academic perspective. As Said himself came to realise, it is impossible to escape the implications of one's institutional base as a researcher working in the Western academy, in a university of a former colonial power.[21] Inevitably, any attempt to formulate an idea of "Indianoceanity," for instance, runs the risk of becoming another Orientalism. The only safeguards are the self-awareness generated by a familiarity with postcolonial theory, not exempt, as we have suggested, from similar accusations; and an attempt to adopt a perspective sanctioned at least in part by those more closely implicated in the field. As it happens, this latter situation is already the case: the idea of the latent unity of the Indian Ocean cultures already has a history, having been developed and propagated by such diverse figures as Camille de Rauville,[22] Jean-Georges Prosper[23] and Jean-Claude Carpanin Marimoutou,[24] all respected intellectuals and literary critics originating from the region.

A-temporal postcoloniality

This question arises from a distinction propagated by the trio Ashcroft, Griffiths and Tiffin, responsible for a series of pioneering publications in the field of postcolonial studies: *The Empire writes back*, *The post-colonial studies reader* and *Key concepts in postcolonial studies*. In the preface to the first of these they propose that the term "post-colonial" need not refer exclusively to writings and situations arising after independence from colonial rule.[25] They argue that it would be appropriately used in relation to cultural manifestations occurring during the colonial period proper, if they represent a reaction or a resistance to the imposition of colonial rule. This led in turn to a rather hair-splitting debate about the status of the hyphen in the term "post-colonial," which concluded that this form should be reserved for situations occurring after independence, whereas the composite form "postcolonial" might be more appropriate refer to earlier situations during the period of colonial rule, or to more a-temporal discourses of colonialism.[26] Our practice here, for the sake of clarity, has been to maintain the composite form "postcolonial," and to use "post-independence" for the strictly chronological usage. The main reason for this is that we shall go on to cover several texts emanating from the colonial period proper which merit consideration under the label "postcolonial", according to the interpretation of Ashcroft et al. A further reason is that it is debatable whether one could use the label "post-colonial" in its temporal sense in relation to Reunion island, which remains a French-administered territory even if it is technically no longer a colony. This paradox will be explored further at the beginning of chapter 6 covering Reunion.

Migration and Diaspora

Although these notions are borrowed from sociology rather than from the writings of postcolonial critics, they are nevertheless important concepts in relation to the literatures that concern us here.[27] All the postcolonial theorists we have so far mentioned (Said, Bhabha, Spivak) have been living displaced from their cultures of origin and work in American universities; many of the writers we shall be studying are similarly expatriates. Migration and diaspora represent the foundational experiences of most of the islands we shall be discussing, several of which were populated very recently as a result of enforced or voluntary migrations (Mauritius, Reunion and the Seychelles) and others still bearing in their cultures the diasporic traces of older migrations (Madagascar and the Comoros). These motifs recur regularly in the literatures of the islands, and even if they do not carry with them the same theoretical baggage as notions such as hybridity, they represent essential terms of reference for the discussions that follow.

"Relation" and relatedness

The Martinican novelist, poet and essayist Edouard Glissant has been only relatively recently inducted into the canon of postcolonial theorists, more perhaps for his essays than for his fiction and poetry. All three are complementary, however, and his theorizing remains very literary and poetic in inspiration. His formulation of "Caribbean-ness" or *antillanité* in his earlier texts such as *Le Discours antillais* [28] has given way in his more recent writing to the notion of *Relation* or relatedness, which takes on a global dimension as part of the *Tout-monde*,[29] of world-consciousness. The significance of this is that, given the durability of the assimilation of the author's island home of Martinique into the French Republic as a *Département d'Outre-Mer*, it becomes difficult to construct an alternative Caribbean identity for the Martinican writer, which manifestly has no immediate prospect of political or institutional fulfilment. This situation has obvious critical parallels with our own postulate of a latent Indian Ocean identity, as well as questioning such a definition of the archipelago in relation to worldwide movements of capital, labor and intellectual exchange. The difference, however, is that four of the five political units covered here have been independent for over a quarter of a century, as against only one out of the four in the Francophone Caribbean: the embattled Republic of Haïti. However wilfully opaque and poetic Glissant's formulations may be, it is clear that for him aspiration to cultural recognition and validation is now to be fulfilled on a global stage, and it will be necessary to bear this in mind when making claims for a marginalized literary field such as the one we are addressing. *Relation* and relatedness are to be achieved internationally rather than within the confines of a particular postcolonial culture, and this is a lesson to be borne in mind when considering the output of what some critics already consider to be a *littérature mineure*,[30] a "minor" literature. Glissant's concept of *Tout-monde*, however, appears effectively to efface distinctions of dominance and exploitation at an economic and social level, in a way which has often been criticized in postcolonial theorising, and which remain relevant in this domain.

The indispensable socio-political context

Some of the criticisms of postcolonial theory formulated by Marxist critics such as Arif Dirlik[31] and Benita Parry[32] also find an echo in this context. As has often been pointed out, a postcolonial theory that remains detached from the socio-political realities of the societies created in the wake of colonialism can scarcely remain credible, and this appears as a concern here. It will be necessary to situate the literary productions and their parallel forms of expression in the very specific context of the societies that produced them, simply because of the often highly contrasted situations that governed their elaboration, their diffusion and their reception. This should be obvious from the attention already paid to these matters in the preceding two chapters. This initial scene setting will be further pursued and refined in the opening section of each subsequent chapter.

A problem arises, however, in terms of methodology and approach, which has not been satisfactorily addressed by the proliferation of postcolonial theory, in spite of its insistence on the all-pervasiveness of colonial ideology. The approach to the literary text has all too often been discursive and textual, at the expense of a more comprehensive attempt to situate it in its social and political context. This probably arises because of the pervasive influence of

French post-structuralism, but it remains a distinct disadvantage in relation to the specific realities of the texts we propose to analyse here. It has to be admitted, however, that very few current approaches have proved capable of articulating the literary text and its socio-political context in general and theoretical terms with any degree of subtlety, so as to avoid the reductive over-simplification of crude Marxist approaches and the vague and impressionistic juxtapositions of traditional literary history. One of the least unsatisfactory attempts has been that of Pierre Bourdieu, in works such as *Les Règles de l'art*,[33] and even this has been far from achieving universal endorsement. It is nevertheless his notion of the "field of cultural production" that I propose to adapt to this context, as a means of situating a work in the context of the national or territorial culture in which it first emerged and has subsequently been interpreted and evaluated. One of the problems with this approach in the context of Francophone literatures is that works and their authors may typically be situated in more than one field: that of the national literature of the country of origin of the author; that of Francophone writing as a whole; and that of French national literature when, as is very often the case, the work has been published in France.[34] The increasing globalization of culture may even add a further literary field, which is that of world literature, in the case of works that are translated and go on to achieve international recognition. The difficulty here is that, given the relative autonomy of the field of literary production from the field of socio-economic and political power, as theorized by Bourdieu, this already elusive relationship is further complicated by the relations between the various other literary fields already mentioned. The approach does nevertheless offer a coherent way of conceptualizing these relationships, going some way to answering the objections of critics such as Dirlik and Parry. It would indeed be ironic if the practice of postcolonial criticism were to ignore relations of political and socio-economic power when, as has often been observed, the broader economic context of recent globalization is accompanied by the most extreme disparity in standards of living across the planet. This disparity is present and perceptible among the islands of the Francophone Indian Ocean, as between the level of development of, for instance, rural Madagascar and urban Reunion. Such observations give an added poignancy to the postcolonial analysis of a literature that remains, in the last instance, the product and the province of an intellectual élite in most of the islands we are concerned with, as well as in metropolitan France, where many of their writers now reside.

Literary history

A variety of approaches have been adopted by earlier critical commentators on the Francophone Literatures of the Indian Ocean, many of them French and working in the Université de la Réunion, others based in the University of Mauritius and the various universities of Madagascar. The traditional one is that of a broad literary history of the region, and the most comprehensive and satisfying example is the work of a metropolitan Frenchman based in Paris: *Littératures de l'Océan indien* by Jean-Louis Joubert, published in 1991. For all its thoroughness—it remains a mine of useful information—it is now fifteen years old and many more recent developments could not be covered. A similar approach of providing basic bibliographical and literary history has been adopted by the journal *Notre Librairie*, notably in its very useful special issues on Mauritian and Malagasy literatures: these were also under the general editorship of Jean-Louis Joubert, although the vast majority of articles were written by locally-based academic specialists.[35] There are forthcoming projects of a literary history of Reunion by Norbert Dodille, and there have already been many histories and anthologies of aspects of Reunionese writing: on poetry, on local folktales, on literature in Creole.[36] The Mauritian poet Jean-Georges Prosper has also published an invaluable and comprehensive literary history of Francophone writing in Mauritius, supplemented in its second edition by an appendix covering writing in other languages such as Creole, Hindi and English.[37] Vicram Ramharai, from the Mauritius Institute of Education, has published a socio-cultural study of writing in Creole from Mauritius.[38] Liliane Ramarasoa has also published two anthologies covering recent Francophone writing from Madagascar, one of them bilingual.[39] Two major conferences at the University of Mauritius in 1997 and 2002, under the direction of Kumari Issur and Vinesh Hookoomsing, brought together many of these figures, and the first collection of these varied and disparate studies has been published,[40] while the second is in press as I write.[41] The present study will inevitably serve as a literary history of postcolonial writing in the region, but the intention is not to be comprehensive in coverage in the way that would suggest: rather it is to explore the relevance of postcolonial themes in this body of writing. This will imply making a selection from the total production of the region, in the light of the significance of particular works in relation to the themes outlined earlier. If certain works have been omitted it is because it seemed that they were not pertinent to this discussion; others have been considered even so, if their relevance seemed at least debatable. It would in any case be rash to attempt a comprehensive coverage of the region's recent literary output in a volume such as this.

Linguistic approaches and diglossia

A considerable body of work has been devoted to the analysis of Reunionese literature by the French CNRS research group at the Université de la Réunion, currently called LCF—"Laboratoire de recherche: langues, textes et communications dans les espaces créolophones et francophones."[42] This has most often approached the literature through the study of its linguistic usage, privileging as a result its linguistic particularities, ranging from regional variations of standard French to the increasing literary use of Creole. The situation of diglossia, the unequal authority attributed to two languages both current in a given social situation, has been adapted by Carpanin Marimoutou to apply to what he calls "literary diglossia," in a situation where Creole writers have been attempting to establish the legitimacy of their language as a vehicle for literary expression.[43] These studies are usually limited to the literature of Reunion island, and do not often cover writing from the other Creole-speaking islands of Mauritius and the Seychelles. The approach has not yet been applied either, to my knowledge, to the situation of literary diglossia in Madagascar, in relation to the rivalry of Malagasy and French as a literary medium. The studies of Reunionese writing inevitably focus on the literature in Creole, and will be referred to in the later chapter on Reunion.

Ethnographic studies

This approach is an appropriate one for literary texts whose form or subject-matter explicitly refers to the culture of a particular ethnic group or society. It has been used by Carpanin Marimoutou as part of a multiple approach to the Reunionese novel, complemented by the more linguistic approaches outlined above.[44] It has also been effectively applied by Valérie Magdelaine-Andrianjafitrimo to analyse the novels of the Mauritian writer Ananda Devi, several of which explicitly draw on Hindu mythology, as well as the family autobiographical novel *Boadour* by the Reunionese author Firmin Lacpatia.[45] These novels are identified as "ethnofictions," a category which could equally well be fruitfully applied to numerous fictional texts emanating from Madagascar, such as *Le Bain des Reliques* by Michele Rakotoson[46] or *Le Pétale écarlate* by Charlotte-Arrisoa Rafenomanjato.[47] Even if it is beyond the scope of this particular study, this would appear to be a fruitful line of enquiry for a large number of texts by Indian Ocean writers.

Psycho-imaginative approaches

In a major study of Reunionese literature, particularly focusing on the prolific poetry of the island, Michel Beniamino has practised what he call the "mythocritique" of this body of writing.[48] This approach attempts to explore the "imaginary of the island" through the recurrent motifs and themes of the poetic literature, which are analysed in terms of the typology established by the critic Gaston Bachelard. The methodology draws on the psychoanalysis of Jung and his notion of the archetype, to establish the way the poetry of the island appeals to certain prevalent myths associated with the island's culture. A similar approach might well be adopted in relation to the poetry of the neighbouring island of Mauritius, equally rich in mythical and imaginative content.

Thematic and comparative approaches

A pioneer in the coverage of the region's literature in the Anglophone context of North America is Françoise Lionnet, with her two works *Autobiographical Voices* and *Postcolonial Representations*. These illustrate a broad comparative sweep, covering a wide range of disparate literary texts from a variety of contexts, in the light of a particular theme: in the first case, that of self-definition through autobiographical writing; and in the second, the position of women's writing in the postcolonial context. Both these studies include incisive chapters on Mauritian women writers: Marie-Thérèse Humbert's *A l'autre bout de moi* in the first[49] and Ananda Devi's *Rue La Poudrière* in the second.[50] These are usefully related to the major themes of postcolonial and post-structuralist thought, such as *métissage*.

Cultural studies

The work of Françoise Vergès, particularly in her study *Monsters and Revolutionaries*, also explores the implications of the notion of *métissage* and the complexity of the postcolonial situation of her native island of Reunion.[51] Although this wide-ranging and very personal study draws occasionally on literary examples, such as Boris Gamaleya or Louis-Timagène Houat, the main thrust of her analysis is socio-political rather than literary, and as such does not really constitute a critical model that might be imitated in this context.

Critical aims and objectives

To recapitulate some of the points made in the Introduction, the principal aim of this study is to provide an introductory overview of the literary and cultural production of the Francophone Indian Ocean region, and in doing so to fill a gap in the English-language coverage of the area. Given the wider interest in postcolonial material currently in evidence, it seems appropriate to use that body of theorizing to provide a coherent framework in which to situate the literary and other material we shall be presenting, which should, in its turn stimulate comparison with other areas already better-documented and studied, such as the Francophone Caribbean. The intention is furthermore to suggest an alternative reading of the literature of the region to the limited body of analysis already published in French, mostly emanating from the Université de la Réunion and the University of Mauritius Even when this analysis is available in published form, as *Un état des savoirs à La Réunion,*[52] or *L'Océan Indien dans les littératures francophones*,[53] it is not widely accessible and well-known to the wider international community of Francophone studies. This work has in any case been completed over a number of years and much of it was developed in the years prior to the emergence of postcolonial theory. This study is not intended to replace such previous work—such an aim would be preposterous—but rather to draw on it, to make it better known and to provide a complementary perspective to it.

Notes

1. See Homi K. Bhabha, *The location of culture* (London and New York: Routledge, 1994), 40-65.
2. See Peter Hallward, *Absolutely postcolonial* (Manchester and New York: Manchester University Press, 2001), 66-125.
3. See Charles Forsdick and David Murphy, eds., "The Case for Francophone Postcolonial Studies" in *Francophone postcolonial studies* (London: Arnold, 2003), 6-9.
4. See Forsdick, Murphy, *Francophone postcolonial studies*, 9-10.
5. See Stephen Slemon, "The Scramble for Post-colonialism" in Chris Tiffin and Alan Lawson, eds., *De-scribing empire: post-colonialism and textuality* (London and New York: Routledge, 1994); reproduced in Ashcroft, Griffiths, Tiffin, eds., *The post-colonial studies reader* (London and New York: Routledge, 1995), 50-51.
6. See, amongst others, Stephen Slemon, "The Scramble for Post-colonialism" in Ashcroft et al., *The post-colonial studies reader*, 45-52; Edward Said, "Orientalism," 87-92; Gareth Griffths, "The myth of authenticity," 237-41; and Linda Tuhiwai Smith "Imperialism, history, writing and theory" in Gaurav Desai and Supriya Nair, eds., *Postcolonialisms* (Oxford: Berg, 2005), 94-115.
7. For a brief review of critical writing in French, see the later sections of this chapter.
8. Bill Ashcroft, Gareth Griffiths and Helen Tiffin, *The Empire writes back: theory and practice in post-colonial literatures* (London and New York: Routledge, 1989).
9. See Bhabha, *The location of culture*, 223-9.
10. See Bhabha, "Of mimicry and man: the ambivalence of colonial discourse," *The location of culture*, 85-92.
11. See Ranajit Guha, ed., *Subaltern studies I and II: writings on South Asian history and society* (Delhi: Oxford University Press, 1982/1983).

12. See Gayatri Chakravorty Spivak, "Can the Subaltern speak" in Cary Nelson and Lawrence Grossberg, eds., *Marxism and the interpretation of culture* (London: Macmillan, 1988); reproduced in Ashcroft et al., *The post-colonial studies reader*, 24-28.

13. See, for instance Edward W. Said, (1978) "Introduction to *Orientalism*" in Gaurav Desai and Supriya Nair, eds., *Postcolonialisms* (Oxford: Berg, 2005), 71-93.

14. See Robert Young, *White mythologies: writing, history and the West* (London and New York: Routledge, 1990).

15. See Edouard Glissant, *Poétique de la Relation* (Paris: Gallimard, 1990).

16. See Bhabha, *The location of culture*, 34-39, quoted in Ashcroft et al., *The post-colonial studies reader*, 206-9. See also Ashcroft et al., "Hybridity," *Key concepts in postcolonial studies* (London and New York: Routledge, 1998), 118-21. For a recent, full-length study of its implications in the Indian Ocean context, see also Prabhu, Anjali. *Hybridity: limits, transformations, prospects.* Albany: State University of New York Press, 2007.

17. See Bhabha "Of mimicry and man. . . ," *The location of culture* 85-92.

18. See Guha, *Subaltern studies.*

19. See Spivak, "Can the Subaltern speak."

20. Edward W. Said, *Orientalism* (New York: Random House, 1978).

21. See Edward W. Said, "Introduction" and chapter 4, "Challenging orthodoxy and authority," in *Culture and imperialism* (London: Chatto and Windus, 1993).

22. See Joubert, *Littératures de l'Océan Indien*, 144, 160; and De Rauville, Camille, *Littératures Francophones de l'Océan Indien* (Saint-Denis: Editions du Tramail, 1990).

23. See Jean-Georges Prosper, *La Créolie indianocániste* (Vacoas, Mauritius: Editions Le Printemps, 1996)

24 See Carpanin Marimoutou and Françoise Vergès, *Amarres: créolisations india-océanes* (Paris: l'Harmattan, 2005).

25. Ashcroft, Griffiths, Tiffin, *The Empire writes back*, 1-2.

26. See Bill Ashcroft, Gareth Griffiths and Helen Tiffin, "post-colonialism/postcolonialism" in *Key concepts in post-colonial studies*, 186-92.

27. See Ashcroft et al., "diaspora," *Key concepts*, 68-70.

28. Edouard Glissant, *Le Discours antillais* (Paris: Seuil, 1987, reprinted Paris: Gallimard).

29. Edouard Glissant, *Tout-monde.* (Paris: Gallimard, 1993); and *Traité du Tout-monde* (Paris: Gallimard, 1997)

30. See Carpanin Marimoutou, quoted in Valérie Magdelaine-Andrianjafitrimo and Carpanin Marimoutou, eds., *Un état des savoirs à la Réunion. Tome II: Littératures* (Saint-Denis: LCF-UMR 8143 CNRS / Université de la Réunion, 2004), 91.

31. See Arif Dirlik, "The postcolonial aura: Third World criticism in the age of global capitalism," *Critical Enquiry,* 20 (Winter 1994), 328-56; reproduced in Desai and Nair, eds., *Postcolonialisms,* 561-88.

32. Benita Parry, "Problems in current theories of colonial discourse," *Oxford Literary Review,* 9 (1987); quoted in Ashcroft et al., *The postcolonial studies reader,* 36-44.

33. Pierre Bourdieu, *Les Règles de l'art: genèse et structure du champ littéraire* (Paris: Seuil, 1992).

34. For a further discussion of this problem, see Peter Hawkins, "*Homo authénegrafricanitus?* Applying Bourdieu to Francophone African Literature," *ASCALF Yearbook,* No. 2 (1997), 28-35.

35. Siméon Rajaona, ed., *Madagascar. 1. La literature d'expression malgache* in *Notre Librairie,* 109, (1992); *Madagascar. 2. La literature d'expression française* in *Notre Librairie,* 110 (1992). Monique Hugon and Jean-Louis Joubert, eds., "Littérature mauricienne," in *Notre Librairie,* 114, (1993).

36. Many of these are summarized in Magdelaine, Marimoutou, eds., *Un état des savoirs à la Réunion.*

37. Jean-Georges Prosper, *Histoire de la littérature mauricienne d'expression française* (Paris and Mauritius: Nathan / Editions de l'Océan Indien, 1978). New edition: Rose Hill, Mauritius: Editions de l'Océan Indien, 1994.

38. Vicram Ramharai, *La Littérature mauricienne d'expression créole. Essai d'analyse socio-culturelle* (Port Louis: Editions Les Mascareignes, 1990).

39. Liliane Ramarasoa, ed., *Anthologie de la literature malgache d'expression française des années 80* (Paris: L'Harmattan, 1994); and Jacques Bourgeacq and Liliane Ramarasoa, eds., *Voices from Madagascar/Voix de Madagascar* (Athens: Ohio University Press. 2002).

40. Kumari R. Issur and Vinesh Y. Hookoomsing, eds., *L'Océan Indien dans les littératures francophones* (Paris and Mauritius: Karthala / Presses de l'Université de Maurice, 2001)

41. Kumari R. Issur and Vinesh Y. Hookoomsing, *Les Discours francophones sur l'Océan indien* (Paris and Mauritius: L'Harmattan / Presses de l'Université de Maurice, forthcoming in 2007).

42. See Magdelaine, Marimoutou, eds., *Un état des savoirs à la Réunion*.

43. Carpanin Marimoutou, "Le Roman réunionnais, une problématique du Même et de l'Autre. Essai sur la poétique du texte romanesque en situation de diglossie" (1990), in Magdelaine, Marimoutou, eds., *Un état des savoirs à la Réunion*, 121-38 (summary of doctoral thesis).

44. See Valérie Magdelaine-Andrianjafitrimo and Carpanin Marimoutou, eds., *Contes et romans: univers créoles 4* (Paris: Anthropos, 2004), sections VI-VIII.

45. Valérie Magdelaine-Andrianjafitrimo, " 'Ethnotexte' et intertextualité: la mise en scène des représentations culturelles dans les 'romans ethnographiques'," in Magdelaine and Marimoutou, eds., *Contes et romans: univers créoles 4*, V, 93-145.

46. Michèle Rakotoson, *Le Bain des reliques* (Paris: Karthala, 1988).

47. Charlotte-Arrisoa Rafenomanjato, *Le Pétale écarlate* (Antananarivo: Société malgache d'édition, 1990). Republished as *Felana* (2007).

48. Michel Beniamino, *L'Imaginaire réunionnais. Recherches sur les déterminations constitutives du rapport entre le sujet et l'île* (Saint-Denis, Editions du Tramail, 1992); summarized in Magdelaine, Marimoutou, eds., *Un état des savoirs à la Réunion*, 27-33.

49. Françoise Lionnet, "Anamnesis and utopia: self-portrait of the web-maker in *A l'autre bout de moi*," in *Autobiographical voices: race, gender, self-portraiture* (Ithaca, NY: Cornell University Press, 1989), 216-44.

50. Françoise Lionnet, "Evading the subject: narration and the city in Ananda Devi's *Rue La Poudrière*," in *Postcolonial representations: women, literature, identity* (Ithaca, NY: Cornell University Press, 1995), 48-68.

51. Françoise Vergès, *Monsters and revolutionaries: colonial family romance and métissage* (Durham and London: Duke University Press, 1999).

52. See the volume of summaries of university studies of Reunionese literature: Magdelaine and Marimoutou, eds., *Un état des savoirs à la Réunion*.

53. See note 40.

Chapter 4

Madagascar

Pre-colonial literary culture

Madagascar is exceptional among the islands of the Indian Ocean, in that it had established its own indigenous written literary culture, using the Malagasy language, well before the French colonization of 1895. There was of course, as in most African cultures, an extensive body of oral literature—folktales, called *angano*, proverbs or *ohobolana*, heroic chants or *antsa*, riddles, songs, etc. but also the speeches of the traditional *kabary*, a form of rhetoric, and the *hainteny*, proverbial poems similar to Japanese Haiku.[1] The language had sometimes been written down on tree-bark, using an Arabic script called *sorabe* by an exclusive society of scribes, the *Katibo*, with an almost sacred status. The very limited diffusion of these texts makes it difficult to identify this body of writing as a literature in the modern sense of the word, but they effectively constituted the royal archives up until the middle of the nineteenth century.

By then Madagascar already had a considerable body of printed literature using Roman script. The origins of this lie in the enterprise of the London Missionary Society to evangelize the newly established centralized monarchy of Radama I in 1820, who was supported by British military aid in completing the conquest of the island by his father. The missionaries Jones and Griffiths persuaded the king to endorse in 1823 their transcription of the Malagasy language into Roman script. The first printing press arrived in Madagascar in 1826. The other major enterprise of the London Missionary Society and its local converts to the Protestant faith was the publication in 1835 of the first translation of the Bible into the newly transcribed Malagasy language.[2] In contrast to the transcription, this was undertaken in the face of considerable persecution by the successor of Radama I, his widow Queen Ranavalona I, who, on acceding to the throne in 1828, reversed her former husband's policy by proscribing foreign influences and brutally punished those Malagasy newly converted to the Christian faith. Despite this the Protestant church in Madagascar was the foundation on which an indigenous literary tradition was to be established later in the century. The reign of Ranavalona I lasted until 1861, but her successors Radama II and Ranavalona II reversed the trend by opening the country to missionaries of all denominations. In 1869, Queen Ranavalona II and her Prime Minister were converted to the Protestant faith. The late nineteenth century saw the flowering of a devotional literature, which laid the basis for individual literary enterprises. During the persecution of Christians under Ranavalona I, it was the hymns that survived better than the written texts, even if their versification was somewhat crude. The anthologizing of these early texts led to the development in 1876 of a form of regular versification adapted from English metric principles and applied to the Malagasy language, thereby creating a form of regular verse, and a more harmonious prosody for hymn lyrics.[3] Thus it was that the Protestant evangelization laid the foundations of a secular written literature in the Malagasy language, which survived the French colonization and is still an important part of the island's cultural production.

Colonial intervention

The French invasion and conquest of 1895 under Gallieni imposed the use of French as an administrative and teaching language, and the early years of colonization saw the beginnings of a literary culture in French. The already established literary culture in the Malagasy language was tolerated as long as it did not undermine the colonial regime: Gallieni even established the *Académie malgache* in 1902 to preserve the Malagasy cultural heritage.[4] One of the first significant events in the Francophone cultural life of the island was the discovery in 1908-1910 by the young Jean Paulhan, posted to Madagascar as a colonial civil servant, of the indigenous form of the *hain-teny*, the texts of which he went on to translate and publish in

France in 1913.[5] These short poetic texts encapsulate ancestral wisdom and poetic vision—their name means "linguistic knowledge"—being close to proverbs and riddles in their form, but without the didacticism of the former or the simple resolution of the latter. They are often based on a dialogue between lovers, yet remain contemplative and mysterious, elliptical and at the same time direct and observational. They have been an influential model for subsequent poets, both in their original Malagasy versions and their French translations: one can recognize their influence in the writings of both Jean-Joseph Rabearivelo and Flavien Ranaivo, who translated and adapted them into French, as well as in the poems of Dox and Esther Nirina.

The Malagasy press in the early years of the French colonial regime was strictly censored, but this paradoxically provided a space for the development of a Malagasy literary culture, and a generation of writers grew up in the 1900s, sometimes called *"les aînés,"* the "older generation." Their aim was the preservation of the ancestral Malagasy culture, but in 1915 those who were members of a strongly nationalist cultural group called the VVS were sent into exile. This effectively suppressed the further development of a literature in the Malagasy language for more than a decade. In the meantime the establishment of French-language schools and the arrival of cultivated civil servants led to the growth of a French colonial literary culture, around figures such as Pierre Camo and Robert Boudry.[6] In 1905, Gallieni's successor as governor, Victor Augagneur, was critical of the brutality of his predecessor's "pacification" program, but was also atheist and anticlerical in his beliefs. 1905 was the year of the separation of the Catholic Church and the French State, and Augagneur discreetly favored the creation of a secular literary culture and sought to resist the dominant hold of the churches on the educational sector.

This complex situation was the context which saw the emergence of major poetic figures such as Jean-Joseph Rabearivelo (1903-1937)[7] and Jacques Rabemananjara (1913-2004),[8] both revealed to an international audience through their inclusion in Léopold Sedar Senghor's celebrated *Anthologie de la nouvelle poésie nègre et malgache* of 1948. Both were born after the French colonization and educated in the French system, in Catholic schools run by missionary priests. Rabearivelo's formal education was less important to him than his noble caste, claiming illegitimate descent from Ralambo, a Merina king of the early seventeenth century. This led to his profound identification with the culture of the traditional Merina monarchy, and a sense of tragic loss, which haunted him until his early death by suicide in 1937. His earliest poems were written in Malagasy and published under a pseudonym in 1915, whereas his first poem in French did not appear until 1921. His identification with traditional Malagasy culture was balanced by his appreciation of the generation of French symbolist poets often called the "poètes maudits"—Baudelaire, Rimbaud, Paul Verlaine, Tristan Corbière. In the 1920s he was very active in the literary milieu of Madagascar, contributing articles to numerous revues, and undertaking translations into Malagasy of poems in French and even in English and Spanish. He was in contact by correspondence with major figures in the French literary world such as André Gide and Paul Valéry. His activity as a bilingual creator and translator makes him a seminal figure and a tragic embodiment of the cultural hybridity typical of the colonial situation. The ambiguity he deliberately created around the status of his writings illustrates well the notion of mimicry as theorized by Homi Bhabha: it was often not clear whether his poems in French were translations of originals in Malagasy, or original compositions. His best-known collections of poems in French, *Presque-Songes* of 1934[9] and *Traduit de la nuit* of 1935[10] are presented as translations from original Malagasy texts, although apparently original creations of their author. Similarly his appropriation of the aesthetics of French Symbolism and its adaptation to the context of colonial Madagascar is typical of the subversion of colonial literary models by indigenous writers. His two novels, *L'Aube rouge*[11] and *L'Interférence*,[12] written in the 1920s but unpublished during his lifetime, are elegiac historical fictions set during the time of the fall of the Merina monarchy; yet they echo the *fin de siècle* melancholy of the decadent late nineteenth-century French poets.

Rabearivelo longed to be able to travel to France and at the time of the Colonial Exhibition of 1937, he had hoped to participate in a Parisian production of a poetic cantata for which he had written the text, *Imaitsoanala, Fille d'oiseau*. But it was not to be. The posthumous *Vieilles Chansons des pays d'Imerina*, of 1939,[13] on the other hand, was based on traditional *hain-teny* texts adapted into French.

Rabemananjara, unlike his predecessor, on the advice of his maternal grandfather, embraced the French language, which he later claimed to have "stolen" from the French, in an influential speech to the Second Congress of Black Writers and Artists in Rome in 1959. In an interview he explained that early exposure to the great writers of the French tradition, such as Lamartine, Baudelaire and Victor Hugo, inspired his preference for French, as well as the desire to reach as wide an audience as possible. He claims, however, to express his Malagasy identity through the medium of French, and certainly this corresponds to his predominant practice: the content of his poetry and drama is always deliberately drawn from the culture of Madagascar, whether it be in the emblematic title of the poem *Lamba*,[14] referring to the cloth worn around the shoulders in traditional Malagasy dress, or *Les Boutriers de l'Aurore*,[15] a play which celebrates the legend of the arrival of emigrants from Southeast Asia in the bay of Antongil, on the east coast of Madagascar, close to where Rabemananjara was born. Thus his poetry and drama again represent an example of the kind of subversive mimicry outlined by Bhabha, in which the colonial language and its literary models are appropriated for anti-colonial literary purposes.

Rabemananjara's career spans the periods of the end of the colonial régime and the early years of independence after 1960. In many ways he is a crucial postcolonial figure in the context not only of Madagascar, but also in relation to the international movement of intellectual resistance to French colonialism in the years after the Second World War. As a young student in Paris in the late 1930s he met Senghor, Césaire, Damas and Alioune Diop, the founder of the revue and publishing house *Présence Africaine*, and was closely associated with that enterprise for most of his later career. Like Césaire and Senghor, at the end of the Second World War he was elected as *Député* to the French National Assembly. As a result of the anti-colonial uprising in Madagascar in 1947 he was tried for treason and imprisoned. He was even threatened with public execution, and this was the circumstance of the composition of one of his most famous poems, *Antsa* (1948). This was drafted secretly in prison when he thought these hours might be his last; it was discovered and seized by the authorities, who eventually consented to its publication. He was given a life sentence, and served eight years in custody before being granted an amnesty in 1956 in Marseille. During this period, most of which was spent imprisoned on the island of Nosy Lava, off the west coast of Madagascar, he wrote several poems and plays, which are amongst his best-known: *Lamba* and *Les Boutriers de l'Aurore*. When he was eventually released, he was forbidden to return to Madagascar, and worked for *Présence Africaine* until the island was finally granted its independence in 1960. It was during this period that he gave a keynote speech to the Second Congress of African Writers and Artists in Rome, in which he laid claim to the French language as a vehicle for the aspirations of all the victims of French colonialism. The colonizer's language had been "stolen" by its former subject peoples, who were now perfectly at home in their acquired tongue and able to use it to further their own ends. Rabemananjara's own work is a testament to this point of view, but its formulation is one which is highly significant in the context of the "independence years" and contrasts strikingly with the linguistic militancy of other anti-colonial theoreticians such as Ngugi wa Thiongo, who regarded a return to one's indigenous language as "Decolonizing the mind." It is significant too in that this point of view has now become one of the principal tenets of *La Francophonie*, the International Francophone Organization, and has in recent years been celebrated even by the French establishment as evidence of the "universal" vocation of the French language.

Post-independence political uncertainty

In 1960 Rabemananjara returned to Madagascar and occupied a variety of ministerial positions in the governments of President Philibert Tsiranana. He eventually rose to the level of Vice-President and was widely regarded as a likely successor to the President, until the regime was overthrown by a left-wing military coup in 1972, under the leadership of General Ramantsoa. Rabemananjara was again forced into exile, and only returned to Madagascar after the collapse of the revolutionary regime. After a period of instability the revolutionary council brought to power in 1975 Admiral Didier Ratsiraka, who was to go on to dominate Malagasy politics until he was overthrown by a popular uprising in 1991.

The revolutionaries of 1972 regarded the regime of President Tsiranana as too neo-colonial, protecting the interests of the former colonial power. Amongst other things, a decree prior to independence in 1958 had instituted French as the teaching language of the Malagasy education system. This was to be reversed by the new revolutionary régime, who adopted a policy of "malgachisation," but in a climate of economic penury that effectively deprived the reform of adequate resources for its implementation. One effect of this policy was to limit drastically the possibilities of publication of works in French, since most diplomatic ties with France had been broken. In practice, most of the significant writing in French was either unpublished, or else was the work of expatriate writers such as Michèle Rakotoson or Esther Nirina. The same was not true of writers whose preferred medium was the Malagasy language, who in any case had little alternative. In general, the revolutionary years led to a chronic impoverishment of the Malagasy economy, with the result that very few publishing houses in Madagascar were able to survive. Literary activity centered around short stories, poems and plays that could be published in the press, submitted for literary prizes and particularly the competitions organized by Radio France Internationale in the areas of short stories and theatre, which gave their first public exposure to writers such as Michèle Rakotoson, David Jaomanoro and Jean-Luc Raharimanana.

The restoration of a more liberal and pro-French régime in 1991 improved the climate somewhat, but the political unrest which led to the impeachment of the newly-installed President Albert Zafy, and subsequently to the return to power of Didier Ratsiraka in the election of 1997 did little to resolve the chronic economic problems of the country. The effect of this was compounded when the refusal of Ratisraka to accept defeat in the elections of 2002 led to a near civil war. In the end the situation was resolved by the recognition of Marc Ravelomanana as President, but only at the cost of a violent disruption of the country's already depleted and run-down infrastructure. Despite its apparently liberal credentials, Jean-Luc Raharimanana's experience in defending his father against trumped-up charges of sedition by the new régime, as recorded in his recent essay *L'Arbre anthropophage*,[16] has done nothing to improve the situation of Malagasy writers and intellectuals who remain in the country. The prospects for a literary renaissance of any kind look none too encouraging: the only way to reach a substantial audience appears to be to go into exile and rely on the publishing institutions of the former colonial power.

Franco-Malagasy poetry

As can be seen from the preceding historical survey, the Malagasy poetic tradition draws extensively on the oral heritage of the *hain-teny*, which is a major influence on the poetry of Rabearivelo and Ranaivo. It is fairly easy to recognize the features of the *hain-teny*, even if a precise definition of the form is elusive: many have been translated into French. They do not appear to obey a regular verse form, with a variable line length that resembles the "vers libre" of the Symbolist generation of French poets. This gives a loose, organic rhythmic structure to the texts. The dialogue format, often between two lovers, gives the shape of a series of questions or propositions and responses, and this provides a sense of linear development of a theme. The propositions and responses are often expressed symbolically, through an implicit metaphor that expresses a situation in terms of the natural environment rather than a direct statement. This aspect is what brings the form close to the proverb or the riddle, which express a general truth in an indirect way, which the listener has to decipher or interpret. The "general truth" in the case of the *hain-teny* is sometimes far from obvious, however, not to say obscure. This combination of portentousness and obscurity, this lack of clear resolution must be what appealed to Jean Paulhan, coming to Madagascar from the post-symbolist ethos of the French literary world in the early 1900s. Here is an example:

> Le destin est un caméléon à la cime d'un arbre:
> Il suffit qu'un enfant siffle pour qu'il change de couleur.
> —Le lac ne voulait pas engendrer la boue.
> Pourtant, si l'on agite l'eau, elle apparaît.
> Nombreux sont les arbres, mais c'est la canne à sucre qui est douce.
> Nombreuses sont les sauterelles, mais c'est l'ambolo qui a les belles couleurs.
> Nombreux sont les gens, mais c'est en vous que mon esprit se repose.[17]

[Destiny is a chameleon at the top of a tree:
It only needs a child to whistle for it to change colour.
—The lake did not intend to produce mud.
Yet if you stir the water, it appears.
There are many trees, but it is the sugar cane that is sweet.
There are many grasshoppers, but it's the *ambolo* that has beautiful colours.
There are many people, but my spirit rests in you.]
(author's translation)

The chameleon, the lake, the sugar cane, the *ambolo* grasshopper are all familiar features of the Malagasy natural environment, but all are endowed here with a symbolic significance, which Paulhan brings out in his footnotes. The two opening lines, for instance, are an oblique enquiry from the woman about the constancy of her lover, to which the later metaphors are a flattering poetic response. Lines three and four, however, contain a slightly threatening warning against the likely effects of inconstancy. The interpretation of the significance each metaphor depends on the reader or listener, even if they carry the authority of a proverbial statement.

Compare this poem by Rabearivelo:

Un oiseau sans couleur et sans nom
a replié les ailes
et blessé le seul oeil du ciel.
Il se pose sur un arbre sans tronc,
tout en feuilles
que nul vent ne fait frémir
et dont on ne cueille pas les fruits, les yeux ouverts.
Que couve-t-il?
Quand il reprendra son vol,
ce sont des coqs qui en sortiront:
les coqs de tous les villages
qui auront vaincu et dispersé
ceux qui chantent dans les rêves
et qui se nourisssent d'astres.[18]

[A bird with no color nor name
folded its wings
and wounded the sole eye of the heavens.
It settles on a tree without a trunk,

all leaves
undisturbed by any breeze
and whose fruits are not for gathering with open eyes.
What is it hatching?
When it takes flight again,
it will be cockerels that appear:
the cockerels of all the villages
who will have defeated and dispersed
those who sing in their dreams
and feed on stars.] [19]

As in the *hain-teny*, the poem is based on an elaborate metaphor, which uses as its motif elements of the everyday décor of Malagasy village life, although here they are not specific to Madagascar. Was that intended by the poet, so that the poem would have a wider relevance? It is certainly a feature of other poems in the collection *Presque-Songes*, which would suggest that Rabearivelo is addressing a readership beyond the island. Yet elsewhere the poet makes great play with the exotic names of the Imerina region, often gallicized, but this too is probably also aimed at a French readership.[20] The question and response form is reminiscent of the *hain-teny*, but here it is not a dialogue between lovers, but a soliloquy. The significance of the symbolism is slightly mysterious, as in the *hain-teny*, but the theme is not a debate about the nature of love, but a more philosophical parable about the romantic isolation of the dreamer. This melancholy meditation on the defeat of the nocturnal dreamer/bird by the cockerel heralds of prosaic broad daylight is reminiscent of the *poètes maudits* of French symbolism: Baudelaire, Corbière or Verlaine. The lines are free in form but musical in their rhythm and sonorities, very like those of the *hain-teny*. The punctuation of the lines is subtly different, however: Rabearivelo has taken a step closer to modernist poetic prose by abolishing the capitals at the beginnings of the lines. What is evident from this comparison is the way Rabearivelo is blending elements from the Malagasy oral tradition with those from French sources.

One should not forget the alternative traditional model of the *kabary*, a form of competitive speech making, which on his own admission was an influence on Jacques Rabemananjara in the composition of his longer poems. Many of Rabemananjara's best-known poems are more discursive in form, rhetorical invocations of the spirit of revolt and aspirations to liberty. It is less easy to demonstrate the influence of the form of the *kabary* on these texts: one can only rely on the poet's own observations:

> Il est certain qu'un certain nombre de mes vers rappelle les *kabary*. Au point de vue rythme, il y a une longueur tout à fait "*kabary*."[21]
> [It is certain that a certain number of my lines recall the *kabary*. From the rhythmic point of view, there is a line length that is typical of the *kabary*.]

Another traditional form of Malagasy oral literature is alluded to in the title of the poem *Antsa*. This is the name of a form of chant to celebrate the glory of the monarchy, often in the military context of a victory.[22] What is interesting here is that this is the label given by Rabemananjara to a poem protesting his love of his country, and written while in prison. In a sense, Rabemananjara is appropriating the traditional form and its noble connotations and adapting it to give resonance and significance to his anti-colonial protest.

At the same time, Rabemananjara makes no secret of his admiration for the poetry of the French Romantic tradition, which he was brought up to appreciate at school, in particular Lamartine, Hugo and Baudelaire, because, as he puts it, in their work "on se sent tout de suite au diapason du monde entier" [one finds oneself in tune with the whole world].[23] The example of Hugo is particularly significant here, as Hugo was a charismatic figure who went into exile for his political beliefs, just as Rabemananjara had to do. Hugo is also a poet with epic scope and ambitions in his poetry, and he may well have provided a model for the epic dimensions of Rabemananjara's work. In *Antsa*, his celebration of his island's aspiration to freedom in 1948 echoes in a quadruple repetition the title of the celebrated poem of Paul Eluard during the French resistance to the German Occupation: *Liberté*.[24] The appropriation of French culture and its use to further the poet's own aims is not restricted to the language: the form of poems such as *Antsa* recalls the rhythmic verset form of the free verse of Paul Claudel, but also that of the Senegalese poet Léopold Sedar Senghor, a figure he knew personally and whose work attempts a similar synthesis of French form and indigenous content.²⁵

However much the form of his poems may be influenced by French models, Rabemananjara insists that their subject matter is rooted in Malagasy life and culture. There is no point, for him, in imitating slavishly the models of French culture. As he declares in an interview with Jean-Luc Raharimanana:

> ... à travers le français, qui n'est pour moi qu'un habit, une parure, c'est la personnalité malgache qui doit être revêtue de cette parure ... ²⁶
> [. . . through French, which is only a clothing, an ornament for me, it's the Malagasy personality which is to be clothed in this ornamentation . . .]

This is certainly true of his poetry: however much the rhetorical flourishes of his poems recall the epic tone of French poetry, the content is always characteristic of Madagascar, with constant allusions to Malagasy culture and traditions, as in the titles of his collections *Antsa* and *Lamba*.²⁷

As a counterpoint to the Francophone poetic ambition of Rabemananjara, it is interesting to evoke briefly the career of one of his contemporaries who followed a very different path. Dox, born Jean Verdi Salomon Razakandraina in 1913, the same year as Rabemananjara, is one of the best-known and widely read poets in Madagascar, whose published output is almost entirely written in Malagasy.²⁸ He did however write some poetry in French, and this was published posthumously in 1991, in a collection called *Chants capricorniens*, and is well represented in various anthologies.²⁹ Thanks to this we can appreciate a poet of considerable stature whose work maintained the independence of spirit characteristic of Malagasy culture and illustrated the autonomy of Malagasy literary institutions, even during the period of colonization and the post-independence economic decline.

The best-known poet of the post-independence period is undoubtedly Esther Nirina, who lived for a considerable proportion of her life in France, where she worked as a librarian in the city of Orleans. Her work illustrates the continuity of Malagasy poetry from the pioneering work of Rabearivelo: like him she was equally at home in French or in Malagasy.[30] She has also undertaken translations of her work, and a posthumous collection of poetry, *Dire par écrit* is in fact a bilingual publication, involving her own texts in Malagasy, under the title *Mirolana an-tsoratra*, along with versions in French by a translator, *Le dire par écrit*, in parallel with her own translations.[31] This unusual emphasis on the finesses of translation is an echo of the ambiguities of Rabearivelo's "translations" of his own texts, and emphasizes her role as an intermediary between the two languages. The elegiac tone of much of her work is reminiscent of Rabearivelo, and like him her use of images of the Malagasy environment makes her an example of the continuity of the influence of the *hain-teny* on Malagasy poetry. As with Rabearivelo, her poetic voice is an intimate, personal one, most often rooted in a sense of her own physical presence in the environment, which is often reflected in a uncompromising light:[32]

> ... Quand je vois la femme
> A chaque pas
> Humiliée
>
> Quand je vois l'enfant
> Se débattre devant
> Une issue murée
>
> Le père au regard
> La mere muette
> A force d'hurler
> L'existence du jour
>
> Oserais-je encore
> Parler d'amour?
>
> [... When I see woman
> Humiliated
> At each step she takes
>
> When I see the child
> Struggle before
> An obstructed exit

The father whose gaze
Has no sockets
The mother mute
From having shouted out
The day's existence

Do I still dare
Speak of love?]

The discreet and lucid realism of Nirina's social observations is very much in keeping with much of the fictional writing of the post-independence era. Writers of the generation of the 1980s and 1990s have turned away from the celebration of traditional Malagasy values to embrace a disenchanted critique of the realities of an impoverished and brutalized society.

Post-independence fiction

In general the novel was not a form favored by Malagasy writers during the colonial period, and even more recently there have been few novels published in Madagascar. Rabearivelo's attempts at the genre, *L'Aube rouge* and *L'Interférence*, both dating from the 1920s, remained unpublished during his lifetime and to date only *L'Interférence* has appeared as a separate publication, in 1987, some 50 years after his death, and published in France.[33] *L'Aube rouge* is now also available in an anthology of texts from the Indian Ocean, which also includes the Malagasy colonial novel by Charles Renel, *Le "Décivilisé."*[34] Fiction has been more often represented by the short story, the *nouvelle*, which has remained a popular and widely practiced genre. The reasons for this are probably that publication is easier, as they are often included in the news and magazine press, and perhaps also that the form is close to the familiar traditional one of the oral folk-tale, called *angano* in Malagasy.[35] Even so, these are most often written in French, and Radio France Internationale has played an important role in organizing competitions that have helped to bring the form to a wide audience beyond Madagascar. Many of the best-known figures of recent Malagasy writing, such as Jean-Luc Raharimanana, started their career with success in these competitions.

The novel has been most commonly the work of expatriate writers using French and publishing their work in France. The best-known figures, Michèle Rakotoson, Charlotte Rafenomanjato and Jean-Luc Raharimanana, appear to use the form to explore the social and political problems of Malagasy society, in a magical-realist vein. It would be wrong to assume that the forms and values of their novels are French rather than Malagasy. All of them use the form to their own ends, and succeed in adapting it in various ways to the demands of their passionate concern for the Malagasy society in which they remain profoundly rooted, even when they are based in France.

Michèle Rakotoson is probably the best known of recent Malagasy novelists, and this she probably owes to her high visibility as a journalist working in Paris for Radio France Internationale, France Culture and other media. Her success began with an apparently autobiographical work, *Dadabé*,[36] which combined a longer principal narrative with other shorter pieces, such as *Complainte d'un naufrage* and *Voyage*; this was awarded the "Grand Prix de Madagascar" in 1985 by the ADELF, an association of Francophone writers. It set a new, personalized tone for Malagasy fiction, the main narrative based on the experiences of a young woman abandoned by her husband, who takes refuge in the childhood memories of her grandfather, the "Dadabé" of the title. The other stories in the collection, such as *Complainte d'un naufrage* are more typical of Rakotoson's later work, however, concerned by the social problems confronting the traditional communities of Madagascar in the face of modernity. *Le Bain des reliques*[37] of 1988 recounts the experiences of a westernized television journalist who is sent to film the traditional Sakalava ceremony alluded to in the title, and who becomes the unwitting victim of a ritual sacrifice.

The theme of the conflict between traditional Malagasy values and the superficial materialism of western societies is picked up again in *Elle, au printemps* (1996).[38] This covers the experiences of a young Malagasy woman migrating to France, and confronted with the inhumane and unfriendly society of the Parisian metropolis, and the abandonment of their traditional values by the expatriate Malagasy community. This exploration of the alienation of a migrant community in metropolitan France illustrates a recurrent theme of

Francophone postcolonial writing. Her novel *Henoÿ. Fragments en écorce* of 1999[39] evokes a nightmarish return of a bereaved husband to what is left of a traditional rural culture devastated by poverty and disease, and the discovery of the fate of country-dwellers reduced to living on waste-tips on the edge of the capital.

Her most recent novel, *Lalana* (2002),[40] tackles a burning contemporary issue, the devastating epidemic of AIDS, in an uncompromisingly realist fashion. The narrative recounts the epic journey of two student friends, one a homosexual dying of the disease, the other a loyal heterosexual friend helping him to find peace and serenity by returning him from the run-down university campus in Antananarivo to his home village on the coast. Along the way they encounter various individuals and groups that reflect the social, material and spiritual distress of an impoverished Malagasy society. All these novels reflect a strong social concern on the part of their author. As she declares in an interview with Monique Hugon:

> La question que je me pose est la question que se posent tous les Malgaches: pourquoi est-ce que nous en sommes arrivés là, dans la situation où nous sommes? . . . Je me demande quels ont été les reflexes qui nous ont été donnés, inculqués, qui font que nous nous sommes empêtrés dans les problèmes économiques présents, dans les interrogations sur notre passé.[41]
>
> [The question I ask myself is the one all Malagasy ask themselves: why do we find ourselves in the situation we are in? . . . I ask myself what are the reflexes which have been given us, inculcated in us, which lead us to get bogged down in the present economic problems, in the questioning of our past.] [42]

She has been described as a "militant" writer, but this does not imply a commitment to any ideology: rather her writing is a way for her to explore fundamental problems in Malagasy culture and its ambivalent relations with the ever more omnipresent Western civilization.

The novels of Charlotte-Arrisoa Rafenomanjato reveal similar preoccupations to those of Michèle Rakotoson, although in a more melodramatic and sensational vein which apparently recalls a certain type of popular novel in the Malagasy language. Like Rakotoson, Rafenomanjato came to prominence in the late 1980s by winning an award in the Radio France Internationale play competition in 1986, for her play *Le Prix de la Paix*.[43] This was followed by two novels, *Le Pétale écarlate*, published in Madagascar in 1990,[44] and *Le Cinquième Sceau* (1993), published in France.[45] Unlike her compatriot, however, she lives and works in Madagascar, where she is an influential literary and political figure who has published political pamphlets such as *La Marche de la liberté*, in 1992.[46] The earlier of the two novels recounts the vicissitudes of the heroine Felana, suffering under a curse that links her to death by fire. Her life is dogged by misadventures apparently caused by the curse, in which her parents and her friends lose their lives. In the end, she is able to exorcize the curse thanks to the loving support of her providential American husband, who himself has to surmount the ordeal by fire. This narrative explores the conflict between the strong sense of the supernatural still omnipresent in Malagasy society and the demands of modernity and international scientific opinion. In this respect, it is similar in theme to *Le Bain des reliques*, although in a racier and less intellectual vein.

Rafenomanjato's second novel *Le Cinquième Sceau* directly reflects her social and political concerns, and represents a more ambitious and wide-ranging portrait of Malagasy society. It was written, according to the author, during the last years of the socialist dictatorship of Didier Ratsiraka, and as such is in some ways prophetic of the overthrow of that regime in 1991. With hindsight, in the preface, the author sees it as an expression of the aspiration of her compatriots towards a more democratic and egalitarian state. The novel evokes a wide range of milieux, although centered on the capital Antananarivo: from the impoverished adoptive family of the visionary hero Andry and the lower depths of the beggar community which he haunts to the cynical and wealthy business milieux dominated by his unrecognized brother Solo. The medical world of Andry's adoptive father, a poorly paid male nurse, is also sketched in, as is the corrupt world of political manipulation and gangsterism. In the course of a mystical and visionary pilgrimage the hero travels to the provinces and rural areas and encounters the hardships, the exploitation and the political corruption that reign there. On his return he leads an apocalyptic march of the city's poor and disenfranchised to demand a profound change of political regime, which is predictably met with violence and repression, as suggested by the title of the novel, drawn from the Apocalypse of St John. The novel is reminiscent of Balzac in its breadth of sociological vision, but also in the verve and melodrama of its rather exaggerated plot devices and characters. Even so, it reflects the deeply felt concerns of the author and draws an uncompromising picture of the evils that beset Malagasy society, which have unfortunately not been vanquished in spite of several changes of government since the heady days of the overthrow of Ratsiraka in 1991.

A similarly anguished concern with the impoverished social fabric of Malagasy life seems to motivate the writing of Jean-Luc Raharimanana. Like Rakotoson, he came to prominence by winning the Radio France Internationale short story competition in 1989 with his story *Lépreux*, subsequently included in his first collection of stories *Lucarne*, published in 1996.[47] He had also, like the two women writers, been the winner of a prize in the same radio station's play competition, in 1990, with his drama *Le Prophète et le Président*.[48] Raharimanana's style is much more experimental, however: his short stories reproduce extreme situations of physical violence and distress, very often from the point of view of a first person narrator and victim, and dramatizing in a shocking and graphic way the realities of life for the down-and-outs of Malagasy society, particularly in the capital Antananarivo. Raharimanana emphasizes the horrific and the squalid aspects of these lives lived at the limits of existence: the child of *L'Enfant riche* desperately trying to recoup a 100 franc coin he has been obliged to swallow to avoid it being stolen; the leper beggar in *Lépreux* attempting to end his miserable existence under the wheels of a passing car. Uncomfortable reading, only bearable because of the dramatic skill and the concision and evocativeness of the writing, but which represents an honest attempt to represent the reality of the poorest inhabitants' lives in a postcolonial city in a run-down third world economy. These stories represent one of the most striking attempts to give a voice to the voiceless "subaltern" evoked by the writings of Gayatri Spivak, through a process of fictional empathy, to create rhetorically a discourse which can go some way towards representing the situation of the destitute victims of the postcolonial city.

Raharimanana's first full-length novel, *Nour 1947*, published in 2001,[49] takes as its subject the Malagasy uprising of 1947, perhaps inspired by the fiftieth anniversary of those events in 1997. It treats them in a poetic and lyrical style, however, which, like *Lucarne*, does not shrink from a graphic representation of the despair, violence and physical suffering of the defeated rebels. The narrative is not a straightforward, linear one, however, but rather a poetic juxtaposition of different threads recounted by a variety of narrators, which flash back to earlier periods in the history of Madagascar so as better to illuminate the tragic nature of the uprising, and its historical resonances. The effect is kaleidoscopic: the narration switches between the stories of the rebel combatants, the memories of a *tirailleur*, a Malagasy colonial soldier in a Vichy French internment camp in 1943, the diaries and letters of two generations of French Catholic missionaries from the eighteenth and nineteenth centuries, and memories of Arab slave trading from "year 970 after the Hejira." The principal narrator is the unidentified lover of Nour, a doomed woman insurgent who gives her name to the novel, and this thread provides a constantly lyrical and mythical commentary on the events of the uprising. This is an ambitious and challenging poetic text but its juxtapositions highlight the tragic ironies of the colonial situation, suggested by the motif of "dziny," a Malagasy notion of the retroactive perversity of fate.

Raharimanana's most recent publication, *L'arbre anthropophage* (2004)[50] is an autobiographical essay rather than a novel, which recounts the writer's disenchanted return to Madagascar to renew contact with his childhood roots, only to find himself embroiled in the defense of his father falsely accused of sedition under the new regime of President Ravelomanana. His body of work represents even so a highly original style of poetic fiction, yoked to a deep preoccupation with the destiny of the humane social values that have not yet been driven from Malagasy society by years of poverty and cynical political opportunism.

Popular theater, classical theater

Most of the leading figures in the Malagasy literary field that we have already discussed have also written plays: it is striking that all three of the major post-independence novelists were in the first instance prize-winners in the Radio France Internationale theater competitions of the 1980s. This suggests how well implanted theatrical culture is in the literary world of Madagascar. There are however several strands in the development of drama in Madagascar. The oldest form is the popular theater in the Malagasy language, called the *hira-gasy*,[51] practiced by troupes of itinerant artists called the *mphira gasy,* or individually the *mpilalao*. These performances mix songs, dance, comic sketches and monologues, and are probably closer to music hall than to literary theater. There is an element of competition in the *hira-gasy* spectacle, with the performers rivaling in eloquence and wit, often practicing the rhetorical techniques of the *kabary*.[52] An interesting comparison would be the "concert party" format of the West African coastal states of Nigeria and Ghana, and similar kinds of popular theater have been developed in Reunion, for example by the Théâtre Vollard troupe. The name *hira gasy* may be translated as "Malagasy song," which suggests that the musical component is the dominant one: this is perhaps the reason why the form is not usually regarded as a genre of theater by Malagasy literary specialists.[53] Theater in the literary sense is thus often regarded as a form brought to the island with French colonization and based on French notions of genre. Thus Rabearivelo could declare in 1933:

> Il faut d'abord se rappeler que le théâtre est étranger chez nous; les Anciens malgaches n'avaient rien qui lui ressemblât, même de loin.[54]
> [One must remember that theater is foreign to us; the Malagasy of former generations had nothing that resembled it, even slightly.]

The early years of the twentieth century saw the development of French-language theater which soon attracted Malagasy authors, who adapted it into the Malagasy language. This is what is generally regarded as "Classical theater" in the Malagasy context, and in the colonial years, between 1922 and 1945, over a thousand such plays were produced.[55]

Rabearivelo himself was commissioned in 1931 to write a "revue" called *Aux Portes de la ville*, which was performed in 1935 in Antananarivo and published in French in 1936. It was Rabemananjara, however, who embraced dramatic writing with the most enthusiasm, publishing several epic and poetic dramas in a tragic mode: *Les Dieux malgaches* (1947),[56] *Les Boutriers de l'Aurore* (1957),[57] *Les Agapes des Dieux* (1962).[58] These treat Malagasy subject matter, drawing on legends and myths of traditional Malagasy culture, but in a stylized form of free poetic verse in French not far removed from his poetry. Dox, on the other hand, applied his poetic talent in the 1960s to adapting classical French tragedies by Corneille and Racine into Malagasy, with versions of *Horace, Le Cid* and *Andromaque*, as well as his own original dramas.[59] Many other authors too numerous to mention composed works for the theater, more often performed than published, so that it is difficult to assess the merits of this abundant output in both Malagasy and French. Even the winning plays from the Radio France Internationale theater competition are not easily accessible, being often published in specialized theater journals, if at all. This is the case with Charlotte-Arrisoa Rafenomanjato's *Le Prix de la Paix* (1986), Michèle Rakotoson's *Sambany* (1978) and *La Maison morte* (1989), and Jean-Luc Raharimanana's *Le Prophète et le Président* (1990).

It does appear, however, that this last body of work represents a break with the more conservative dramas that had hitherto dominated the French-language theater in Antananarivo. This new style of theater, probably inspired by the avant-garde drama of Beckett, Ionesco and Genêt, is more freewheeling in form and style, is not afraid of abrupt changes of tone and linguistic register, and above all is concerned with the social and political problems of post-independence Madagascar. It remains a minority taste, however, being essentially an intellectual theater popular in the university milieux, or else appealing to an international taste and well suited to performances in festivals such as the Festival International des Francophonies in Limoges.[60] Broadly speaking, then, literary theater in Madagascar draws on French models for its form, even when it is written in Malagasy, but the themes and content are usually drawn from the history and culture of the island, or else its contemporary social and political problems. In the meantime the traditional *hiragasy* continues as a popular theatrical form, apparently little affected by the aspirations of francophone literary modernity.

A highly exportable musical production

However significant the recent literary production of Madagascar, its audience is restricted by the cost and limited availability of books in Madagascar, and by the marginality of most Francophone writing within the French literary scene, in spite of some commercial successes by African authors like Ahmadou Kourouma. It is interesting to compare this situation with the lively music scene in Madagascar, which has produced some remarkable musicians who are well known in international world music circuits, and have enjoyed considerable success, although not at the level of African international superstars such as Youssou N'Dour or Salif Keita. Homegrown Malagasy popular music is an extraordinarily rich and distinctive field, with many different styles and several unique instruments particular to the island.[61] It is essentially a dance music, with a range of different rhythms, from the rolling 6/8 tempo of the *salegy* from the North of the island to the frenetically fast *tsipika* from the South. The best-known indigenous instruments are the *valiha*, a bamboo harp with strings along the length of a wide diameter hollow tube of bamboo, which acts as a soundbox. Another is the *kabosy*, a kind of homegrown guitar with a square soundbox, four or five strings and partially fretted neck. Despite the popularity of home-grown music in Madagascar, there are very limited recording facilities in the island and no effective distribution network for CDs. Audio cassettes, most often pirated, are the most common means of diffusion of the music, apart from local television and radio; but this means there is no properly structured system of performing rights for artists, which makes them dependent on live performances for their income.

In this situation it is hardly surprising that they have had to go abroad for recording purposes, and to try to supplement their income from the international market. The most successful at this have been Rossy, a singer and multi-instrumentalist who has recorded several albums for American labels;[62] Justin Vali, who is based in Paris and was launched by Peter Gabriel's RealWorld label in the United Kingdom;[63] and Tarika, who shuttle between London and Antananarivo and have released several albums in the United Kingdom and America.[64] Some artists have not gone so far afield, and have used the better recording facilities of France or nearby Reunion to promote their careers: these include the *salegy* star Jaojoby, recorded by the French world-music specialist *Label Bleu*,[65] the singer-songwriter Tiana,[66] and the group Fenoamby[67] and its lead singer/songwriter Marius Fontaine, whose records are produced in Reunion. At the time of writing a singer-guitarist called Modeste Hugues is building a career in the United Kingdom, and there are many more notable figures who enjoy an enviable international reputation, such as the guitarist D'Gary[68] and the accordionist Régis Gisavo,[69] even if they are not often seen outside of Madagascar.

The strength of Malagasy popular music lies in its immediately recognizable style. It usually involves a very infectious and danceable up-tempo rhythm, simple but catchy tunes expressing an irrepressible vitality, and some striking sounds, vocal as well as instrumental, from instruments such as the *valiha*. There is a strong tradition of choral singing in Madagascar, which is probably attributable to the well-established Christian church traditions, both Protestant and Catholic, and this has made close harmony a common feature of the Malagasy style. Western instruments such as the accordion feature strongly, and more recently the synthesizer and the electric guitar, but without detracting from the distinctiveness of the Malagasy sound. The lyrics are almost always in Malagasy, although sometimes a translation into English and/or French is provided in the CD booklet. It is hard to judge their merits from a translation, but in general the appeal of this music lies most often in the sound and the rhythm, especially for international audiences.

A rich postcolonial culture

In conclusion, it is clear that Madagascar is home to an extraordinarily rich and varied culture, whose roots go back well beyond the properly colonial period. Colonial influences transformed it profoundly, however, and in the post-independence period we have to recognize the complexity of the situation of Malagasy culture. On the one hand the Malagasy language is the vehicle for a considerable proportion of the cultural output of the island: plays, short stories, songs, poetry; but this indigenous tradition has assimilated colonial influences from French literature, as well as from the ecclesiastical traditions of the Christian churches, both Protestant and Catholic. The championing of the Malagasy vernacular by the Protestant churches has had a decisive impact on the development of the Malagasy language, and this influence is noticeable even today in the strongly Protestant-inspired regime of President Ravelomanana. On the other hand the French language has also been assimilated by a sizeable proportion of the country's intellectual élite, who are entirely at home in using it to express sentiments and ideas which are deeply rooted in Malagasy culture. Madagascar is a keen participant in the institutions of *La Francophonie*, and the education system has re-adopted French as its principal international language for teaching and intellectual exchange. For better or worse, Madagascar belongs in the orbit of the French-speaking world for the foreseeable future. This complex picture is further complicated by the survival of regional identities within the island, so that musical styles and poetic traditions are not uniform from one region to another. Madagascar's superficial political and linguistic unity hides a considerable ethnic and cultural diversity that occasionally surfaces in unexpected ways in the writing and performing of the island, so that the culture is a hybrid one despite its apparent distinctiveness and homogeneity. All these factors make it a fascinating case study for the exploration of post-colonial theorizing in a practical context.

Notes

1. See "Introduction" in *Voices from Madagascar*, ed. Jacques Bourgeacq and Liliane Ramarasoa (Athens: Ohio University Press, 2002), xii.

2. See M. Ratrimoarivony-Rakotoanosy, "Evolution de la culture écrite," in *Notre Librairie*, 109 (1992), 15-16.

3. See H. Rakotoandrianoela, "1820-1915: naissance des arts littéraires" in *Notre Librairie*, 109 (1992), 40-41.

4 See Bourgeacq and Ramarasoa, *Voices from Madagascar*, xii; and Jean-Louis Joubert, *Littératures de l'Océan Indien* (Vanves, France: EDICEF / AUPELF, 1991), 39.

5. Jean Paulhan, *Les Hain-tenys merina* (Paris: Librairie orientaliste Geuthner, 1913).

6. See Joubert, *Littératures de l'Océan Indien*, 49-50.

7. Rabearivelo is probably the most widely studied of Malagasy writers: for a general introduction, see Joubert, *Littératures de l'Océan Indien*, 59-71.

8. For a useful introduction to the work of Rabemananjara, see Joubert, *Littératures de l'Océan Indien*, 73-86.

9. Jean-Joseph Rabearivelo, *Presque-Songes* (Tananarive, Madagascar: Henri Vidalie, 1934). Reprinted in *Poèmes* (Paris: Hatier, 1990).

10. Jean-Joseph Rabearivelo, *Traduit de la Nuit* (Tunis: Editions du Mirage, 1935). Reprinted in *Poèmes* (Paris: Hatier, 1990).

11. Jean-Joseph Rabearivelo, "L'Aube rouge" in *Océan indien— Madagascar, La Réunion, Maurice*, ed. Serge Meitinger and J.-C. Carpanin Marimoutou (Paris: Omnibus, 1998), 101-96.

12. Jean-Joseph Rabearivelo, *L'Interférence* (Paris: Hatier, 1987).

13. Jean-Joseph Rabearivelo, *Vieilles Chansons des pays de l'Imerina* (Tananarive, Madagascar: Imprimerie officielle, 1939).

14. Jacques Rabemananjara, *Lamba* (Paris: Présence africaine, 1956).

15. Jacques Rabemananjara, *Les Boutriers de l'Aurore* (Paris: Présence africaine, 1957).

16. Raharimanana, *L'Arbre anthropophage* (Paris: Editions Joëlle Losfeld, 2004).

17. From Jean Paulhan, *Hain-teny merina: poésies populaires malgaches* (Antananarivo, Madagascar: Foi et Justice, 1991), 13.

18. From the collection *Traduit de la Nuit* (1934); in *Anthologie de la literature malgache d'expression française des années 80*, ed. Liliane Ramarasoa, (Paris: L'Harmattan, 1994), 221.

19. Author's translation.

20. For a discussion of Rabearivelo's use of proper names, see Liliane Ramarasoa, "Les (en)jeux des noms de lieux dans la poésie malgache d'expression française. Cas de Jean-Joseph Rabearivelo," in *La littérature malgache* (Lecce, Italy: Argo, *Interculturel/Francophonies*, 1/2001), 21-32.

21. From interview in Jean-Luc Raharimanana, "Jacques Rabemananjara, poète et dramaturge," *Notre Librairie*, 110 (1992), 26.

22. See Bourgeacq and Ramarasoa, eds., *Voices from* Madagascar, 291, note 3.

23. In an interview with Raharimanana, *Notre Librairie*, 110 (1992), 23.

24. In Bourgeacq and Ramarasoa, eds., *Voices from* Madagascar, 5; from Jacques Rabemananjara, *Antsa* (Paris: R. Drivon, 1948).

25. Examples can be found in Senghor, ed., *Anthologie de la nouvelle poésie nègre et malgache* (Paris: Presses Universitaires de France, 1948), 149-76.

26. See interview with Raharimanana, *Notre Librairie*, 110 (1992), 24.

27. Jacques Rabemananjara, *Antsa* (1947); reprinted (Paris: Présence africaine, 1956); and *Lamba* (Paris: Présence africaine, 1956).
28. See José De Rossi, "Dox, la tradition rénovée," *Notre Librairie*, 109 (1992), 100-101.
29. See Ramarasoa *Anthologie de la literature malgache*, 226-30 and Dox, *Chants capricorniens* (Antananarivo, Madagascar: Editions du Centre Albert Camus, 1995).
30. See Esther Nirina, *Lente Spirale* (Antananarivo, Madagascar: Madprint/Revue de l'Océan Indien, 1990).
31. Esther Nirina, *Mirolana an-tsoatra / Dire par écrit / Le dire par écrit* (Saint-Denis de la Réunion: Grand Océan, 2004).
32. *Rien que lune* (Saint-Denis de la Réunion: Grand Océan, 1998).
33. Rabearivelo, *L'Interférence*.
34. Rabearivelo, "L'Aube rouge."
35. See Bourgeacq and Ramarasoa, eds., *Voices from Madagascar*, 291, note 4.
36. Michèle Rakotoson, *Dadabé* (Paris: Karthala, 1984).
37. Michèle Rakotoson, *Le Bain des reliques* (Paris: Karthala, 1988).
38. Michèle Rakotoson, *Elle, au printemps* (Saint-Maur: Sepia, 1996).
39. Michèle Rakotoson, *Henoy. Fragments en écorce* (Avin/Hannut, Belgium: Editions Luce Wilkin, 1999).
40. Michèle Rakotoson, *Lalana* (La Tour d'Aigues: Editions de l'Aube, 2002).
41. Monique Hugon, "Entre deux langues. Entretien avec Michèle Rakotoson," *Notre Librairie*, 110 (1992), 77.
42. Author's translation.
43. Text unpublished, but it was made into a telefilm in 1988.
44. Charlotte-Arrisoa Rafenomanjato, *Le Pétale écarlate* (Antananarivo, Madagascar: Société malgache d'édition, 1990).
45. Charlotte-Arrisoa Rafenomanjato, *Le Cinquième Sceau* (Paris: L'Harmattan, 1993).
46. Charlotte-Arrisoa Rafenomanjato, *La Marche de la Liberté* (Saint-Denis de la Réunion and Paris: Azalées / L'Harmattan, 1992).
47. Raharimanana, *Lucarne* (Paris: Le Serpent à Plumes, 1996).
48. Text unpublished.
49. Raharimanana, *Nour, 1947* (Paris: Le Serpent à Plumes, 2001).
50. Raharimanana, *L'Arbre anthropophage* (Paris: Editions Joëlle Losfeld, 2004).
51. See Danielle Andriajafy, "Le theatre: une aubaine . . . pour une élite," *Notre Librairie*, 110 (1992) 69-70, note 2.

52. See Joubert, *Littératures de l'Océan Indien*, 24.

53. The *hira gasy* is barely mentioned in the issue of *Notre Librairie* No. 109 (see Rajaona, 1992) devoted to literature in the Malagasy language.

54. From *Ny Fandrosoam-baova*, "*Le nouveau progrès*," 25 octobre 1933, No 110; quoted by Ramiandrasoa (see note below).

55. See Jean-Irénée Ramiandrasoa, "Le théâtre malgache classique: 1922-1945," *Notre Librairie*, 109 (1992), 71.

56. Jacques Rabemananjara, *Les Dieux malgaches* (Gap, France: Ophrys, 1947).

57. Jacques Rabemananjara, *Les Boutriers de l'aurone* (Paris: Présence africaine, 1957)

58. Jacques Rabemananjara, *Les Agapes des dieux* (Paris: Présence africaine, 1962)

59. See Ramarasoa, *Anthologie*, 238; and Joubert, *Littératures de l'Océan Indien*, 30.

60. See Andriajafy, Danielle, *Notre Librairie* (1992), 69-75.

61. For an overview, see the section by Ian Anderson, "Madagascar," in *World Music*, vol. I, ed. Simon Broughton, Mark Ellingham and Richard Trillo (London: The Rough Guides, 1999), 523-32.

62. Such as Rossy, *One eye on the future, one eye on the past* (USA: Shanachie records, 1993), CD No. 64046.

63. Justin Vali, *The Truth* (Box, UK: Real World, 1995), CD No. CDRW 51.

64. Such as Tarika, *Soul Makassar* (London: Sakay, 2001), CD No. SAKD7037.

65. Jaojoby, *e tiako* (Amiens, France: Indigo/Label bleu, 1997), CD No.LBLC2533.

66. Tiana, *Miharina / Renaissance* (Réunion: JBE Musik, 2005), CD No. JBE008.

67. Fenoamby, *Fanajana /Respect* (Réunion: Discorama), CD 93.05.

68. D'Gary, *Mbo Loza* (Amiens, France: Indigo/Label bleu).

69. Régis Gizavo, *Mikea* (Amiens, France: Indigo/Label bleu).

Chapter 5

Mauritius

Is there a specifically Mauritian culture?

This might seem a provocative way to begin a study of the complexity of the Mauritian literary and cultural field, but it is based on a detached observation of the dynamics of the social reality that underpins the field.[1] The various ethnic, linguistic and religious communities of Mauritius seem to cling to communalist notions of their pre-colonial origins, and use them to define their social identity. Thus there are Franco-Mauritians, Indo-Mauritians, Sino-Mauritians, Creoles (which in the context of Mauritius usually means of African or mixed ancestry) and Muslims; and even within these categories there are subdivisions, between Indo-Mauritians who claim Tamil ancestry, or membership of the Brahmin caste, for instance. The difficulty with all these labels is that of determining what the Mauritian element is actually composed of, apart from citizenship of and residence on the island of Mauritius. Even this definition of Mauritianity is problematic, however, since there is an extensive diaspora of Mauritians in the United Kingdom, the United States, Australia, France and the European Union, and whose effective nationality is often that of their host state. This complexity applies even to the major creative writers and artists, and to the language they choose as the vehicle for their work. Thus there is a substantial body of Mauritian literature written in French, in spite of 150 years of British colonisation; but also a significant literature in Hindi,[2] in Mauritian Creole, for which some writers claim the status of *morisien*; in English,[3] in Tamil[4] and even in Mandarin Chinese[5] and in the creolised Indian language called Bhojpuri.

A complex political and social evolution

The fundamental reason for this fragmented and paradoxical situation is that, unlike Madagascar, Mauritius can lay claim to no pre-colonial culture of its own. The island was uninhabited until it was claimed by the Dutch in 1598, colonized in the mid-seventeenth century, in 1638, only to be abandoned by them some decades later, in 1710. It was many years after the French annexation of 1715 and the arrival of the first French settlers in 1722 that a literary culture first began to emerge. The first major French literary text to be associated with the island was Bernardin de Saint-Pierre's famous novel *Paul et Virginie*, published in 1788, and this is still regarded as the foundational text of the Franco-Mauritian literary tradition, even if it was written after a brief visit by its author to the island in 1768-1770 and the publication of his highly critical account *Voyage à l'Ile de France* in 1773.[6] The first printing press arrived in the island in 1768 [7] and, apart from the development of a local press, the French literary culture of the island first grew up in the context of political societies inspired by the French revolution, such as the Jacobin *Club de la Chaumière* [8] and this naturally enough used the French language of what was then called "L'Ile de France."

The British conquest of the island in 1810, during the Napoleonic wars, brought to an abrupt end the direct dependency of the island on France, although it probably focused the sense of identity and the political resistance of the land-owning Franco-Mauritian élite, around the literary society *La Table Ovale*, Bonapartist and revolutionary in inspiration.[9] But by this time they were vastly outnumbered by the slave population who had been brought in by them from a variety of African homelands, including Madagascar, during the previous century. The vehicular language of this community was not French, but Creole, a language developed for everyday communication between the slaves, who often had no other common African tongue, and their immediate masters, who themselves often spoke a regional, non-standard French. This predominantly African population was to be freed progressively from 1835 onwards, when slavery was finally abolished by the British colonial authorities, and the Franco-Mauritian plantation-owners proceeded to recruit a replacement work-force from the Indian sub-continent, who were scarcely better treated than the former slaves. This group brought with them their Hindu religion, and Indian languages such as Hindi, but also Tamil and Bhojpuri, which are still practised in some communities on the island. This community gradually conquered the right to full citizenship and the respect of their cultural traditions, as described in Abhimanyu Unnuth's epic novel *Lal Pasina*, recently translated into French as *Sueur de sang*.[10] In modern-day Mauritius, their descendants form a numerical majority of the population, with the result that Indian culture and Hindu religious beliefs permeate all sectors of the island's political institutions and social life.

Subsequent waves of immigration brought in workers from China, fleeing the upheavals of Chinese society in the early years of the twentieth century; and Muslim traders from the Indian region of Gujerat and what is today Pakistan. These groups have also maintained their distinct social identity, including the practice of their traditional languages and religions, with the result that in modern-day Mauritius their children can choose to learn Urdu or Mandarin Chinese as well as Hindi at primary school. There is also a substantial Muslim minority and a smaller Buddhist community alongside the well-established Hindu, Catholic and Protestant religious groups.

The island remained a British colony until independence in 1968, and English is still the dominant language of the administration and government. It is also the teaching language of the education system, but French is also taught as a compulsory second language from primary school onwards. The effective *lingua franca* of the island is in fact Mauritian Creole, spoken by 95 per cent of the population, and used on a daily basis by most Mauritians. Paradoxically, it has no official recognition in the school system, although since the 1970s there has been a movement to use the language for literary expression, notably by the dramatist Dev Virahsawmy. This is most significant in the areas of oral culture: theatre and popular music, as in the neighbouring island of Reunion; but several novels in Creole have also been published, the first being René Asgarally's *Quand montagne prend difé* in 1977.[11] In the early years of the twenty-first century there has finally been a semblance of an official recognition of Creole, with the appointment of a national commission to standardise its written form and grammar, but it is still far from being an officially approved language on a level with English and French.

Cultural separatism and co-existence

Since independence was negotiated in 1968, Mauritius has remained a secular state with British-style parliamentary institutions. The British monarch even remained as the titular Head of State until 1992, when after a constitutional reform, a republican regime was introduced. The function of President, under the new constitution, is similar to that of the former monarch: a figurehead with little executive power, rather than an American or French-style presidency. The parliamentary system ensures an effective alternation of power, as has happened in the most recent elections of 2005. The constitution guarantees even so the rights to parliamentary representation of ethnic minorities such as the Chinese community, but also religious minorities such as the Muslims, thus enshrining ethnic and religious differences at the level of the political system. In a similar way the state-funded school system offers teaching of minority languages such Mandarin or Urdu, even at primary school level, and maintains schools with religious affiliations, such as Catholic and Hindu-based schools. Attendance at these schools is not limited, however, to children practising these religious beliefs.

Mauritian society is thus a fragmented one, with different interest groups vying for political and economic influence, usually based on ethnic and religious communities. The Franco-Mauritian community, traditionally Catholic, is still the dominant land-owning group, and the large sugar estates still control large sectors of the island's economy. Indo-Mauritian and Chinese entrepreneurs have also contributed to the economic dynamism of the island, with trading links to the Indian sub-continent, as well as to South-East Asia. The non-skilled workforce of the island is generally divided between Indo-Mauritian, Hindu groups and Creole, usually Catholic ones. In general, these sub-groups have little social contact with each other, and tend to marry among themselves. They co-exist and work together peacefully on a day-to day basis, in spite of a latent rivalry and competition for influence and prestige. Inter-community disputes do occasionally erupt, however: the most famous example in recent times was the riots that broke out in 1999 after the death in police custody of the Creole reggae singer Kaya, a hero of the Creole community. This provided the subject-matter for a recent novel by Carl de Souza, called *Les jours Kaya*.[12] Another example of such tensions was the attempt by the Hindu community to censor the publication of Lindsey Collen's novel *The Rape of Sita* in 1993, on the grounds that its title and plot were an affront to traditional religious portrayals of Sita, a mythical figure of purity in the Hindu religion.

A strongly Francophone literary heritage

In the light of the social, cultural and linguistic fragmentation of Mauritian society, it is all the more surprising that French has maintained its dominance as the principal vehicle of literary and cultural expression. This remains the case in spite of the fact that English is the teaching language of the school system, and the official language of parliament and government; and this during a period when English has reinforced its dominance as the world-wide international language of science, business and diplomacy. Mauritius is certainly an active member of the International Francophone organization as well as the Commonwealth, and hosted the annual Francophone summit in 1993. What are the factors which have contributed to this unexpected situation?

The first must be the need to cling to a tradition, to establish a heritage, a continuity in this far-flung territory: the first newspapers and literary publications of the island in the late eighteenth century were in French, and have remained so A second factor must be the generative link between French and the effective *lingua franca* of the island: Mauritian Creole. This means that French is not as "foreign" to the Creole-speaking reader as, say, Hindi: there are many shared idioms and elements of vocabulary. A final element must be the social prestige of the Franco-Mauritian community, who constitute a kind of unofficial "aristocracy" of the island by virtue of their land-owning status, and in spite of the hardships their ancestors inflicted on generations of slaves and indentured labourers. For well over a century it was only in that privileged social group that the conditions for the production of literary works existed, and where a literary culture could survive. Even so, towards the end of the nineteenth century a Creole writer of mixed race origin such as Léoville L'Homme could succeed in achieving national recognition as a poet, journalist and newspaper editor. The rising generation of Creole intellectuals were keen to display their literary credentials through an enthusiastic endorsement of the French tradition, in the face of the growing influence of the Hindu community. The elitist associations of the use of French in the context of Mauritian culture are no doubt also the reasons for the more recent revolt of writers choosing to use Creole or Hindi as the vehicle for their literary works. Even so, there is an element of aesthetic preference in the decision of many Mauritian authors to adopt the French language, based on its rich intellectual and artistic heritage and its expressive possibilities.

So the vast majority of literary works published by Mauritians since the late eighteenth century have been written in French, regardless of the ethnic background of their authors. Indeed, many of them were educated in France, and even when they were not, as in the case of Ananda Devi, who studied in the United Kingdom, they still choose to write in French. It has been common for Mauritian writers to make their careers in France: this was the case for figures such as Loys Masson, novelist and resistance poet, who arrived in France in 1939, on the eve of the Second World War and became a leading French literary figure in the post-war years, remaining there until his death in 1969. Even when writers do not settle in France, the principal publishing opportunities for their work exist in France rather than in Mauritius. The island has only relatively recently developed locally-based publishing houses, such as the Editions de l'Océan Indien; for over 150 years the production of books was most often in the hands of printing houses, commissioned by the authors themselves, rather than professional publishers, which gave added weight and prestige to the rare privilege for a Mauritian writer of being published in metropolitan France.

A rich Francophone poetic tradition

The two major figures of Mauritian literature in the twentieth century are undoubtedly Robert-Edward Hart (1891-1954) and Malcolm de Chazal (1902-1981). The major part of their career is thus dated during the colonial period, and only Chazal's later years can be situated in the post-independence period. The question which then arises in this context is to determine to what extent their work can be considered postcolonial, if at all. However influential, are they not both colonial writers, by the predominant chronology of their work? Both can be seen as tributaries of metropolitan French literary traditions: Symbolism, in the case of Hart, and Surrealism in the case of Chazal. In neither case is the principal thrust of their work a critique of the colonial situation, yet neither do they endorse it directly. Rather their preoccupations are properly poetic and transcendent, questioning the status of man in the universe, exploring the potential of the poetic imagination. Although they both travelled away from Mauritius, both remained steadfastly loyal to the island and identified profoundly with it: their Mauritianity is in both cases unassailable.

Using as a touchstone some of the principal themes of postcolonial theory, let us examine briefly the characteristics of each poet's writing. Hart was born into a culturally hybrid family: his father was a British-born solicitor, and his mother a French aristocrat descended from a minor poetic figure of the Pléiade in the French sixteenth century, Pontus de Tyard.[13] This is perhaps the reason for his cultural open-ness to cosmopolitan influences, and his poetry celebrates the cultural richness of the Mauritian context, as well as its natural beauty. He adapted into French extracts from the Bhagavad-Gita,[14] as well as translating some classics of English poetry into French.[15] He published a collection of "Poèmes védiques" based on Hindu mythology[16] and, inspired by visits to Madagascar and contacts with Malagasy writers such as Rabéarivelo and French expatriates such as Pierre Camo, he also celebrated traditional Malagasy culture in a series of poems.[17] It is this cosmopolitanism and his receptiveness to indigenous cultures which marks him out as different from many of his colonial contemporaries. His quest for an elusive spiritual fulfilment and the melancholia of its ever-postponed realisation makes him a representative example of the influence of French Symbolism. In this respect he is typical of his generation of poets and less distinctively Mauritian, less obviously postcolonial. In a way he seems to relish the opportunities offered by the complex colonial networks of influence, and is far from denouncing its abuses. On the contrary, he appears to have taken advantage of the cultural links they facilitated with the other colonies of the region, such as Madagascar, India and Reunion.

Malcolm de Chazal was the descendant of one of the first French families to settle in Mauritius. At an early age he was sent to train as an agricultural engineer in the sugar industry, in Louisiana, USA. After a brief stay in Cuba, he returned to Mauritius in 1925, never again to leave the island. The sugar industry was not for him, and he eventually found a niche as a civil servant in the telecommunications sector. His writing has little to do with this rather prosaic reality, however: it is mostly concerned with the formulation of a cosmic vision of the universe and man's place within it, the origins of the magical island of Mauritius in a mystical and surrealist cosmology which he elaborated in a prolific series of publications between 1940 and his death in 1981

His early texts were formulated as a series of poetic aphorisms, which collected together in the volume *Sens plastique* came to the attention of the influential French literary figure Jean Paulhan. The volume was published by Gallimard in Paris in 1948[18] and Chazal was hailed as a primitive mystic and surrealist. Subsequent volumes of his prolific output were published only in Mauritius, as the cosmology they expressed became increasingly centred on the origins of the island as a fragment of a submerged continent called Lémurie, a myth first propagated by the Reunionese writer Jules Hermann. This "myth of origins," a strange mixture of Christian and Swedenborgian theology involving the notion of the primeval fall of man, was developed in various treatises and collections of poetic texts, the most important of which is probably *Petrusmok* of 1951.[19] Jean-Louis Joubert attributes the origins of this mythology to the need for a foundational myth for a Creole culture which is otherwise condemned to acknowledge its transitory, problematic origins. In other words, it can be seen an elaborate, eloquent and fantastical way of avoiding any confrontation with the colonial realities of Chazal's own background. This delusional subterfuge does not imply, however, that Chazal endorses the colonial situation into which he was born: on the contrary, in the preface to *Petrusmok*, he has some pungent comments to make, as he was often given to do on many other topical issues in the Mauritian press:

> L'île Maurice est un pâté de roches dans l'Océan Indien, où sur un fond de colonialisme négrier, vivote une pseudo-civilisation dont chaque communauté revendique le monopole.

> ... Ce pays cultive la canne à sucre et les préjugés.[20]

> [Mauritius island is a pâté of rocks in the Indian Ocean on which, against a backdrop of slave-trading colonialism, a pseudo-civilisation survives, over which each community claims to have a monopoly.
>
> ... This country cultivates sugar cane and prejudices.][21]

Such a statement is almost enough to ensure him a place in the pantheon of postcolonial writers, but such denunciations are not the main thrust of his writing, which is more concerned with the propagation of his particular mystical alternative reality.

Expatriate writers

A third more recent figure completes the picture of the major figures of Mauritian poetry in the twentieth century. Edouard Maunick, unlike his illustrious predecessors, has spent the best part of his career away from the island. In many ways he is a more obviously postcolonial writer than the two older poets. In his own words, his own ancestry and birth (in 1931) symbolize the hybridity of the various communities of the island:

> l'homme blanc qui prit ma grand-mère
> dans son lit refusa de donner son nom à ma mere
> ainsi ma mere put épouser
> mon père lui-même petit-fils de coolies venant des Indes
> que voulez-vous que j'y fasse [22]

> [The white man who took my grandmother
> into his bed refused to give my mother his name
> and so my mother was able to marry
> my father himself son of coolies from India
> what do you expect me to do about it] [23]

His early career was as a teacher and librarian in Port-Louis, but in 1960 he moved to Paris, where he worked as a journalist and broadcaster, and was associated with the journal and publishing house *Présence africaine*. He worked briefly as a radio presenter in Saint Lucia in 1962, he held a visiting post at the University of California in Los Angeles in 1970. From 1980 he held various posts as an international civil servant, with the International Francophone Organisation, as a member of its Supreme Council, and with UNESCO. He was awarded prizes and medals by the Académie française and other French literary institutions. Under the first presidency of the Republic of Mauritius in the 1990s, he was appointed Ambassador to South Africa. This brilliant, nomadic career is reflected in his disparate and fragmented body of work, in which the theme of his problematic identity resurfaces regularly as a motif:

> moi cet enfant de mille races
> pétri d'Europe et des Indes
> taillé plus profondément
> dans le cri du Mozambique
> reconnaissant les racines
> je me tais en signe de deuil
> sur la part non partagée
> je suis nègre de preference [24]

> [myself this child of a thousand races
> moulded from Europe and the Indies
> more profoundly carved
> from the cry of the Mozambican
>
> recognizing the roots
> I fall silent as a sign of mourning
> For that part unshared
> I am a negro by preference] [25]

His poetry is usually more dense and elusive, however, like the later poetry of the Martinican poet Aimé Césaire, to whom he dedicated a collection as a tribute.[26]

Exile has been a recurrent temptation for Mauritian writers, more so than is perhaps the case with writers in general, who in any case often need to place themselves at a distance from their home society, from their origins. This was certainly the case with Loys Masson, who, as mentioned earlier, left Mauritius as a student immediately prior to the Second World War and never returned. Although he carved himself out a place in the French literary world, first as a resistance poet and subsequently as a radical left-wing and Christian writer, several of his post-war novels return to Mauritian subject matter, treated from a highly critical perspective. Among the most significant of these were *L'étoile et la clef*,[27] which takes its title from the Latin motto of the Mauritian coat of arms, "Stella clavisque mari indici" [The star and the key of the Indian Ocean]. This autobiographical evocation of Masson's youth and adolescence is set in the context of the social unrest of Mauritius in the 1930s, and the struggle of the Indian cane workers for political representation. Other texts relating to the Indian Ocean include *Le Notaire des noirs* of 1960,[28] which recounts the tragic destiny of an idealistic young lawyer whose career is jeopardised by his sympathy for the underprivileged black population; and *Les Noces de la vanille*,[29] a family drama set on a vanilla plantation in Réunion island. Jean-Louis Joubert analyses the significance of Masson's tragic family intrigues, in which the recurrent motif of a child victim and the alienation and repression of the black population are linked, as a representation of the collective guilt of the Franco-Mauritian community and the inability of Masson to accept his own social background, which prevented him from returning to the island.[30] This situates Masson's fiction, however obliquely, as a significant element in the postcolonial representations of the island's social history, and identifies its author as belonging both to the French and the Mauritian literary heritage.

Another well-known figure in recent French fictional writing is similarly situated astride the two literary fields. Jean-Marie Gustave Le Clézio was born in Nice into a well-established Franco-Mauritian family, but his early career as a writer was clearly situated in the context of the experimental fiction of France: his first novel *Le Procès*[31] was awarded the prix Renaudot in 1963. Much of Le Clézio's writing concerns the instability of travel, of exile, and many of his narratives are set in exotic locations such as Onitsha in Nigeria, Mexico, etc. It was not until the publication of *Le Chercheur d'or*[32] in 1985 that his readership became aware of the Mauritian background of its author. The novel recounts a magical and idyllic journey to the peripheral Mauritian island of Rodrigues, retracing the steps of an uncle who went there in search of a buried treasure. This has since become a classic of Mauritian literature, and its author an influential figure in the island's recent literary development,[33] even though his more recent texts have resumed their nomadic subject-matter and have little direct relevance to his publicly declared Mauritian identity. In this respect he is probably representative of the extensive Mauritian diaspora, and his work symbolically opens up the postcolonial questioning of the relevance of national identification.

Similar expatriate Mauritian writers include Marie-Thérèse Humbert, whose first novel *A l'autre bout de moi*, published in France in 1979,[34] expresses in fictional terms many of the underlying social tensions of the multi-ethnic and multi-cultural society of Mauritius. The novel was awarded a literary prize by the women's magazine *Elle*, and enjoyed considerable commercial success in France and in Mauritius. It recounts the personal drama of twin sisters in a middle-class Creole family, tempted by relationships with members of the Franco-Mauritian and Indian communities, against a background of social prejudice and the stigma of illegitimate pregnancy and abortion. Humbert's later novels usually abandon the Mauritian setting, and are probably better situated in the context of metropolitan French writing.[35]

The poet Khal Torabully, on the other hand, is clearly situated in a postcolonial Mauritian context through the content of his verse, which explores questions of ethnic identity through the neologism of "coolitude," probably inspired by the celebrated Negritude movement of Aimé Césaire and Léopold Sédar Senghor. His collection *Cale d'étoiles* of 1992 [36] explores the cultural heritage of the Indian indentured labourers brought to Mauritius during the nineteenth century, as they were to the islands of the Caribbean and elsewhere. Yet Khal has made his home in metropolitan France, which places him at one remove even from this problematic identity, making him a symbolic figure of the migration of cultures typical of the postcolonial era.

The most recent expatriate novelist stands in striking contrast to figures such as Masson and Le Clézio. Although she has settled in France for some time now, the fictional writings of Ananda Devi [37] are almost exclusively focused on the social dynamics of Mauritian society, and in particular the Indo-Mauritian community. Her prolific output of novels and short stories, which began with the collection *Solstices* in 1977 [38] and continued with the collection *Le Poids des êtres* in 1987 [39] mostly feature female heroines who are often also narrators. This is the case with her first full-length novel, *Rue La Poudrière*,[40] a daring first-person narration by a prostitute in the slum quarters of the island's capital Port-Louis. Since then several novels have appeared, many of which explore various forms of suffering and alienation of women figures, often outcasts from a repressive society and victims of various kinds of mental and emotional and even physical abuse. This is the case in texts such as *Le Voile de Draupadi*,[41] in which the heroine resorts to Hindu mysticism through the mythical figure of Draupadi to resolve her traumatic loss of both her child and her husband; in *L'Arbre fouet*,[42] the heroine tries to exorcise a curse by which she is doomed to commit a murder; in *Pagli*[43] the heroine is ostracised by her conformist Hindu community because of her affair with a Creole fisherman, thereby breaking the taboo of inter-community relations. With these novels exploring various kinds of female alienation, she has successfully moved from a local audience and the limited publishing outlets of Mauritius, first to L'Harmattan, one of the best-known French publishers of Francophone material, and more recently to Gallimard, probably the most prestigious Parisian publishing house. Whatever one may think about the neo-colonial implications of such a trajectory, the fact remains that the Gallimard imprint is still likely to ensure a wider audience in the Francophone world, and France in particular, than a local publication in Mauritius. The success of her work has probably drawn on the popularity in recent decades of feminist writing, and in particular it explores the predicament of women in what are conventionally called "Third World" societies. Much of her writing also illustrates an ethnographic dimension, exploring the power of traditional and religious myths in the postcolonial society of Mauritius.[44]

Insular novelists

The novel is relatively recent development in Mauritian writing: in the nineteenth-century poetry and drama were the favoured genres. The dominance of the form in nineteenth and twentieth century French literature eventually led to its adoption by Mauritian writers, and even the novel of cyclical and epic proportions, such as the *Cycle de Pierre Flandre* by Robert-Edward Hart.[45] By general assent, a landmark which ushers in the postcolonial novel in Mauritius is *Namasté*, published locally by Marcel Cabon in 1965.[46] This is a Mauritian version of the peasant novel in the manner of Giono, but celebrating the values of the Hindu community in a language which integrates creolisms and local detail, and expressing for the first time a solidarity between the Creole peasant community and the Indo-Mauritian one. This makes the novel yet another example of the subversive mimicry of an established French genre, adapted as a vehicle for the postcolonial ambitition of celebrating hybridization. Cabon himself was of Creole background, but used his considerable literary talent in celebration of the multi-cultural richness of the island's culture.

A contemporary novelist who has continued in the socially inclusive vein of Cabon is Carl de Souza. His first novel, *Le Sang de l'Anglais* [47] was awarded the prize of the Francophone organisation the ACCT (Agence de co-opération culturelle et technique) in 1989. This is ostensibly a novel written from a purely Franco-Mauritian perspective: the narrator Saint-Bart describes with affection and condescension the misplaced loyalty of his school-friend Hawkins to his partly British ancestry. This first-person narration is heavily laced with irony, however, as the novel effectively describes the twilight of the colonial era, the transfer of power to the Indian majority at independence, the exodus of the other ethnic communities to Australia, to Canada, to the United Kingdom. This first fictional text carried no hint of the range of diversity of the subsequent novels. *La Maison qui marchait vers le large* [48] recounts the rearguard defence of an ageing Franco-Mauritian landlord against the encroaching multi-racial society in a suburb of the capital Port Louis. The collapsing colonial mansion of the title is symbolic of the decline of the pretensions of the Franco-Mauritian community to the colonial domination of Mauritian society, as its owner is obliged to come to terms with his Indo-Muslim tenants, and eventually to depend on their generosity and support. The novel sympathetically describes in parallel the conflicts of the Muslim family, whose son is abandoning their traditional religious values for the cynical realism of modern urban youth culture. De Souza's subsequent works have been surprising departures: *Les jours Kaya*[49] offers a nightmarish fictional account of the violence and looting which followed the death in police custody of the reggae singer Kaya. The hero and heroine are not Creoles, like the singer and his rioting supporters, but a young Indo-Mauritian couple caught up in the demonstrations and the violence they unleashed. Yet another surprise came with the most recent novel: *Ceux qu'on jette à la mer* [50] is a harsh and uncompromising tale of the living conditions of a group of Chinese boat-people trying to reach the paradise of North America (by way of Haïti!) with the help of unscrupulous people-traffickers. The range and diversity of the subject-matter of De Souza's novels make them a series of vignettes of the tensions between the various ethnic communities of Mauritius, usually described from a first-person standpoint. His broader ambition seems to be to document the social dynamics of the emerging multi-cultural community in Mauritius, and to represent these from within the worlds of particular individuals and their values. The complexities of these social relations are sensitively and perceptively handled and this makes De Souza one of the most satisfying postcolonial writers in contemporary Mauritian literature.

Creole poetry, theatre and music

As mentioned earlier, the post-independence years in Mauritius have seen the growth of a literature written in Mauritian Creole.[51] In the first instance this was part of a left-wing inspired political nationalism, during the years following independence in 1968, and was resisted by the largely Francophone or Anglophone establishment. The legitimation of the Creole language was also challenged by the Indo-Mauritian community who championed the claims of Hindi as an official language. This stalemate situation has effectively blocked any attempt to give the Creole language any official status until very recently, when an official commission has been looking into the standardisation of its written form. This is necessary since the written form of Creole is a hotly disputed question. Should it be written as a variant of French, using French-based spelling? This would be to downgrade the language to the status of a *patois*, an incorrect variety of regional French. Its partisans favour a strictly phonetic transcription of "kreol"; but this proves difficult to read for the non-initiated Francophone or Anglophone, and even for the semi-literate creolophone. Even then there are disputes as to the best way of transcribing phonetic vowels, for instance, or whether to use accents, as in French.

The major Creole writer of in recent years has been an important contributor to these debates. Dev Virahsawmy regards "kreol" as a national language, referring to it as "morisien." His first published work was poetry, polemical verse written while in prison for his political activities: *Disik sale* (1974)[52] *Lafumé dâ Lizié* (1977)[53] and *Mo rapel* (1980).[54] He has since become best known for his prolific output of plays. The earliest of these continue the militant and political vein of his poetry, such as *Li* (1979),[55] also written while he was in prison. His early plays also reveal a practice he was to develop in much of his later work: the adaptation into the Mauritian context of classic dramas from the Anglophone theatre, most often by Shakespeare. Thus the story of *Macbeth* is adapted into a satire of arbitrary military coups in *Zeneral Makbef* (1981)[56] and Ben Jonson's *The Alchemist* becomes *Dokter Nipat* (1983).[57] His strategy is to demonstrate that the Creole language can handle sophisticated dramatic texts and to appropriate for it some of the prestige of classic literary theatre: thus *Dokter Nipat* contains allusions to Molière's *L'Avare* as well as Ben Jonson. He also draws on other cultural heritages, notably Indian mythology in the musical drama *Dropadi* (1982).[58] His best-known play, the only one to have been translated into English, is *Toufann* (1991),[59] a freewheeling adaptation of *The Tempest* which ironically includes characters called "Poloniouss," "Kordelia" and even "King Lir." These "in-jokes" depend on cultural allusions and the knowing complicity of a sophisticated audience, and the inter-text of the Shakespeare play is re-written in a satirical vein to refer to the political and social situation of Mauritius, featuring the central motif of the conflict between Prospero and Kaliban for the domination of the island. Virahsawmy's adaptations are not always as autonomous and creative, however: he has also published relatively faithful versions of *Much ado about nothing* as *En ta senn dan vid* (1995),[60] *Macbeth* as *Trazedji Makbess* (1997*)*,[61] as well as adaptations of musical comedies such as *Joseph and his Amazing Technicolour Dreamcoat* as *Zosef ek so paletot l'arc-en-ciel*.[62] Many of his texts illustrate again the working of a certain subversive mimicry in Mauritian postcolonial literature, appropriating classic texts from British and French dramatic literature and using them for his own ends, in much the way suggested by Homi Bhabha.

Apart from theatre, the other area of expression where Mauritian Creole is the dominant mode of expression is in popular music. Mauritius shares with Réunion and Seychelles the traditional music of the sega, which is the musical heritage of the former slaves brought to the islands to work on the plantations. They improvised songs on a simple chant/response format and accompanied themselves with percussion instruments such as the *ravanne* a kind of tambourine, the *maravanne*, in Réunion called the *caïamb* or *kayanm*, a tray of hollow cane stems filled with grains of rice which produce a rustling rhythm similar to the maracas, and the triangle, in resonant metal.[63] This original form, called the *sega ravanne*, at first outlawed by the plantation owners, was gradually accepted as a local dance form in European society and instruments such as the violin, the guitar, the banjo and sometimes the accordion were added: this variety is called the *sega salon*. One of the most famous exponents of the traditional *sega* was Ti-frere, whose songs composed in Creole were sung by all sectors of the Mauritian community. Only at the end of his life Ti-Frere was recorded commercially and for the radio and his songs are still available on a tribute CD.[64] The *sega* is still alive, although most often in a somewhat commercial form, performed as a show for tourists in the many hotels in Mauritius.

As in many "third world" countries, and especially island cultures, Jamaican reggae has been adopted and acclimatized as a form of popular song. Mauritius is no exception, and has several reggae groups who have achieved an international reputation in the region. The best known reggae singer is the late Kaya, who used the rhythm as a vehicle for social protest prior to his death in police custody in 1999, in circumstances still not fully elucidated, provoking riots in protest on the part of the Creole community. His recordings survive,[65] however, and remain very popular as an expression of revolt against the conditions of the poor and disenfranchised in Mauritian society. They express in Creole sentiments of the aspiration of a return to traditional African values, as propagated by the Rastafarian religion.

The influence of Hindu culture

The influence of the Indo-Mauritian community increased as it grew in number, but it was only in the years after the Second World War, a period of aspiration to independence and democratic representation, that the

Hindu cultural values began to assert their presence in Mauritius. The pioneering figures of Basdeo Bissoondoyal and the brothers S. M. and B. K. Bhagat are largely responsible during this period for the diffusion and development of a literature in Hindi during the post-war years.[66] Since independence in 1968, Abhimanyu Unnuth has emerged as a major novelist, achieving considerable success in India with novels written in Hindi, and being awarded several literary prizes. It has taken some time for his work to become known to the Francophone public, thanks to some translations of his work into French. Thus a collection of his short stories, *Les Empereurs de la Nuit*, translated by Aslakha Callikan-Proag, appeared in 1983.[67] This was followed in 1997 by a full length novel, *Ek Bigha Pyar*, originally published in 1972, and translated as *Le Culte du Sol*.[68] More recently *Lal Passina*, a major novel first published in India in 1977, was published in translation Paris in 2001 under the title *Sueurs de sang*, with a preface by Jean-Marie Le Clézio.[69]

Even though the bulk of the work by Unnuth is not available to non-readers of Hindi, it is clear that his fiction represents a major contribution to postcolonial writing in Mauritius. Its recurrent theme is the depiction of the life of the ordinary Mauritian of Indian background, and his narratives are often set in the peasant community descended from the indentured labour force brought in during the nineteenth century. Its ethos is to celebrate the sacrifices and achievements of this community in conquering their civil rights, their material well-being, their right to religious and cultural expression. This is best embodied in the most recent publication, *Sueurs de Sang*, which recounts in an epic vein the struggle of several generations of Indian immigrants to Mauritius to improve their barbaric working conditions and force the respect of the colonial masters for their family and community values and their religious beliefs.

The inescapable presence of English

Given that English is the teaching language of the education system in Mauritius, as well the official language of the government and administration, it is surprising that there is not a greater use of English for literary purposes. Added to this, one might have expected that the status of English as a world language of communication and the vast potential readership that it implies might have persuaded more Mauritian writers to embrace the language. In practice, however, literature in English is clearly a minority activity and it has only been in relatively recent times, since the 1960s, and surprisingly, since independence in 1968, that there has been a substantial quantity of publications in English. These have remained almost exclusively local publications, thereby limiting severely their access to a wider Anglophone readership. One wonders why Mauritian authors have rarely succeeded in publishing their work with major metropolitan publishing houses in the United Kingdom, the United States or the Commonwealth: after all, there are many Mauritian writers who have been taken up by French publishers in France. Mauritian literature in English has remained on the whole an unfulfilled potential, in spite of anthologies promoted by the British Council, such as Ron Butlin's *Mauritian Voices*. [70]

The nearest to an exception to this general rule is provided by Lindsey Collen, for whom English is her mother tongue, since she was born and educated in South Africa. Mauritius has become her adopted home and she has been active in left-wing politics in the island, along with her husband, Ram Seegobin. To date she has published five novels, the second and fifth of which have been awarded Commonwealth prizes for literature: *There is a tide* (1990),[71] *The Rape of Sita* (1993),[72] *Getting rid of it* (1997),[73] *Mutiny* (2001)[74] and *Boy* (2005).[75] The latter text is an English version of a novel she first published in Mauritian Creole, called *Mision Garson* (1996).[76] She has also published some poetry in Creole, notably *Vizit labalenn* (1995).[77] It is interesting that she has remained loyal to the left-wing publishing house Ledikasyon pu Travayer for all her works except the most recent ones: perhaps the chance of European exposure was too tempting! In general her writing focuses on the situation of women, and depicts the ambivalence of their situation on the revolutionary Left with considerable verve and directness. With *The Rape of Sita* this led to the book being banned by the Mauritian government, and to her receiving death threats: she had offended the orthodox Hindu community by the suggestion that Sita as the symbolic figure of female purity could be the victim of a rape, even if the name was simply that of a fictional contemporary figure involved in radical politics.

Many Mauritians have been educated in British universities, and sometimes this leads to writers adopting English as their preferred medium. This certainly the case of Régis Fanchette, who has published several collections of poetry and novels in English. He is equally at home in French, however, and several of the short stories collected in a restrospective anthology, *A Private Journey*,[78] show this. The musicality of his verse reflects the optimism of his lyrical and philosophical outlook, and transforms the cosmopolitan subject-matter. Fanchette's open-ness and multi-culturalism make him a representative postcolonial figure, even if his writing is limited in its audience.

Anther poet choosing English as a medium of expression is the Indian poet Sakuntala Hawaldar, who was born in Bombay but settled in Mauritius. The personal, intimate lyricism of her collections of poetry, such as *I have seen strange things*[79] and *Moods, Moments and Memories*,[80] reveal a romantic sensibility. She has also tackled contemporary political issues in her poems, such as *Biafra* and *The Birth of Bangla Desh*, and the meditative introspection of her earlier verse has given way in her later work, such as *You*[81] and *Hymns from Beau Bois*,[82] to a mature feminine and meditative outlook on the world.

A disparate multicultural field

It can be difficult to see such a diverse literary output as belonging to a single literary field. Even so, in spite of the variety of languages, it would appear that all these literary ambitions can be situated within the fabric of a limited social space, that of an island of a little over a million inhabitants. In terms of the Bourdieusian conception of a field, one is therefore obliged to take into account the choice of language as an element of the positioning of a literary work. The competition of the literary field simply reflects the rivalry of the various ethnic groups for the dominant habitus of Mauritian society. If one needs evidence of the coherence of the Mauritian literary field, one can look to the way, in critical accounts of Mauritian literature, individuals identified with one or other linguistic or cultural grouping regularly endorse the work of another. Thus the Franco-Mauritian Jean-Marie Le Clézio, writing in French, is happy to endorse the work of the Indo-Mauritian Abhimanyu Unnuth, writing in Hindi;[83] the Indo-Maurician linguist Vinesh Hookoomsing will defend the writing in English of Lindsey Collen;[84] the Indo-Mauritian educationalist Vicram Ramharai will devote a detailed study to writing in Creole,[85] etc. In spite of the linguistic and cultural diversity the literary field of Mauritian writing does effectively function as a field. A final confirmation is provided by the admirable inclusiveness of the special number of the Francophone journal *Notre Librairie*, which covers most of the disparate tendencies of Mauritian writing in French, in Creole, in Hindi, in English, in Chinese.[86] Yet this is a French journal officially funded by the French government and promoting the literary field of "La Francophonie." Such are the paradoxes of the postcolonial situation: the very diversity of the cultural output of Mauritius is sanctioned and endorsed through one of the oldest of its colonial ties, with French metropolitan culture.

Notes

1. I have already explored this question in an article in French; see Peter Hawkins, "Y a-t-il un champ littéraire mauricien?" in *Les Champs littéraires africains*, ed. Romuald Fonkoua and Pierre Halen (Paris: Karthala, 2001), 151-60.
2. See Jean-Georges Prosper, *Histoire de la littérature mauricienne de langue française*, nouvelle édition (Rose Hill, Mauritius: Eds. de l'Océan Indien, 1994), 319-21.
3. See Prosper, *Histoire de la littéature mauricienne*, 321-23.
4. See Joubert, *Littératures de l'Océan Indien*, 105.
5. See Josiane Fievez, "La littérature chinoise. Entretien avec Joseph Tsang Mang Kin" in *La Littérature mauricienne, Notre librairie*, 114 (1993), 79-83.
6. See Prosper, *Histoire de la littéature mauricienne*, 27-28. Extracts from Bernardin's *Voyage à l'Ile de France* have been re-issued in an anthology: Serge Meitinger and J.-C. Carpanin Marimoutou, eds., *Océan indien—Madagascar, la Réunion, Maurice* (Paris: Omnibus, 1998), 753-821.
7. See Prosper, *Histoire de la littéature mauricienne*, 13; Joubert, *Littératures de l'Océan Indien*, 106.
8. See Joubert, *Littératures de l'Océan Indien*, 106.
9. See Prosper, *Histoire de la littéature mauricienne*, 19-20.
10. Abhimanyu Unnuth, *Sueur de Sang*, translated from the original Hindi by Kessen Budhoo and Isabelle Jarry (Paris: Stock, 2001). Original title *Lal Pasina* (1993).

5. See Josiane Fievez, "La littérature chinoise. Entretien avec Joseph Tsang Mang Kin" in *La Littérature mauricienne, Notre librairie*, 114 (1993), 79-83.

6. See Prosper, *Histoire de la littéature mauricienne*, 27-28. Extracts from Bernardin's *Voyage à l'Ile de France* have been reissued in an anthology: Serge Meitinger and J.-C. Carpanin Marimoutou, eds., *Océan indien—Madagascar, la Réunion, Maurice* (Paris: Omnibus, 1998), 753-821.

7. See Prosper, *Histoire de la littéature mauricienne*, 13; Joubert, *Littératures de l'Océan Indien*, 106.

8. See Joubert, *Littératures de l'Océan Indien*, 106.

9. See Prosper, *Histoire de la littéature mauricienne*, 19-20.

10. Abhimanyu Unnuth, *Sueur de Sang*, translated from the original Hindi by Kessen Budhoo and Isabelle Jarry (Paris: Stock, 2001). Original title *Lal Pasina* (1993).

11. Renée Asgarally, *Quand montagne prend difé* (Mauritius: Mascarena University Publications, 1977).

12. Carl De Souza, *Les jours Kaya* (Paris: Eds. de l'Olivier, 2002).

13. See Joubert, *Littératures de l'Océan Indien*, 134.

14. Robert-Edward Hart, *Bhagavad-Gita* (Port Louis, Mauritius: Standard Printing, 1936).

15. Robert-Edward Hart, *Poèmes anglais* (Port Louis, Mauritius: La Typographie moderne, 1929).

16. Robert-Edward Hart, *Poèmes védiques* (Port Louis, Mauritius: Standard Printing, 1941).

17. Robert-Edward Hart, *Sensations de route* (Port Louis, Mauritius: General Printing and Stationery, 1918).

18. Malcolm de Chazal, *Sens plastique* (Paris: Gallimard, 1948).

19. Malcolm de Chazal, *Petrusmok* (Port Louis, Mauritius: Eds. de la Table Ovale, 1951).

20. De Chazal, *Pétrusmok*, v.

21. Author's translation.

22. From Edouard Maunick, *Fusillez-moi* (Paris: Présence africaine, 1970).

23. Author's translation.

24. From Edouard Maunick, *Les Manèges de la mer* (Paris: Présence africaine, 1964).

25. Author's translation.

26. Edouard Maunick, *Toi laminaire* (Mauritius and Reunion: Editions de l'Océan Indien / CRI, 1990). The title echoes that of Aimé Césaire's collection *Moi, laminaire*.

27. Loys Masson, *L'Etoile et la clef* (Paris: Gallimard, 1945).

28. Loys Masson, *Le Notaire des noirs* (Paris: Robert Laffont, 1961). Reprinted (Mauritius: Eds. de l'Océan Indien, 1985). The full text is also included in the anthology: Serge Meitinger and J.-C. Carpanin Marimoutou, eds., *Océan indien—Madagascar, La Réunion, Maurice* (Paris: Omnibus, 1998)

29. Loys Masson, *Les Noces de la vanille*. (Paris: Robert Laffont, 1962). Reprinted (Mauritius: Editions de l'Océan Indien, 1981).

30. See Joubert, *Littératures de l'Océan Indien*, 176.

31. Jean-Marie Gustave Le Clézio, *Le Procès* (Paris: Gallimard, 1963).

32. Jean-Marie Gustave Le Clézio, *Le Chercheur d'or* (Paris: Gallimard, 1985).

33. Le Clézio has recently championed the recognition of the Indo-Mauritian writer Abhimanyu Unnuth, providing a preface for the French translation of his novel *Sueur de sang* (2001). Several articles on his Mauritian-inspired texts are included in *L'océan Indien dans les littératures francophones*, ed. Kumari R. Issur and Vinesh Y. Hookoomsing (Paris and Mauritius: Karthala / Presses de l'Université de Maurice, 2001).

34. Marie-Thérèse Humbert, *A l'autre bout de moi* (Paris: Stock, 1979). For an in-depth study of the work see Françoise Lionnet, *Autobiographical voices: race, gender, self-portraiture* (Ithaca, NY: Cornell University Press, 1989), 216-44.

35. See Joubert, *Littératures de l'Océan Indien*, 181-82.

36. Khal, *Cale d'Etoiles—Coolitude* (Reunion: Editions Azalées / Editions du Flamboyant, 1992). For a discussion of his work, see Véronique Bragard, "Transoceanic echoes: coolitude and the work of the Mauritian poet Khal Torabully," *International Journal of Francophone Studies*, 8:2 (2005), 219-33.

37. She is sometimes referred to by her full name Ananda Devi Nirsimloo.

38. Ananda Devi, *Solstices* (Mauritius: Regent Press, 1977). Reprinted (Mauritius: Editions de l'Océan Indien, 1997).

39. Ananda Devi, *Le Poids des êtres* (Mauritius: Editions de l'Océan Indien, 1987).

40. Ananda Devi, *Rue la Poudrière* (Dakar and Abidjan: Nouvelles Editions Africaines, 1989). For an analysis of this work see Françoise Lionnet, *Postcolonial representations: women, literature, identity* (Ithaca, NY: Cornell University Press, 1995), 48-68.

41. Ananda Devi, *Le Voile de Draupadi* (Paris: L'Harmattan, 1993).

42. Ananda Devi, *L'Arbre fouet* (Paris; L'Harmattan, 1997).

43. Ananda Devi, *Pagli* (Paris: Gallimard, "Continents noirs" series, 2001).

44. For a reading of Ananda Devi's novels as "ethnotextes," see Valérie Magdelaine-Andrianjafitrimo, "'Ethnotexte' et intertextualité: la mise en scène des représentations culturelles dans les 'romans ethnographiques'" in *Contes et Romans: Univers créoles 4*, ed. Valérie Magdelaine-Andrianjafitrimo and Carpanin Marimoutou (Paris: Anthropos, 2004), chapter 5. For the mythical and religious dimension, see Véronique Bragard, "Cris de femmes maudites, brûlures du silence: La symbolique des elements fondamentaux dans l'oeuvre d'Ananda Devi," *Notre Librairie*, No. 142 (2000), 66-73.

45. Robert-Edward Hart, *Le Cycle de Pierre Flandre* (Port Louis, Mauritius: la Typographie Moderne, 1928-1934), comprising 4 novels: *Mémorial de Pierre Flandre*, 1928; *Respiration de la vie*, 1932; *La Joie du monde, vols. I and II*, 1934.

46. Marcel Cabon, *Namasté* (Port Louis, Mauritius: Le Cabestan, Royal Printing Co., 1965). Reprinted (Rose Hill, Mauritius: Editions de l'Océan Indien, 1981). The full text is included in the anthology *Océan indien—Madagascar, la Réunion, Maurice*, ed. Serge Meitinger and J.-C. Carpanin Marimoutou (Paris: Omnibus, 1998), 943-1011.

47. Carl de Souza, *Le Sang de l'Anglais* (Paris: Hatier, 1993).

48. Carl de Souza, *La Maison qui marchait vers le large* (Paris: Le Serpent à plumes, 1996).

49. Carl de Souza, *Les jours Kaya* (Paris: Editions de l'Olivier, 2000).

50. Carl De Souza, *Ceux qu'on jette à la mer* (Paris: Editions de l'Olivier 2001).

51. For a detailed analysis of this development, see Vicram Ramharai, *La littérature mauricienne d'expression créole. Essai d'analyse socio-culturelle* (Port Louis, Mauritius: Editions Les Mascareignes, 1990).

52. Dev Virahsawmy, *Disik sale* (Port Louis, Mauritius: MMMSP / Olympic printing, 1974).

53. Dev Virahsawmy, *Lafumé dâ Lizié* (Port Louis, Mauritius: MMMSP / Olympic printing, 1977).

54. Dev Virahsawmy, *Mo Rapel* (Port Louis, Mauritius: MMMSP / Olympic printing, 1980).

55. Dev Virahsawmy, *Li* (Port Louis, Mauritius: MMMSP/Olympic printing, 1979). Trilingual version in Mauritian Creole, Reunionese Creole and French (Saint-Denis: Les Chemins de la Liberté, 1979).

56. Dev Virahsawmy, *Zeneral makbef* (Port Louis, Mauritius: Bukié Banané, 1981).

57. Dev Virahsawmy, *Dokter Nipat* (Rose Hill, Mauritius: Bukié Banané, 1983).

58. Dev Virahsawmy, *Dropadi* (Terre Rouge, Mauritius: Bukié Banané, 1982).

59. Dev Virahsawmy, *Toufann* (Port Louis, Mauritius: La Sentinelle, 1991). Translation into English by Nisha and Michael Walling in *African Theatre; Playwrights and politics*, ed. Martin Banham, James Gibbs and Femi Osofisan (Oxford, Bloomington and Johannesburg: James Currey / Indiana University Press / Witwatersrand University Press, 2001). For an analysis of Virahsawmy's strategy in adapting Shakespeare, see Françoisee Lionnet, "Creole Vernacular Theatre: Transcolonial Translations in Mauritius." *MLN*, 118, No. 4 (Sept. 2003) 911-32.

60. Dev Virahsawmy, *Enn Ta senn Dan Vid* (Port Louis, Mauritius: LPT, 1995).

61. Dev Virahsawmy, *Trazedji Makbess* (Port Louis, Mauritius: LPT, 1997).

62. See Dev Virahsawmy, "Quand le theatre nourrit sa langue" in *Notre Librairie*, 114 (1993), 116-18.

63. For a full account of the development of the Mauritian sega, see Jacques K. Lee, *Sega: the Mauritian folk-dance* (London: Nautilus Publishing, 1990).

64. Ti-frère, *Hommage à Ti-Frère* (Paris: Radio France / Ocora, 1991), CD No. C 560019.

65. Kaya, *Zistoir Revoltan* (Réunion: Discorama, 1996), CD 96.16.

66. See Prosper, *Histoire de la literature mauricienne*, 320.

67. Abhimanyu Unnuth, *Les Empereurs de la Nuit*, translated into French by Aslakha Callikan-Proag (Moka, Mauritius: Editions de l'Océan Indien / Mahatma Gandhi Institute, 1983).

68. Abhimanyu Unnuth, *Le Culte du Sol*, translated into French by Kessen Budhoo and Shakuntala Boolell (Vacoas, Mauritius: Editions Le Printemps, 1997).

69. Abhimanyu Unnuth, *Sueurs de sang*, translated into French by Kessen Budhoo and Isabelle Jarry (Paris: Stock, 2001).

70. Ron Butlin, ed. *Mauritian Voices—new writing in English.* (Newcastle, UK: Flambard, 1997).

71. Lindsey Collen, *There is a tide* (Port Louis, Mauritius: LPT, 1990).

72 Lindsey Collen, *The Rape of Sita* (Port Louis, Mauritius: LPT, 1993).

73. Lindsey Collen, *Getting rid of it* (London: Granta, 1997).

74. Lindsey Collen, *Mutiny* (London: Bloomsbury, 2001).

75. Lindsey Collen, *Boy* (London: Bloomsbury, 2005).

76. Lindsey Collen, *Mision Garson* (Port Louis, Mauritius: LPT, 1996).

77. Lindsey Collen, *Vizit labalenn* (Port Louis, Mauritius: LPT, 1995).

78. Régis Fanchette, *A Private Journey . . . itinéraire privé* (Mauritius: Editions de l'Océan Indien, 1996).

79. Shakuntala Hawaldar, *I have seen strange things* (Port Louis, Mauritius: Mauritius Printing Co., 1971).

80. Shakuntala Hawaldar, (*Moods, Moments and Memories* (Beau Bassin, Mauritius: the Triveni, 1972).

81. Shakuntala Hawaldar, *You* (Port Louis, Mauritius: Lem Wee Graphics, 1981).

82. Shakuntala Hawaldar, *Hymns from Beau Bois* (n.p., 1994).

83. Jean-Marie G. Le Clézio, "Préface" in Unnuth, *Sueurs de Sang*, (2001).

84. See back cover of Lindsey Collen, *There is a tide* (1990).

85. See Vicram Ramharai, *La littérature mauricienne d'expression créole* (1990).

86. *Littérature mauricienne*, special issue of *Notre Librairie*, 114 (1993).

Chapter 6

La Réunion

A postcolonial society?

One cannot help wondering whether Reunion island can legitimately described as postcolonial.[1] It is after all a *Département d'Outre-Mer*, a term usually abbreviated to the acronym "DOM," to designate the non-European territories with a full departmental status integral to the French Republic, which also involves membership of the European Union. These include the Caribbean islands of Guadeloupe and Martinique, the South American enclave of Guyane française, and Reunion. The status of "DOM" is not accorded to all French overseas territories: Mayotte, for instance, in the Comorian archipelago, is currently a "Collectivité départmentale," and is in the process of becoming a *DOM*; Tahiti is part of La Polynésie française, a *Territoire d'Outre-mer*, a "TOM," as is Nouvelle Calédonie, with a greater degree of political autonomy. Reunion has always been a French territory, since the first inhabitants settled there permanently in 1665, except for a brief period of occupation by the British from 1810 to 1815, during the Napoleonic wars. The discussion turns on the implication of the law passed by the French National Assembly in 1946, which assimilated the territories now called "DOM" as fully-fledged and integral parts of the French Republic, under the same political and administrative regime as the metropolitan French departments. Reunion is thus politically and administratively a part of France, and the Reunionese population are citizens of France.

Technically and constitutionally, therefore, La Réunion ceased to be a colony in 1946. It is obviously postcolonial in the temporal sense, but remains very heavily dependent on metropolitan France for its economic prosperity and its high standard of living. The high levels of unemployment and the presence of oppositional groups critical of its dependent status give the island some of the characteristics of a colony, even after over fifty years as a *DOM*. Its writers and artists are often highly critical of the effects of this dependency, and some champion the autonomy of its culture and aspire to a greater degree of independence from the centralized French government. One of the points of tension has been the status of the Creole language, which, in spite of being widely spoken by many native Reunionese, was until very recently accorded no official recognition. The moves towards regionalisation in the French state and the Charter for regional and minority languages promulgated by the European Union have led since the turn of the century to a change in the status of Creole, which is now acknowledged in the school and university system as a regional culture.

The strength of French presence and resources

The positive side of Reunion's integration into French culture lies in the generously endowed cultural institutions that the island benefits from. The local and regional authorities derive their revenue from a tax on imports called the *octroi de mer* that, although it contributes to the high cost of living in the island, also provides them with a source of public finance beyond the more usual local taxation. This is reflected in the island's numerous sports facilities, arts centres, theaters, galleries, concert venues, etc., which provide a home for a thriving cultural and artistic activity. The result of this is that the island supports several theater troupes, numerous local musical groups and a thriving local publishing industry, which features several indigenous publishing houses. This contrasts strikingly with the neighboring island of Mauritius, which is far from possessing such a rich cultural infrastructure. This is accompanied by numerous grants and administrative bodies designed to foster the arts, with the result that the island's population enjoys a standard of cultural activity that compares favourably with any French regional city such as Bordeaux, Lyon or Marseille. It is also home to a large, modern, well-equipped university with an attractive campus on the edge of the capital Saint Denis and a second campus in the south of the island in Le Tampon. These naturally provide a focus, besides the extensive municipal facilities, for visiting musicians, theater groups and gatherings of writers and artists.

Reunion is thus a kind of "shop window" for the presence of French culture in the Indian Ocean region, and attracts artists and writers from the other islands of the zone. It also attracts students to its university and higher education colleges, and in spite of the high levels of local unemployment there is a steady stream of immigration from the poorer societies of the region such as Madagascar and the Comoros.

A model for a multi-cultural France?

Reunionese society is much more ethnically diverse than that of metropolitan France. No statistics are permitted, under French republican law, which would discriminate between groups of citizens on racial grounds. The composition of Reunionese society is generally similar to that of Mauritius, however, with recognisable groups of metropolitan French expatriates, often civil servants and teachers, locally called by the Creole name "zoreys"—there are many apocryphal stories about the origin of the nickname. There is a sizeable minority of inhabitants of Indian origin, not as numerically dominant as in Mauritius, who are familiarly called "Malbars" and usually practice Hindu religious beliefs. There is a black population of African or Malagasy origin, sometimes designated as "cafre," a term which does not carry the same denigrating charge as the word "kaffir" in the South African context: they are often Catholic, sometimes covertly practising animist beliefs such as ancestor worship and sorcery, and if of recent Malagasy origin, sometimes of Protestant faith. There is a Chinese population, originally brought in as indentured laborers and independent immigrants in the late nineteenth and early twentieth century, who have traditionally taken over the small-scale retail sector of local shops.[2] They are increasingly present in the professions; they are sometimes Buddhist in their religious allegiances. Finally there are Islamic traders of Indo-Pakistani background, misnamed "zarabes," who are very present in the retail sector of textiles and electrical goods.

One of the justifications for the ban on any ethnically-based census in Reunion is that in many cases it is very difficult to determine what background an individual may come from, such has been the degree of racial intermarriage in the island. Family names are often completely misleading in this respect, and often do not correspond to the apparent ethnicity of their bearers. Reunion is thus well on the way to becoming an ethnically mixed society where stereotypical notions of racial groupings are irrelevant. This is far from being the case in metropolitan France, as the riots of October 2005 have demonstrated, and indeed, Reunionese moving to mainland France often find it extremely difficult to deal with the racist attitudes prevalent there. It is difficult to determine why such relative harmony should be the case in Reunion: it has been attributed to the egalitarianism of French republican institutions, but if this were the case why would it not be so in mainland France? It has also been traced back to the periods in the fairly recent history of the island where communal solidarity was forced on the disparate population by periods of extreme scarcity, as during the Second World War or epidemics of diseases such as malaria and cholera, in the second half of the nineteenth century. It is certainly in marked contrast with Mauritius, where ethnic and cultural differences are much more clearly defined and reinforced. Social conflict is by no means absent from Reunion, but it is typically a symptom of marked differences in wealth and standard of living, and is not usually defined in terms of ethnic rivalry. The island thus represents a potent symbol of the positive values of French republicanism in a context where French influence is dominant.

Postcolonial precursors

As in the other islands, Reunion can boast a certain number of writers who, while writing during the period of colonisation, were ideologically at odds with its values, and in particular its dependency on slavery. For Ashcroft, Griffiths and Tiffin, the label "postcolonial" refers not to the chronological period after the end of colonial rule, but rather to an ideological position of reaction to the colonial situation.[3] Thus one can consider an eighteenth century writer such as the poet Evariste de Parny as a postcolonial writer, by virtue of his opposition to the institution of slavery. Parny was born in what was then called the "Île Bourbon" in 1757, and grew up there before being sent to metropolitan France at the age of nine to complete his education. He returned to the island in 1773 for a period of three years, during which a love affair provided the inspiration for his early literary success in France, with a collection of elegies published under the title of *Poésies érotiques* in 1778 (the title does not carry the connotation of eroticism in the modern sense). Apart from his occasional denunciations of the evils of slavery in letters and speeches, his most remarkably postcolonial work is the collection of *Chansons madécasses* of 1787, which he presented as prose translations of the songs of a Malagasy slave woman in Bourbon. These early prose poems are almost certainly his own work rather than translations, and quite apart from the unusual fiction of adopting the lyrical voice of a slave, they evoke, among other things, the deceptiveness of the early French colonial settlers in Madagascar, parodying their warnings not to trust the natives.[4] Some of these texts were controversially set to music by the French composer Maurice Ravel in the 1920s, at the peak of French colonialism.

Another significant anti-colonial writer is Louis Timagène Houat, born in the island in 1809, tried, condemned and exiled to mainland France because of his anti-slavery views in 1838. He is also the island's first novelist, with *Les Marrons*, published in 1844.[5] This is a sympathetic portrait of the society of runaway slaves who had lived continuously in the inaccessible mountains of the island since the earliest colonial settlements. It also celebrates mixed-race relationships and criticizes the abuses of colonial society, albeit in a somewhat naïve and clumsy style.

The romanticisation of the *marrons* or runaway slaves was to continue in the work of the chronicler of early Bourbon society Eugène Dayot, who serialised his fictional account of the early settlers of the island in his *Bourbon pittoresque*, first published in the local newspaper *Le Courrier de Saint-Paul* in 1848. Because of leprosy contracted in his youth he was unable to complete his picture of the early colonial society, which turned the battle between the runaway slaves and slave hunters such as the legendary Mussard into a popular adventure story. The unfinished text was republished in his collected works in 1878 and 1977 and in its own right in 1967.[6]

Another notable nineteenth century figure, Auguste Lacaussade, of mixed-race parentage, made his reputation as a poet of the exotic charms of the landscape of his native island. He also used the rhetorical skills developed in imitation of his hero Victor Hugo to denounce the abuses of its slave-owning society, and published several collections of poetry between 1839 and 1876, including *Les Salaziennes* and *Poèmes et paysages*.[7] After a childhood and youth spent in Reunion, his literary career was almost entirely Parisian, as was the case of many poets of subsequent generations. Most of the numerous poets inspired by the beauty of the island during the nineteenth and twentieth centuries celebrated its exotic charms in fairly conventional verse, even when in their other writings they were critical of the faults of colonial society. This is the case with such major figures as Leconte de Lisle, a major French poet born on the island but who left it at an early age, only returning for short stays in his youth. Although he is often celebrated as a Reunionese writer, only a relatively small number of his poems evoke the memory and the décor of his island origins.[8]

Other notably influential figures in the development of Reunionese literature include the colonial apologists Marius and Ary Leblond, cousins and joint authors of a stream of colonialist novels, essays and histories between 1902 and 1953, date of the death of Marius.[9] They celebrated in their significantly-titled novel of 1914, *Le Miracle de la race*, the fictionalised portrait of Jules Hermann, a dynamic local politician and intellectual, author of *Les Révélations du grand océan* of 1927,[10] a posthumously-published treatise on the origins of the Mascarene islands as part of the lost continent of "La Lémurie," during the earliest dramatic movements of the tectonic plates of the earth's crust. This was to have a considerable influence on the Mauritian writers Robert-Edward Hart and Malcolm de Chazal.[11]

Créolie and *Créolité*

The first authentically postcolonial Reunionese poetry was the work of an expatriate Reunionese writer, as had been so often the case in the past. Jean Albany first published his own slim volumes of verse in Paris from 1951 onwards, beginning with *Zamal*.[12] Although his work was often nostalgic and exotic in inspiration, like his predecessors, this title suggests what is different about it: "zamal" is the Reunionese Creole word for cannabis. The familiar tone and Verlainian lyricism of Albany's song-like verse incorporates elements of Creole as well as authentic and evocative allusions to the particularities of the island's flora and fauna. In the process Albany breaks away from the traditional French versification of his predecessors and succeeds in creating a genuinely popular poetry eventually appreciated by his compatriots who had remained back home in Reunion. In 1968, with the collection *Bleu mascarin*,[13] he began to compose his poems entirely in Creole, 1972 he mentioned in a text called *Vavangue* [14] that he inhabited a mental universe he called "Créolie" and this term became a controversial rallying-call for a new literary movement that was to gather pace in the 1970s. In 1974 he published a glossary of Creole terms, *P'tit glossaire, le piment des mots créoles*, [15] and although using the etymological French-based spelling gave a new impetus to the rediscovery of the popular vernacular of the island. Another significant development was his collaboration in 1979 on a cassette recording called *Chante Albany*[16] in which local artists such as Alain Peters composed and performed popular sung versions of his poems in between his own recitations, and this was to mark the beginning of the militant championing of the autonomy of the island's language and culture in poetic songs by artists such as Ziskakan and Danyel Waro.[17]

Albany's notion of "Créolie" was taken up by the poet and Catholic Archbishop of Reunion Gilbert Aubry, for whom it took on the meaning of a celebration of the island's mixed-race culture in his poem *Hymne à la Créolie* of 1978.[18] Aubry had already begun his celebration of the island's distinctive environment and culture in his first collection of poems *Rivages d'Alizé* of 1972.[19] He was joined in his public declaration of principle by the poet and novelist Jean-François Sam-Long, and the two published a series of annual collections of literary texts under the collective title of *Créolie*. They were supported in this venture by Albany and by the long-exiled poet Jean-Henri Azéma who, after a chequered career as an extreme nationalist compromised by partisan collaboration with the Vichy government during the Second World War, had subsequently settled in Argentina. Only in his later years did he rediscover his Reunionese identity through the Créolie movement, having renounced his previous ideological affiliations, and by publishing some memorable poetic collections such as *Olographe* (1978),[20] *D'Azur à perpétuité* (1979),[21] *Le Pétrolier couleur antique* (1982),[22] *Le Dodo vavangueur* (1986).[23] These celebrate his revaluation of the island's characteristic culture, but also exorcise the painful legacy of the slave trade and trace the island's maritime heritage through legends of pirates, bandits and runaway slaves. The *Créolie* movement was specifically non-political, however, and in this respect appears somewhat conservative in relation to other more militant groups. It does constitute, however, a clear but unacknowledged precursor, by over ten years, of the Caribbean Créolité movement launched in 1989 in Martinique by Jean Bernabé, Patrick Chamoiseau and Raphaël Confiant, with their manifesto *Eloge de la créolité*.[24]

Militancy and bilingualism in poetry

A more radical current of poetry emerged in the 1970s, beginning with the collection *Matanans et langoutis* of 1971 by Anne Cheynet, documenting the poverty and deprivation of the island's underprivileged population.[25] This vein was developed by Alain Lorraine's landmark collection *Tienbo le rein* of 1976,[26] a celebration of social solidarity and resistance, written in French in spite of the Creole title. In the meantime one of the masterpieces of modernist poetry in Reunion was published in 1973: Boris Gamaleya's *Vali pour une reine morte*.[27] This long, complex poetic text, composed in enforced exile by its revolutionary militant author, whose parents were a Russian émigré father and a Reunionese Creole mother, incorporates many different conventions and styles, ranging from regular verse and stylised dramatic dialogue to free verse passages using Creole and Malagasy vocabulary as well as standard French. It celebrates the Malagasy heritage of the runaway slaves who settled in the inaccessible mountains of the centre of the island, through the couple Cimendef and Rahariane and their conflict with the French colonial slave hunter Mussard. The title contains an allusion to the Vali, the traditional Malagasy bamboo harp, and gives the poem the dimension of an epic, dedicated to the roots of the island's authentic identity which for the poet lie in the resistance of the maroons to the encroachment of a slave-owning colonial culture, symbolised by the demonized figure of Madame Desbassayns, an emblematic slave plantation owner. The poem is a difficult and obscure text in a modernist poetic style, and Michel Beniamino has devoted an exhaustive early study to the diversity of the vocabulary used in it, using this as a basis for an interpretation of the text in terms of its modulation of the themes of exile and the search for identity.[28] The poem is clearly a major postcolonial text, as much by its linguistic texture as its themes, and sustains comparison with Aimé Césaire's celebrated *Cahier d'un retour au pays natal*. Gamaleya has maintained his output of dense, multiple-genre texts, celebrating the complexity of the island's heritage. A text of a similar epic character, *Ombline ou le Volcan à l'envers*,[29] a reworking as an oratorio of an earlier dramatic text *Le Volcan à l'envers ou Mme Desbassyns le Diable et le Bondieu*,[30] was eventually performed and republished in 1998.

Another radical figure equally at home writing in French and Creole is Jean-Claude Carpanin Marimoutou, who published his first collections of poetry *Fazèle*[31] and *Arracher cinquante mille signes*[32] in 1979 and 1980 respectively . His militant defence of the Creole language and autonomist political positions, close to those of the independent Parti Communiste Réunionnais, are usually expressed in short, dense and elliptical texts which lend themselves to popular musical settings: he has also been one of the lyricists closely associated with the group Ziskakan. In parallel he has developed a successful career as an academic and literary critic, pioneering the introduction of Creole studies in the university, and in recent times has published bilingual collections of poetry, such as *Romans pou la tèr ek la mèr*,[33] and a CD of recited poems alternating between French and Creole.[34]

The earliest texts published by the novelist Axel Gauvin were a pioneering manifesto in favour of the literary use of Creole: *Du créole opprimé au créole libéré* in 1977,[35] some twelve years earlier than the *Éloge de la créolité* of Bernabé, Chamoiseau and Confiant. He also published a collection of early poems in 1983: *Romans po detak la lang demay le ker*,[36] which includes, amongst other things, the lyric of the celebrated anti-colonial anthem performed by the group Ziskakan, *Bato fou*. Several other militant poets who also published their first collections of poems during this period also double as lyricists for Ziskakan, such as Alain Armand[37] and Patrice Treudhardt.[38]

Social novels in French and Creole

The late 1970s and early '80s also saw the publication of a number of populist novels written in French or in Creole, and, in the unusual case of Axel Gauvin, both languages. One of the earliest was *Les*

Muselés by Anne Cheynet in 1977,[39] describing the lives of ordinary Réunionnais, their struggle to make a living, their political voice stolen by corrupt politicians. Daniel Honoré was among the first to attempt to write novels documenting individual histories in Creole, the mother tongue of their protagonists, in *Louis Redona*,[40] *Cemin Bracanot'*[41] and *Marceline Doub'kèr*.[42]

Axel Gauvin's first novel is best situated in this context: *Quartier trois lettres*[43] recounts the daily lives of fishermen and their families in Saint-Leu, the coastal town with the "three-letter name" of the title. What is distinctive about this text is the attempt to creolize standard French in the narration by introducing Creole vocabulary, such as "fait-noir" for "nuit," and not simply in the exchanges of dialogue of the protagonists. This experiment is to go further in 1984 with the publication of a fully Creole version of the novel, *Kartyé trwa lèt*.[44] Gauvin's second novel, *Faims d'enfance*[45] takes as its subject a similar micro-universe, that of children attending a school canteen, and the resistance of a Hindu child narrator to the compulsory French diet. This highlights the difficulty of the imposed French culture of the island in coming to terms with cultural difference: and yet the narrator hero falls in love with an exotically red-headed French girl, emphasizing the ethnic mixing which is also a characteristic of Réunionnais society. Here again, Gauvin also publishes a Creole version some years later, under the title *Bayalina*,[46] the conflation of the nicknames of his two protagonists. Gauvin's third novel, *L'Aimé*,[47] probably his most successful, goes much further in integrating creolisms into the text of a novel written in French, and to a much more substantial text. The subject matter is again a very specific micro-universe in an obscure corner of Reunionese society: the adoption and nurturing of her sickly and abandoned grandson by a grandmother and her ageing, cantankerous second husband. The style, sustained throughout a long narrative, adopts the familiar creolized turns of phrase of a narrator who is a sympathetic observer of the protagonists' everyday predicaments, often apostrophizing them as would a close friend, neighbour or relative. The novel evokes in this way the particularities of popular everyday life in Reunion, the community solidarity, social problems such as alcoholism, the deep social divisions and the island's heritage of colonialism in Madagascar. As such it is one of the finest postcolonial novels to have emerged from Réunion, deeply rooted in the island's culture and yet permeated with universally humanist warmth. Gauvin's more recent novels, *Cravate et fils*[48] and *Train fou*[49] have been generally less successful, and he seems to have abandoned the pattern of publishing a parallel text in Creole, perhaps because of the limited market for such texts.

The historical novel and the anxiety of identity

Novels about the history of the island have been particularly prolific and popular in recent years, for reasons that one can well understand: they provide fictional interpretations of the origins of the complex identity of the island's multi-ethnic and multi-cultural population. Some of these are ethnically based, such as Firmin Lacpatia's *Boadour—du Gange à la Rivière des Roches*,[50] which recounts in fictional terms the arrival in the island of the first Indian indentured labourers in the mid-nineteenth century. Other writers range widely across the different communities and periods, as does Jean-François Sam-Long in novels such as *Terre arrachée*,[51] the story of the Antandroy of southern Madagascar brought to the island as indentured labourers in the 1920s; the story of *Madame Desbassayns*,[52] the mythical eighteenth century slave-owner; or the story of the Reunionese recruits in the First World War in *Pour les bravos de l'Empire*.[53] One of the most prolific writers in this genre is Daniel Vaxelaire, who, although not born in Réunion, has settled in Saint-Denis and made it his home for several decades. His novels cover many of the crucial moments in the history of the island and the Indian Ocean region, and probably result from his editorial work on the monumental *Mémorial de la Réunion*. His historical fictions provide tableaux from the broad sweep of the development of the islands: the runaway slave hunters of the eighteenth century in *Chasseur de noirs*,[54] the social aspirations of a freed slave in *L'Affranchi*;[55] Pierre Poivre and the competition of the eighteenth century spice trade in *Chasseurs d'Epices*;[56] the traumatic effect of the Napoleonic wars and the British conquest on the colonial society of Mauritius in *Grand Port*[57] and *Cap Malheureux*;[58] the legendary exploits of the seventeenth century pirates Misson and Caraccioli in attempting to found a utopian republic called Libertalia in Northern Madagascar in *Les Mutins de la liberté*.[59] These are all conventionally well-constructed, psychologically subtle linear narratives, but a playful and ironic complicity with his readers has been the characteristic of his more recent work, such as the portmanteau historical fantasy *Bleu nuit*,[60] his biography of Bernardin de St. Pierre and the origins of his fictional protagonists Paul and Virginie in *Une si jolie naufragée*,[61] or his pirate romance *Supplique pour ne pas être pendu avec les autres pirates*.[62] All these represent satisfying and entertaining fictional accounts of the roots of the island's and the region's culture, through an evocation of its most mythical and most determining figures and situations.

In a sense, the trilogy of comic novels published by Dhavid Huet, *Ti-Kréver*,[63] *Tienbo l'kèr*[64] and *Doboute Tanbi*,[65] belong all three in this historical section, for between them they cover the last years of the colonial period, beginning in the 1930s and bringing their story up to 1946, after the Second World War. They are a probably a romanced and humorous autobiography of their author, for they recount the schooldays, adolescence and early adulthood of a young boy nicknamed "Ti-Kréver" by his entourage in the east of the island near Saint-Benoit. Their charm lies in their creolised French and their nostalgic evocation of the "good old days" of the colonial society when Reunion was a picturesque backwater of the French colonies. The escapades of the hero are played for laughs and nostalgic recognition, appealing principally to an audience who shared the experiences of that generation, but they are equally attractive to a younger audience keen to acquire through laughter a sense of shared community. The colonial nostalgia and the somewhat folklorized Creole language and culture make the novels a less radical and sharp evocation than Monique Agénor's comparable *Bé-Maho*, but they do present a convincing portrait of everyday hardships and community solidarity in colonial Réunion.

In a similar vein, but with a growing formal sophistication, Monique Agénor has also exploited the rich resources of the region's history in a way that explicitly dramatizes the cultural issues of the postcolonial society of Reunion. Her first novel, *L'Aïeule de l'île Bourbon*[66] recounts as a first-person narrative the tumultuous life of a social outcast woman transported from a French jail in the seventeenth century in order to populate the island as one of its very first inhabitants. Her second, more adventurously, presents as a comic novel the vicissitudes of the island's society and politics during the Second World War, when they moved dramatically from Vichy repression to Gaullist and Allied conquest. *Bé Maho*[67] is set in a thinly disguised Hell-Bourg, a resort in the Salazie mountain valley, and the interactions of its inhabitants are recounted in a deliciously creolized French that undercuts the pretensions of the political establishment of the period. *Comme un vol de papang'*[68] attempts a double, framed narrative, in which a Creole-speaking Reunionese girl of Malagasy extraction is trying to recover the missing manuscript of her own account of the life of one of her ancestors, a lady in waiting at the court of the last Queen of Madagascar, Ranavalona III. The symbolic importance of the Malagasy narrative has been "stolen" from her by unknown persons, and it is perhaps that illicit manuscript in French, stolen from her just as the independence of Madagascar was stolen by the French, which we are now reading. This effectively represents the hegemony of French culture over all the rival and diverse cultures of the region, and the dispossession of the Reunionese from other aspects of their own cultural heritage. As such it represents one of the most successful attempts to incorporate into a literary text, both in form and content, the paradoxical situation of postcolonial Reunionese culture.

Postcolonial theater, neo-colonial subsidies

At around the same time as the Creole revival at the end of the 1970s, Emmanuel Genvrin, of metropolitan French origin, and Jean-Luc Trulès, a Reunionese returning to his native island, decided to launch a theater company, which they named after Ambroise Vollard, the art dealer of Reunionese extraction who was a friend of Alfred Jarry, and continued the series of Jarry's *Ubu roi* with his own *Ubu colonial*, after the original author's death. The first production of the Théâtre Vollard, appropriately enough, was a staging in 1979 of Jarry's *Ubu roi* at the Luc Donat Theater in Le Tampon, on a shoestring budget and making use of masks, sacks and packing cases as its décor. This was followed by an adaptation of Aimé Césaire's *Une Tempête*, itself adapted from Shakespeare's celebrated *The Tempest*. It took until 1981 for the troupe to come up with an original play, written and directed by Emmanuel Genvrin, called *Marie Dessembre*.[69] This was a drama of transgressive relations between a plantation-owner's son and a slave girl, who falls pregnant just prior to the abolition of slavery in 1848. Her illegitimate, mixed-race daughter is born as the abolition is announced in December 1848, hence the name of the heroine, who becomes a symbol of liberty. The play was performed at the municipal theater in the former covered market in Saint-Denis, the *Théâtre du Grand Marché*, where the Vollard troupe were to become intermittently resident. This was followed by *Nina Ségamour*[70] in 1982, the story of a "Miss Réunion" of 1940 who travels to Paris under the German Occupation. Their next original show, again written by Genvrin, was called *Etuves*,[71] and incorporated a performance by slaves of the revolutionary drama *L'Esclavage des Nègres* by Olympe de Gouges in 1792, at the time when the French Revolution was proposing to abolish slavery. But the Colonial Assembly avoids the issue and the slaves are not granted their freedom. These early productions set the pattern of dramatizations of crucial moments in Reunionese history, using a mixture of French and Creole dialogue, and featuring songs and musical interludes; but their radicalism was not popular with the municipal authorities of Saint-Denis, and the company was obliged to take over a disused cinema in the neighbouring town of La Possession. *Etuves* was also performed in mainland France at the Festival des Francophonies in Limoges. Their next major creation, *Lepervenche chemin de fer*[72] in 1990, was a drama about the beginnings of trade unionism on the railways in Réunion in the period of the Popular Front in 1936, and the rivalry between the left-wing politicians Léon de Lepervanche and Raymond Vergès, architects of the 1946 law introducing "Départementalisation." This show began the policy of the company using non-theatrical locations for their productions: the play was staged at a disused railway halt between La Possession and Saint-Denis and the old diesel train was brought back into service to bring in the audience. When the play was produced in metropolitan France, it was similarly staged in disused railway sheds near Paris, at Trappes, and at Vitry-sur-Seine. Another feature of the company's productions from this point onwards was the provision of a typically Creole meal and refreshments as an integral part of the show.

Their next major independent production, *Votez Ubu Colonial*[73] in 1994 was a freewheeling adaptation of Ambroise Vollard's *Ubu colonial* after Jarry, targeting the well-documented political corruption in Reunion by presenting the island's politics as those of an African dictatorship. It was performed at the disused factory of Jeumon in Saint Denis, the home provided for the company by the local authorities. The latter were none too pleased at this corrosive satirical attack, however, and this marked the beginning of their withdrawal of financial support for the company. The show was a considerable popular success, however, and toured in France under a circus big top.

Genvrin was not the only author working with the Vollard troupe during this period: Reunionese playwright Jean-Louis Rivière also wrote and directed *Garson* in 1987, *Carousel*[74] in 1992 and *Emeutes*[75] in 1996, the latter a dramatisation of the notorious riots of the Chaudron district of Saint-Denis in 1991. Genvrin's last production in Réunion for the Vollard troupe was the much more literary and traditional *Baudelaire au Paradis*[76] of 1997, which embroidered on the story of the youthful poet's visit to the islands of Reunion and Mauritius in 1842.

Despite the prolific output of original plays, inventive and innovative productions and popular success, the local authorities eventually withdrew their subsidies and the local representatives of the French Ministry of Culture publicly criticized Genvrin and the troupe and also withdrew financial support. The company was obliged to go into liquidation at the end of 1999.[77] Since then the French Ministry of Culture has set up an "Indian Ocean Centre for Drama" at the sometime home of the Vollard company in the Théâtre du Grand Marché in Saint-Denis, where its programming has been considerably less controversial and more conservative. Vollard, unbowed by this reverse in their fortunes took a lively show, *Sega Tremblad*, a musical comedy about the tribulations of Reunionese immigrants in metropolitan France, to the Divan du Monde theater in Paris in 2000. The company still re-surfaces from time to time but, having lost their institutional base and support, are less able to maintain their former creativity.[78]

In the 1990s a very different theater company established itself in the south of the island. Working as a group since 1986, conducting ethnographic fieldwork in the islands of the region, the Théâtre Talipot company eventually found a home in the disused sugar factory at Pierrefonds, between Saint-Louis and Saint-Pierre. After several smaller touring productions, their most ambitious event was a multi-cultural, multi-media drama of 1996 called *Mâ*, written by Philippe Pelen.[79] This used all the resources of theater—music, dance, mime, visual effects—to produce a synthesis of myths of procreation and maternity drawn from the disparate cultures of the region—Malagasy, Indian, African—and employing dialogue in various languages: French, Creole, Malagasy, Hindi. The show toured extensively in the region, and drew many appreciative critical articles, not least from the agents of UNESCO. Philippe Pelen theorized the practice of the company in an article published in the same volume as the play, called "Théâtre et métissage." Their aim was clearly to develop a synthesis of archetypal myths by juxtaposing stories drawn from indigenous folk cultures. This approach was deployed to great effect in their next, even more successful 1997 production *Les Porteurs d'eau*. This relied more on music, dance and mime than dialogue, and was able to appeal to worldwide audiences in its extensive tour. It developed simple elemental responses to notions of thirst, the need for water, and the fear of water shortage. Amongst other successes it was presented at the Edinburgh Fringe Festival in 1998 and won a "Fringe First" award. Philippe Pelen was responsible for the over-all conception of the show, but the music by Ricky Randimbiarison, in a very Malagasy style, was an important element in the show's success, and it has been published on a CD.[80] Talipot's subsequent show *Passages* (2000) followed a similar aesthetic approach to myths of rites of passage; but despite prestigious performances in Paris seems to have been less successful.

In their different ways, the two companies Vollard and Talipot illustrate contrasting strategies for a postcolonial theater practice, the one rooting itself in the complexity of a particular island culture, the other attempting to transcend cultural differences to achieve a broad-based humanism.[81]

A cross-fertilized musical field

The indigenous musical production of Réunion has been extraordinarily rich in recent years, and it is surprising that so little of it has come to the attention of the international world music circuits, with the possible exception of those based in France. With the revival of interest in Creole culture in the 1970s came the rediscovery of the traditional form of the *maloya*. As in Mauritius, the *sega* had existed for well over a century and had been assimilated and adapted into the consensual colonial culture of the islands, losing some of its distinctiveness in the process, so that it had become a rather predictable and sanitized form of popular entertainment. The *maloya*, a related form of percussion-based chant-response music, had been banned by the authorities as a threat to public order, as it was associated with secret traditional ceremonies of ancestor worship, the "servis kabaré," in which it was used to induce a trance-like state in the participants. This music was re-discovered in the 1970s by left-wing activists such as the poet Boris Gamaleya and brought to the attention of the public by the Reunionese Communist Parrty as an authentically popular indigenous musical form. Its ageing lifelong practitioners rapidly became stars, such as Firmin Viry,[82] Le Rwa kaf[83] and Gramoune Lélé.[84] Firmin Viry could be heard performing on a souvenir LP published by the Reunionese Communist Party for its twentieth anniversary congress in 1978, along with an interminable Castro-style policy speech by the party's leader Paul Vergès. The most commercial of the trio of senior *maloya* originals was Gramoune Lélé, who performed with an extensive troupe of percussionists and backing singers who were all members of his own family. Until his death in 2004 he toured extensively with them in Europe and even as far away as Brazil and Japan. He also published several albums recorded by the French specialist company Label bleu.[85] His effervescent and dynamic style made him the most accessible of the popular *maloya* pioneers and his lyrics, in a Malagasy flavoured Creole, are often spontaneously poetic and evocative, as well as occasionally expressing social criticism of the effects of colonialism.

The ternary 6/8 rhythms of the *maloya* were an inspiration to the Creolist poets of the 1970s, and many of them alluded to them in their writings. Some went further, however, and adopted the form as their own. This was the case with Danyel Waro who, after a period in jail for refusing to complete his French military service, began to write politicized protest songs in the *maloya* style;[86] he also developed the skills to construct the typical percussion instruments of the form, amongst others the *kaïamb*, a tray made of cane stalks filled with grains; or the *roulèr*, a large barrel-like bass drum. Waro's lyrics are inspired by a poetic revolt against the neo-colonial aspects of Reunionese society, whether it be the imposition of standard French or the bureaucratic French administration. He is himself a living example of the *Batarsité*[87] he proclaims in a famous song: he is white, but of mixed-race origin typical of the "hauts," the mountainous zones of the island where runaway slaves and poor whites once fraternized to eke out a precarious living. Musically his songs have a "blues" feel which suggests a covert influence of black American music, but in all other respects he remains true to the pure musical form of the *maloya*, with no European harmonic instruments other than the chant / response of the human voice. He has toured extensively in Europe and elsewhere, and several further CDs have been issued, the booklet usually containing the Creole lyrics and sometimes a translation into English and / or French.[88]

At roughly the same time as Daniel Waro's first publications in the late 1970s, a number of his fellow Creole poets formed a live performance group called Ziskakan. This included Gilbert Pounia, now the lead singer, but also Carpanin Marimoutou, Patrice Treuthardt, Axel Gauvin, Alain Armand and others. Ziskakan's earliest recordings were rather like agitprop cabaret performances, with polemical texts in Creole declaimed as well as sung. The personnel of the group has changed over the years, some of the early writers developed their careers in different directions, but many still write for the group. The constant has been Pounia, who was usually responsible for the musical settings, but who has since developed into a poet in his own right.[89] Not surprisingly Ziskakan's musical style was based on the *maloya*, but combined this with acoustic and harmonic instruments in a folk-rock style, often incorporating elements from other genres.[90] It has been suggested that one of the sources of the *maloya* might well be the drumming associated with Tamil religious rituals, as well as the more obvious Afro-Malagasy roots of the form, and more recently Indian-style instruments and percussion have been a feature of the group.[91] The musical arrangements have been consistently rich and inventive, incorporating sometimes a chorus of Corsican polyphony,[92] at others a Breton bagpipe[93] into their complex rhythmic and instrumental textures. The Creole lyrics have always been of a sustained poetic quality, celebrating the beauty of the island, as in *Romans la o*,[94] but also its political and social contradictions, as in the celebrated anthem *Bato fou*,[95] written by Axel Gauvin, in which the "crazy boat" of the island has been forcibly towed and moored off the coast of France. More often the lyrics are personal and lyrical, as in the touching *Mariaz sekre*.[96] In recent years Ziskakan has toured extensively, and have released a concert video which gives a good idea of the high quality of their live performances.[97]

A paradoxical richness

The richness of the postcolonial output of Reunion is evident from the density of reference in what precedes. It is clear that Reunion's writers and artists do benefit considerably from the excellent material facilities the island's authorities can offer them: many of the publications in Creole, for instance, are subsidized by the island's Conseil général, and it would be difficult to conceive of the lively theatrical activity of the island without the assistance of local authority sponsorship. As we have seen, the independence of the island's Creole culture can sometimes be under threat in this situation, and artistic autonomy can sometimes be compromised. The island maintains a delicate balance between its economic dependency on metropolitan France and French institutions, and its strong indigenous, hybrid culture in which many strands come together to produce a very individual synthesis, not reducible to any one element in its composition, whether French or other. In some ways it is the most postcolonial of the cultures of the Francophone Indian Ocean, and yet in a context which constantly emphasizes a neo-colonial dependency on France. This paradox is one that is not unique, as most postcolonial cultures seem to maintain a symbiotic relationship with their former colonial rulers, in which the traffic of influence is often a two-way one. In the broader context of globalization, the aspiration to national independence is becoming increasingly an unrealisable utopia: multiple international influences always permeate the most tightly controlled national frontiers. The question is rather to determine whether a distinctive culture is able to maintain its distinctiveness, without being reduced to slavish imitation of the most economically influential models. My judgement is that Reunionese culture does succeed in doing this: remaining open to outside influences yet managing to maintain its particular savour, its complex identity.

Notes

1. I have explored in some detail the implications of the question in an article: see Peter Hawkins, "How appropriate is the term "post-colonial" to the cultural production of Reunion?" in *Francophone post-colonial cultures,* ed. Kamal Salhi (Lanham, MD: Lexington, 2003), 311-20.

2. See Sonia Chane-Kune, *Aux Origines de l'identité réunionnaise* (Paris: L'Harmattan, 1993), 188-90.

3. See Bill Ashcroft, Gareth Griffiths, and Helen Tiffin, eds., "General Introduction" in *The post-colonial studies reader*, (1995), 2.

4. Evariste de Parny, *Chansons madécasses* suivies de *Poésies fugitives* (London: n. p. 1787). The texts are reproduced in the anthology: *Océan indien—Madagascar, La Réunion, Maurice,* ed. Serge Meitinger and J.-C. Carpanin Marimoutou (Paris: Omnibus, 1998), 73-80. See also Jean-Louis Joubert, *Littératures de l'Océan indien* (1991), 208-10 and 218-19.

5. Louis-Timagène Houat, *Les Marrons* (Paris: Ebrard, 1844). Reprinted (Sainte-Clotilde, Reunion: CRI, 1988); and (Piton Sainte-Rose, Reunion: Editions AIPDS, 1998). The full text is also included in the anthology *Océan indien—Madagascar, La Réunion, Maurice*, eds. Meitinger and Marimoutou, (1998), 403-506.

6. Eugène Dayot, *Bourbon pittoresque* (1848). Reprinted in *Oeuvres choisies* (Paris: Challamel, 1878). Reprinted (Saint-Denis de la Réunion: Imprimerie Croix-Sud, 1967). Republished (Saint-Denis de la Réunion: Nouvelle Imprimerie Dionysienne, 1977). See Joubert, *Littératures de l'Océan Indien*, 225, 237.

7. See Joubert, *Littératures de l'Océan Indien,* 211-12, 220.

8. See Joubert, *Littératures de l'Océan Indien,* 212-14, 221-23.

9. See Joubert, *Littératures de l'Océan Indien,* 228-32, 239-41.

10. See Joubert, *Littératures de l'Océan Indien,* 226-28.

11. See chapter 4.

12. Jean Albany, *Zamal* (Paris: Bellenand, 1951). Reprinted, Paris: chez l'auteur, 1980.

13. Jean Albany, *Bleu mascarin* (Paris: chez l'auteur, 1969).

14. Jean Albany, *Vavangue* (Paris: chez l'auteur, 1972).

15. Jean Albany, *P'tit'glossaire—le piment des mots créoles* (Paris: chez l'auteur, 1974).

16. Jean Albany et al., *Chante Albany* (Saint-Denis de la Réunion: Editions Goutte d'eau dans l'océan, 1979) cassette. Reissued on CD: (Saint-André, Reunion: Piros, 1999).

17. See later section in this chapter.

18. In Gilbert Aubry and Jean-François Sam-Long, *Créolie* (Saint-Denis de la Réunion: UDIR, 1978).

19. Gilbert Aubry, *Rivages d'Alizé* (Saint-Denis de la Réunion: chez l'auteur, 1971). New edition (Saint-Denis: Nouvelle Imprimerie Dionysienne, 1980).

20. Jean-Henri Azéma, *Olographe* (Buenos Aires: Trois Salazes, 1978).

21. Jean-Henri Azéma, *D'Azur à perpétuité* (Buenos Aires: Trois Salazes, 1979).

22. Jean-Henri Azéma, *Le Pétrolier couleur antaque* (Saint-Denis: Trois Salazes, 1982).

23. Jean-Henri Azéma, *Le Dodo vavangueur* (Saint-Denis: Trois Salazes, 1986).

24. Jean Bernabé, Patrick Chamoiseau, and Raphaël Confiant, *Eloge de la créolité / In praise of creoleness*. (Paris: Gallimard, 1989). For an earlier, alternative reading of the relation between *Créolie* and *Créolité*, see Françoise Lionnet, "*Créolité* in the Indian ocean: two models of cultural diversity," *Yale French Studies*, 82 (1993), 101-12.

25. Anne Cheynet, *Matanans et langoutis* (Saint-Denis: R.E.I. 1972).

26. Alain Lorraine, *Tienbo le rein, Beaux visages cafrines sous la lampe* (Paris: L'Harmattan, 1976).

27. Boris Gamaleya, *Vali pour une reine morte* (Saint-Denis: Réunion Edition Impression. 1973). Reprinted, Saint-André, Reunion: Imprimerie Graphica, 1986.

28. Michel Beniamino, *Lecture de "Vali pour une reine morte" de Boris Gamaleya* (Sainte-Clotilde, Reunion: Institut de Linguistique et d'Anthropologie de la Réunion, 1985).

29. Boris Gamaleya, *Ombline ou le Volcan à l'envers* (Saint-André and Saint-Denis: Océan Editions / Conseil général de la Réunion, 1998).

30. Boris Gamaleya, *Le Volcan à l'envers ou Mme Desbassyns, le Diable et le Bondieu* (Saint-Leu, Reunion: Presses du Développement, 1983)

31. Carpanin Marimoutou, *Fazèle* (Saint-Denis: Les Chemins de la Liberté, 1979).

32. Carpanin Marimoutou, *Arracher cinquante mille signes* (Saint-Denis: Editions Goutte d'eau dans l'océan, 1980).

33. Carpanin Marimoutou, *Romans pou la tèr ek la mèr* (Saint-Denis: Grand Océan, 1995).

34. Carpanin Marimoutou, *Koz langaz* (Marseille: DCC, 1999) CD, poet la Rénion, no. 1.

35. Axel Gauvin, *Du créole opprimé au créole libéré* (Paris: L'Harmattan, 1977)

36. Axel Gauvin, *Romans po detak la lang demay le ker* (Saint-Leu, Reunion: Presses du Développement, 1983).

37. Alain Armand, *Zordi* (Saint-Denis: Les Chemins de la Liberté, 1978).

38. Patrice Treudhardt, *20 désanm et d'entre tous les Zanzibar* (Saint-Denis: les Chemins de la Liberté, 1979).

39. Anne Cheynet, *Les Muselés* (Paris: L'Harmattan, 1977).

40. Daniel Honoré, *Louis Redona* (Saint-Denis: Les Chemins de la Liberté, 1980).

41. Daniel Honoré, *Cemin Bracanot'* (Saint-Leu, Reunion: Presses de l'I.L.R., 1984).

42. Daniel Honoré, *Marceline doub'kèr* (Saint-Denis: UDIR, 1988).

43. Axel Gauvin, *Quartier trois-lettres* (Paris: L'Harmattan, 1980).

44. Axel Gauvin, *Kartyé trwa lèt* (Saint-Denis: Editions Ziskakan, 1984).

45. Axel Gauvin, *Faims d'enfance* (Paris: Seuil, 1987).

46. Axel Gauvin, *Bayalina* (Saint-Denis: Grand Ocean, 1995).

47. Axel Gauvin, *L'Aimé* (Paris: Seuil, 1990).

48. Axel Gauvin, *Cravate et fils* (Paris: Seuil, 1996)

49. Axel Gauvin, *Train fou* (Paris: Seuil, 2000).

50. Firmin Lacpatia, *Boadour—Du Gange . . . à la Rivière des Roches* (Saint-Denis: A.G.M., 1978).

51. Jean-François Sam-Long, *Terre Arrachée* (Saint-Denis: Nouvelle Imprimerie Dionysienne, 1982).

52. Jean-François Sam-Long, *Madame Desbassayns* (Le Tampon, Reunion: Editions Jacaranda, 1985).

53. Jean-François Sam-Long, *Pour les bravos de l'Empire* (Le Tampon, Reunion: Editions Jacaranda, 1987).

54. Daniel Vaxelaire, *Chasseur de noirs* (Paris: Lieu commun, 1982). Reprinted (Paris: Gallimard, 1988) "Folio Junior" series, No. 421.

55. Daniel Vaxelaire, *L'Affranchi* (Paris: Lieu Commun, 1984) Reprinted (Paris: Phébus, 1986).

56. Daniel Vaxelaire, *Les Chasseurs d'épices* (Paris: J.-C. Lattès, 1990). Reprinted (Saint-Denis: Orphie, 2001).

57. Daniel Vaxelaire, *Grand Port* (Paris: Phébus, 1993).

58. Daniel Vaxelaire, *Cap Malheureux* (Paris: Phébus, 1994).

59. Daniel Vaxelaire, *Les Mutins de la Liberté* (Paris: Lieu commun, 1986).

60. Daniel Vaxelaire, *Bleu nuit* (Paris: Flammarion, 1996).

61. Daniel Vaxelaire, *Une si jolie naufragée ou Le roman vrai de Paul et Virginie* (Paris: Flammarion, 2001).

62. Daniel Vaxelaire, *Supplique pour ne pas être pendu avec les autres pirates* (Saint-Denis: Orphie, 2003).

63. Dhavid, *Ti Kréver—l'enfant bâtard* (Saint-André, Reunion: Océan Editions, 1990).

64. Dhavid, *Tienbo l'kèr* (Saint-André, Reunion: Océan Editions, 1993).

65. Dhavid, *Doboute tanbi* (Saint-André, Reunion: Océan Editions, 1994).

66. Monique Agénor, *L'Aïeule de l'Isle Bourbon* (Paris: L Harmattan, 1993).

67. Monique Agénor, *Bé-Maho* (Paris: Le Serpent à plumes, 1996).

68. Monique Agénor, *Comme un vol de papang'* (Paris: Le Serpent à plumes, 1998).

69. Emmanuel Genvrin, *Marie Dessembre* (Saint-Denis: Eds. Théâtre Vollard, 1987).

70. Emmanuel Genvrin, *Nina Ségamour* (Saint-Denis: Eds. Théâtre Vollard, 1986).

71. Emmanuel Genvrin, *Etuves* (Saint-Denis: Eds. Théâtre Vollard, 1988).

72. Emmanuel Genvrin, *Lepervenche chemin de fer* (Saint-Denis: Grand Océan, 1991).

73. Emmanuel Genvrin, *Votez Ubu colonial* (Saint-Denis: Grand Océan, 1994).

74. Jean-Louis Rivière, *Carousel* (Saint-Denis: Eds. Théâtre Vollard, 1992).

75. Jean-Louis Rivière, *Emeutes* (Saint-Denis: Grand Océan, 1997).

76. Emmanuel Genvrin, *Baudelaire au Paradis* (Paris : L'Harmattan, 1998).

77. For a further discussion of this development, see Peter Hawkins, "Ubu in the tropics: the rise and fall of the Théâtre Vollard," in *African Theatre: playwrights and politics*, ed. Martin Banham, James Gibbs and Femi Osofisan (Oxford, Bloomington and Johannesburg: James Currey / Indiana University Press / Witwatersrand University Press, 2001), 144-54.

78. For a review of their twenty-year career, 1979-1999, see the illustrated album: Théâtre Vollard, *Vingtième: 20 ans d'un theatre réunionnais* (Saint-Denis: Band' décidée, l'Autre Hémisphère, 1999).

79. Philippe Pelen, *Mâ* (Saint-Denis: Grand Océan, 1996).
80. Théâtre Talipot, *Les Porteurs d'eau / The water carriers* (Saint-Pierre, Reunion: Théâtre Talipot. 1998), CD No MP9901.
81. For a further development of this comparison, see Peter Hawkins, "Two contrasting strategies for a postcolonial theatre in Reunion," *International Journal of Francophone Studies*, 2, 1 (2000), 45-50.
82. Firmin Viry, *Ti mardé* (Amiens, France: Label bleu / Indigo, 1998), CD LBLC 2548.
83. Lo Rwa kaf, *Somin galisé* (Saint-Denis: Discorama, 1992), CD 9209.
84. Gramoune Lélé, *Namouniman* (Amiens, France: Label bleu / Indigo, 1993), CD LBLC 2508.
85. Gramoune Lélé, *Soleye* (Amiens, France: Label bleu / Indigo, 1995), CD LBLC 2528; and *Dan kèr Lélé* (1998) CD LBLC 2558.
86. For Danyel Waro's earliest texts, see Danyel Waro, *Romans ekri dans la zol en Frans* (Saint-Denis: Les Chemins de la liberté, 1978); and *Gafourn* (Saint-Denis: Editions Ziskakan, 1987). The latter has also been issued as a cassette and CD, distributed by Piros.
87. Danyel Waro, *Batarsité* (Saint-André, Reunion: Piros, 1994), CD CDP5198. The text of the song can be found in the CD booklet and in Danyel Waro, *Demavouz la vi* (Saint-Denis: Grand Océan, 1996), 104-6.
88. Danyel Waro, *Foutan fonnker* (Paris: Cobalt, 1999), CD No. 09293-2; and *Bwarouz* (2001), CD No. 09351-2.
89. Gilbert Pounia, *Somin Granbwa* (Saint-Denis: Grand Océan, 1997).
90. See the compilation album Ziskakan, *Ziskakan 20 tan* (Saint-Denis: Discorama. 1999)
91. The Indian influence is particularly visible on Ziskakan, *Rimayer* (Saint-Denis: Discorama, 2001), CD 2001.09, even including the design of the CD sleeve.
92. On Ziskakan, *Soley glasé* (Paris: Sankara / Mercury, 1996), CD 532 410-2.
93. On Ziskakan, *Kaskasnikola* (Paris: Mango / Island, 1993), CD 514 974-2.
94. In Ziskakan, *Kaskasnikola*.
95. In Ziskakan, *Soley glasé* and Ziskakan, *Bato fou* (Saint-André, Reunion: Piros / Sonodisc, 1991). The song is so well-known and popular in Reunion that the group re-recorded it in 1996, well over ten years after its original release.
96. In Ziskakan, *Soley glasé*.

97. Ziskakan, *Ziskakan live* (Saint-Denis: Discorama, 2004), DVD 2004.12.

Chapter 7

The Comoros, the Seychelles

Ambiguity and contrast in the Comorian archipelago

The four islands of the Comorian archipelago have in common a problematic political and economic status, but for very different reasons. Ngazidja, known in French as "La Grande Comore," the largest of the islands and the most populated, tends to regard itself as the natural centre of the Comorian state: this has been one of the main grievances of the other islands, Moheli (Mweli), and Anjouan (Ndzwani), and the main reason for the latter's recent attempts to secede from the Comorian federation. The other reason is probably the proximity of the example of Mayotte (Maore), which has reaped the benefits of its adherence to the French Republic in terms of its much higher standard of living and its vastly better social and educational facilities. Even so, the Comorian federation still in theory lays claim to the renegade island of Mayotte, and has been supported in this in the past by the African Union. On the other hand Mayotte has recent taken one more step towards the status of full Overseas Department of the French Republic, projected at some time in the next decade, by moving from an "Overseas Territory" (*TOM*, or *Territoire d'Outre-Mer*) to a "Departmental Collectivity" (*Collectivité départementale*) in 2001.

This situation looks like a rather fragile compromise, and as a consequence the postcolonial culture of the islands is a similarly problematic and disparate affair. There is, for instance, a gulf between the level of access to cultural facilities available to the Mahorais in Mayotte, and what is available to the inhabitants of the other three islands. The level of education, the access to books, to cinemas, theatres, publishers and other cultural facilities is simply not comparable. Most of the small number of authors from the Comorian federation are living overseas, part of an extensive Comorian diaspora on which the islands' economy increasingly depends, whereas some of the pioneering writers of Mayotte have at least been able to work for a time in the island in the educational sector of the French civil service.

A disastrous decolonization

In the round of decolonisation inaugurated by General de Gaulle on his return to power in 1958, the Comoros islands voted to remain part of the French Republic in a referendum.[1] Some fifteen years later, in 1973, Ahmed Abdallah, elected President of the Governing Council, began negotiations for the independence of the islands. In a referendum in 1974, 95 per cent of voters pronounced in favour of independence, except in Mayotte, where 65 per cent voted against it. When, a year later, in July 1975, President Ahmed Abdallah declared the independence of the Comoros, Mayotte seceded and chose to remain French. A month later, in August 1975, Ahmed Abdallah was overthrown by Ali Soilih, the leader of the opposition, who installed a Marxist and revolutionary regime intent on destroying the deeply rooted Islamic religious traditions of the island. Three catastrophic years later the new leader was himself overthrown by the intervention of mercenaries led by the notorious Bob Denard, and Ali Soilih was killed while trying to escape. The story of the Comorian revolution is recounted in satirical terms by the islands' first novelist, Mohamed Toihiri, in *La République des imberbes*, published in 1985.[2] Ahmed Abdallah's Federal Islamic Republic was not to fare much better, however, being dependent on the goodwill of Bob Denard and his mercenaries and supported by the Apartheid regime in South Africa. It nevertheless survived until 1989, when again Ahmed Abdallah was overthrown and this time killed, with the complicity of the power broker Bob Denard. The effective omnipotence of the mercenaries in the islands' political regime is a principal target of Toihiri's second satirical novel *Le Kafir du Karthala*, published in 1992.[3] A period of chronic political instability followed the demise of Abdallah, leading up to the declaration of secession by the island of Anjouan, who appealed to the French government for their support, applying to be granted a comparable status to Mayotte. This led to protracted negotiations which brought about the new constitution of the Union des Comores in 2001,[4] intended to guarantee equitable power-sharing between the three islands and recognising at the same time the aspiration of Mayotte to achieve full Departmental status within the French Republic.

The uneasy assimilation of Mayotte

Mayotte proudly proclaims that it has been French since 1841.[5] The last Sultan of the island, Andriantsuli, a Malagasy nobleman who had converted to Islam, sold the island to the French, who then used it as a base from which to consolidate their colonial designs on the other islands of the Comoros, as well as neighboring Madagascar, where their rivals, principally the British but also the Germans, were attempting to gain a foothold. In a treaty of 1886, the French government imposed the status of protectorate on the other three islands. After the French annexation of Madagascar in 1895, the Comoros were governed from 1908 onwards by the colonial administration in Tananarive, having previously been administered since 1896 from Reunion. In 1943, during the Second World War, the British occupied the islands briefly so as better to oust the pro-Vichy administration of Madagascar, but the Comoros reverted to France in 1946, with the status of Overseas Territory, administered separately from Madagascar, with a degree of internal autonomy. The fortress town of Dzaoudzi in Mayotte became the capital of the Comoros until 1966, when the local administration of Saïd Mohamed Cheikh decided to transfer the administration to Moroni, in Grande Comore. This was not welcomed by the Mahorais, and this was the beginning of their move towards autonomy which was confirmed by the result of the 1974 referendum. Since independence several Comorian heads of state have laid claim to Mayotte, but the French have maintained their presence in Dzaoudzi, bolstered by the garrison of the French Foreign Legion stationed there. Despite the negotiated settlement of the 1997 crisis of the secession of Anjouan, resulting in the creation of the Union des Comores, there has been a constant stream of illegal immigration from the other islands into Mayotte, mostly coming from the nearby island of Anjouan. Even if the French government has avoided taking on responsibility for Anjouan, its inhabitants are finding their own ways of returning to the fold of the French Republic: almost a third of the population of Mayotte, some 160,000 inhabitants, are believed to be illegal immigrants, mostly from Anjouan.[6] The French state has been obliged to take measures to prevent this flow of illegal immigration, by restricting contacts between the islands to air traffic and banning sea crossings; they have also limited the access to free health care to paid-up subscribers to the French social security system.

The society of Mayotte is becoming rapidly Europeanised, with the arrival of the Euro, cash dispensers, hypermarkets and an increasingly consumerist lifestyle. The roots of Mahorais society are profoundly Islamic, however, and the local population more readily speaks a variety of local languages rather than French. French secular institutions seem to be artificially grafted onto a society whose traditional values are Muslim ones: the madrassas still thrive alongside French primary schools and throughout the Comoros there has been a strong and ancient tradition of Sunni Islamic holy men whose cultural ties were stronger with Zanzibar than with France.

The Arabic and Swahili heritage

Unlike the other groups of islands, the Mascarenes and the Seychelles, the Comoros have been inhabited since the dawn of time, by a population of varied origins. Their geographical position in the Mozambique Channel, between the African mainland and the large land mass of Madagascar, made them a natural port of call for traders. Long before the arrival of the European explorers, the East African coast was home to a trading culture of dhows coming from as far away as Arabia and the Persian Gulf. The common language of East Africa is of course Swahili, which is still widely used in the Comoros alongside local languages, French and a variety of Malagasy, the latter particularly in Mayotte. The Comoros became Islamic as early as the tenth century AD, under the influence of Mohamed ben Othman. In the sixteenth century the islands were annexed by Mohammed ben Haïssa, establishing a dynasty of Shirazian sultans who introduced Arabic script, which was used to write in both Swahili and Comorian as well as Arabic.

Thus the chronicles of the Comoros are documented from then onwards, and represent a substantial pre-colonial culture, even if the islands were in effect a dependency of their Persian Gulf rulers. It was only when the islands were repeatedly attacked by Betsimisaraka raiders coming from Madagascar in the late eighteenth century that the sultanates of the islands began to seek the protection of the European naval powers. This was the beginning of a growing intervention of the French and other colonial powers in the affairs of the archipelago during the nineteenth century. It is clear from this that the culture of the Comoros is predominantly Islamic, and that the relevance of French is of very recent origin and fairly superficial. Even so, Carole Beckett, a South African scholar has published a pioneering anthology of the Islamic devotional poetry of the Comoros written in French.[7] The folktales, chronicles and praise-songs from the islands' oral tradition have also been collected, transcribed, translated into French and studied by Moussa Saïd Ahmed;[8] this is just one example of a considerable body of ethnographic scholarship studying the rich archive of records of the Comoros written in Arabic script.

Postcolonial novels in French

The first novel written in French emanating from the Comoros has already been mentioned: *La République des imberbes* is a devastating satirical attack on the excesses of the revolutionary regime of Ali Soilih between 1975 and 1978. Its tone is that of an ubuesque farce, shot through with irony and black humour, and in many ways reminiscent of the African version of magic realism practised by the Congolese novelist Sony Lab'ou Tansi in novels such as *La Vie et demie*.[9] There is a significant difference, however, in that the events recounted in *La République des imberbes* remain close to well-documented facts, even if the names of the protagonists have been disguised: it is thus a *roman à clef* in a way which Sony Lab'ou Tansi's novels are not. The anti-hero Guigoz, a thinly-disguised Ali Soilih, is presented as an immature would-be firebrand intent on a rapid and forced transformation of his country's ancestral culture, with its flamboyant "Grands mariages," its holy men and their supernatural powers, its veiled womenfolk, etc. Part of the bleak comedy of the book lies in the unexpected consequences of this revolutionary zeal, as well as the sheer absurdity of the revolutionary policies themselves, imposed on a bewildered population by a cohort of young "zazis," red guards modelled on those of the China or Cambodia.

Toihiri's second novel *Le Kafir du Karthala* adopts a somewhat more serious and personal tone: the hero is a doctor who, diagnosed with a terminal cancer, plans to rid his beleaguered country of the baleful influence of the mercenaries of Bob Denard, (here designated by the euphemism of "Partenaires" and the fictional name of Prosper Barnabée) by infiltrating the government under the cover of his medical reputation, so as better to assassinate them as a suicide bomber. This wish-fulfilment narrative is laced with satirical comments on the French expatriates and the local bourgeoisie in the neo-colonial high society of the capital Moroni; and some bitter observations of the apartheid system in neighbouring South Africa, where the hero is despatched as a conference delegate.

A more serious novel, *Le Sang de l'Obéissance* by Salim Hatubou,[10] paints a similarly negative portrait of a corrupt and exploitative society where the worst elements of neo-colonialism combine with the most retrograde and hypocritical façade of traditional customs and beliefs. Hatubou's models are explicitly those of North African novelists: Tahar Ben Jelloun, Driss Chraïbi, Mehdi Charef, Azouz Begag, according to an appreciative critical article by Danielle Nivo Galibert.[11]

Mayotte has not been left behind in creating a body of postcolonial fiction in French. The first, pioneering Mahorais novelist was Abdou S. Bacou, who published *Brulante est ma terre* in 1997 in Paris. In a more radical and clearly postcolonial vein, the dramatist Nassur Attoumani published not one but two novels in 2001, *Nerf de Boeuf*[12] and *Le Calvaire des Baobabs*.[13] The former was intended, according to its author, as a de-mystification of one of the great taboos of the Comoros islands: their involvement in the slave trade. It is an uncompromising tale of the misfortunes of an African slave who attempts, unsuccessfully, to escape and return to his mainland home. The second is a drily ironic tale reminiscent of Mongo Beti in which an Islamic holy man and healer is unable to cure his own infected foot, resulting from a misdirected axe blow; a well-meaning but naïve French doctor tries to cure him by taking him to hospital, where he dies, in spite of the resources of Western medicine. Attoumani has also published a collection of folktales of Mayotte, translated into French: *Contes traditionnels de nos ancêtres . . . les menteurs: recueil de contes mahorais*.[14] His provocative and iconoclastic attitude, already clear in this title, has not endeared him to the French authorities of his native island, so that he was no longer allowed to remain a French civil servant and member of the teaching profession.[15]

Postcolonial theater in Mayotte

Nassur Attoumani is better known as a dramatist than as a novelist, especially in his native island of Mayotte. He made his name with the Théâtre M'Kakamba—the name means "rainbow"—from 1989 onwards, and began to write plays for the group. His first published work, *La Fille du Polygame* of 1991, the first published play from Mayotte, is a mordant satire on the sexual behaviour of the Islamic society of the island, and in particular the double standards implicit in the practice of polygamy. The intertext is clearly that of Molière's plays, in particular *L'Ecole des Femmes*. The naïve heroine of the play, Fatiha Bahouili, rejects her parents' plans to marry her off to a wealthy cousin who will pay the parents a handsome bride price. Fatiha has other ideas and wants to marry a poor disabled immigrant. After the wedding the latter turns out to be polygamous like her father, so she divorces him and marries the cousin originally betrothed to her. At the end of the play, however, she is seen talking on the 'phone to her new lover and walking out on her traditionalist and male chauvinist second husband. The influence of feminism is obvious, but so too are the manifest contradictions between the Islamic traditions of the island and the French legal system, not least in the non-recognition of local languages. Like the novel *Le Calvaire des Baobabs*, the play refuses to suggest a neat conclusion, ending on an ambiguous note suggesting perhaps that women are as incapable as men of respecting the law of monogamy and fidelity, and that the imposition of the French legal system is farcical in a society so dominated by traditional Islamic values.

Attoumani has so far published two further plays, *Le Turban et la Capote* in 1997 and *Interview d'un macchabé* in 2000. These are both corrosive social satires in a similar vein to *La Fille du Polygame*. *Le Turban et la Capote* is based on Molière's *Tartuffe*, in which Pessoiri, a credulous and polygamous Muslim in dispute with his latest wife Maborcheti, takes his grievances to the Cadi, Mabawa, a local figure of traditional Muslim authority, who attempts to seduce his wife instead of helping to resolve the problem. The Cadi is in conflict with the French-trained local doctor, Hachafati, who is campaigning for the use of contraceptives to prevent the spread of AIDS, and is in favour of abortion as a way of containing the galloping birthrate in Mayotte.

Interview d'un Macchabé is also a satirical comedy about the judgement day of an ordinary Mahorais, who is interrogated by two angels, Moun'kar and Nakir, representing Good and Evil, under the supervision of the Archangel Djibril. The dead man is hypocritically befriended by Sheytwani, the devil disguised in a French tricolour sash, who eventually brings about his downfall. Attoumani's scepticism is all too clear about the imposition of French republican values on the strongly Islamic society of Mayotte.

Attoumani is obviously a writer of great talent and he will probably go on to surprise and shock his audiences further by pointing up the absurdities and contradictions of the neo-colonial situation of his island. His work so far can be seen as a significant opening-up of a postcolonial literary field in an island culture which had previously been a prisoner of its conservative Islamic traditions and its economic dependency on France.

Musical traditions in the Comoros

The *Rough Guide to world music* gives a useful account of the complex musical heritage of the Comoros, in which the Swahili styles of East Africa are dominant, such as the *twarab*.[16] These are often mixed with other influences from Madagascar, and from the ubiquitous reggae styles, and these often feature western electronic instruments alongside traditional ones. Comorian artists such Maalesh[17] and Mikidache[18] work in the Paris world music scene rather than in the islands. Although there seems to be a distinctive variety of topical songwriting practised in the Comorian island of Moheli,[19] this does not seem to have been much recorded and exported. There is little to suggest any strong literary content to these musical productions, however, as in the example of Réunion.

The Seychelles: the assertion of Creole identity

In comparison to the Comoros, the decolonisation of the Seychelles has been a story of relative success. As in the Comoros, within a few months of independence in 1976 the islands were the victim of a coup d'état, but the revolutionary regime of France-Albert René, Prime Minster turned President in 1977, proved more stable and durable than those of the Comoros. The standard of living of the Seychelles population improved so much that they enjoyed one of the highest per capita incomes among the states of the African Union. In the last decade, however, since the mid 1990s, the strategy of René's government has faltered, and since his retirement in 2003, his successor James Michel has been struggling to redress the country's ailing economy.[20] Even so, the Seychelles still benefit from an enviable stability and a relative prosperity, and this has been achieved, as in Mauritius, by an astute management of the country's limited resources: principally its huge fishing reserves and the cultivation of an up-market ecological tourism. The country is suffering at the time of writing from a chronic shortage of foreign currency resulting from an over-reliance on international loans, and it is struggling to service its debt payments.

One of the earliest policy decisions of René's government in the late 1970s was the elevation of Creole, the local vehicular language, to the status of an official language, alongside English and French: this made the islands the only state in the world where this was the case. This was accompanied by the extension of the use of Creole as a teaching medium in the primary sector of the education system. These measures, accompanied by the creation of a Creole Institute —*Lenstiti kreol*—have established the Seychelles as a centre of Creole culture, celebrated in an annual festival.[21] The islands have seen the development of a local literature written in Creole, mostly consisting of short stories and poetry, but also including the long-standing tradition of popular songs and folk-tales. There are limits, however, to this assertion of national identity that has helped to unify a geographically scattered country, where the population is of a very mixed origin. As in Mauritius, great emphasis is placed on the learning of English and French, and English replaces Creole as the principal teaching language in the secondary sector. The result is that most Seychellois are able to converse both in French and English as well as Creole. It is noticeable, however, that despite its official status, there are scarcely any public notices written in Creole: English and French are much more visible. The effect of these policies has been to diversify the very limited literary production of the Seychelles between three languages: Creole, French, and English.

The growth of literature in Creole

The earliest literature in Creole emanating from the Seychelles dates back to the late nineteenth century, when a primary school teacher, Rodolphine Young, attempted a translation of the fables of La Fontaine into Seychellois Creole,[22] closely following in this the example of Marbot, an author from Martinique who published *Les Bambous* in 1826.[23] This translation was eventually published in 1983 in Germany, thanks to the good offices of two researchers, Annegret Bollée and Ingrid Neumann, who were studying the local Creole and collecting the traditional folk-tales of the islands.[24] Other linguistic researchers also working on Seychellois Creole also produced collections and studies of folk-tales at around the same time, such as Michel Carayol and Robert Chaudenson, who were based in Reunion and covered the whole Indian Ocean region.[25] The Caribbean linguist Lambert-Félix Prudent also included poetry in Creole from the Seychelles in an anthology published in Paris in 1984.[26] The first novel written in Creole was eventually published in 1985: Leu Mancienne's *Fler Flétri*.[27] This was preceded by the attempt of the already well-known Francophone writer Antoine Abel to publish a novel locally: *Montann en leokri* of 1981.[28] In a similar vein, the official state publishing house put out a tri-lingual anthology of recent Creole poetry in 1986: *Leko bann ekriven*.[29]

Since then the Creole Institute has published numerous novellas and collections of poems in Creole, often intended for use in schools, but which also represent a considerable body of Seychellois popular literature in Creole. An example of the former category, the educational text, would be *Mang Lalin* by Sherrell Pitt-Kennedy,[30] a reworking of the celebrated tale of General Gordon, the martyr of the siege Khartoum and a Victorian visitor to Praslin island, who on discovering the suggestive shapes of the seed and the stamen of the "coco de mer" was convinced he had found the site of the biblical Garden of Eden. This idea is woven into a successful and humorous "children's story for adults" in a bilingual Creole / English edition, by an expatriate English writer. The other category of locally-written novellas is made up of apparently autobiographical accounts of personal relationships, disguised and transposed for dramatic effect, and expressing the difficulties and tensions of ordinary Seychellois in their everyday lives. A typical example of this would be *En kado nwel* [A Christmas present] by Benediste Hoareau,[31] the story of an unhappy love affair between a black girl of modest background and a middle-class white boy who emigrates to Australia. As the blurb describes it: "En fiksyon ki amen ou dan en monn lemosyon, lanmour, persekisyon, soufrans, traison me osi senserite" [A fiction which takes you to a world of emotion, love, persecution, suffering, betrayal but also sincerity]. Sometimes the subject matter is a serious social problem such as incest and child sexual abuse, as in the novella *Mwan Florans* [I, Florence] by Jeris Dogley.[32] Other texts take on the trappings of the thriller, as in the mystery story *Letranze Dan Mwan* [The Stranger in me] by Lise Morel.[33] Interesting as these texts may be, they remain at the level of popular fiction rather than serious literature, and are clearly aimed at a local readership rather than an international one. The emergence of this Creole literature has been extensively explored by the French researcher Pascale Canova, in an authoritative study of *La Littérature seychelloise*.

Poetry, fiction and essays in French

The Seychelles have not been particularly prolific in their production of literature in French, but their best-known contemporary Francophone writer, Antoine Abel, first published a collection of poems, *Paille-en-queue* in 1969.[34] His poetry has been appreciated for its simplicity of style and poetic evocation of the beauties of his native island,[35] in a manner reminiscent of the Reunionese poet Jean Albany. He went on to establish an international reputation as a fictional writer in the 1970s with his novellas *Coco sec* and *Une Tortue se rappelle*, both published in Paris by a small publishing house which has since disappeared.[36] His work is thus difficult to obtain, but Abel also published collections of folktales and poems in French from the Seychelles,[37] as well as a later novel in Creole, mentioned earlier.

In 1984 the Reunionese writer Jean-François Sam-Long compiled an anthology of poetry in French and Creole from the Seychelles, published in Reunion.[38] This included figures from the early twentieth century, "Les Aînés," such as Daniel Varigault de Valenfort and Marie Guénard, as well as the more familiar verse of Antoine Abel. The poetry of "Les plus jeunes" is of greater postcolonial interest, since most were writing since the independence of the island and several in Creole. Those using French included Daniel Ally, Patrick Mathiot, Marie-Cécile Médor and Elva Pool; those preferring Creole were Bernard Valentin and June Vell. In general their lyricism is somewhat naïve, however, and limited in scope.[39]

The historian and scientist Guy Lionnet, of Mauritian background but settled in the Seychelles, has written several historical accounts in French of the islands' development: such as *Par les Chemins de la mer*,[40] a chronicle of the most famous visitors to the islands. He also published scientific studies, such as that of the famous *Coco de mer* in 1986, as well as historical dramas which, although performed locally, have not been published. An exception to this was the play *Bonjour Monsieur de Quinssy*, which was broadcast by Radio France Internationale in 1978.[41]

Fiction in English

As in Mauritius, English is not often used for literary expression in the Seychelles, in spite of its potential for a world-wide audience: in recent times Creole tends to be the preferred medium for personal expression, with French used where an international audience is envisaged. Exceptions to this general rule are usually attributable to expatriate British writers, such as Sherrell Pitt-Kennedy, mentioned earlier. A further successful example is the collection of short stories published by the long-term islander Glyn Burridge, under the rather banal title of *Voices*.[42] These tales skilfully and evocatively recreate the atmosphere of the outer islands of the Seychelles archipelago, and recount in a gripping but humane way the closeness to life and death of their inhabitants, surviving on some of the most beautiful but fragile and isolated territories of the planet.

Creole music and songs

The heritage of traditional music and songs in the Seychelles bears many similarities with the other Creole islands of the region. The *sega* style popular in Mauritius and Reunion is also well established in the Seychelles and its history is similar: a slave music assimilated by the local European population and adapted by them to include European harmony instruments. One difference is that the original vocal / percussion form in the Seychelles was called *moutia*, rather than *sega ravanne* as in Mauritius, or *maloya* as in Reunion. The instruments are very similar however: the tambourine-style drum and the *bombe*, elsewhere called a *bobre*, a one-stringed percussive bass instrument; and a rattle called a *cascavelle*. There are other subtle differences, however: the traditional European dances such as the *contredanse*, the quadrille and the Scottish reel still survive and have been assimilated into Seychellois folklore: they feature in local entertainments for tourists and are still widely practised. These styles are also common in Rodrigues, the offshore dependency of Mauritius.[43] Recordings of the Seychelles varieties are still available on CD[44] and have also featured on ethno-musicological radio programmes on BBC Radio 3.[45]

In recent times the Seychelles have seen the influence of reggae, which, as in Mauritius and Reunion, has been mixed with the local *sega* rhythms to produce a composite form of local popular dance music, using electronic instruments, sometimes called *seggae*. This genre has thrown up a generation of local singer-songwriters, whose lyrics in Creole often combine social commentary with the more usual love stories, in a style sometimes reminiscent of the Trinidadian calypso. One of the best-known exponents of this is Jean-Marc Volcy, a local super-star for several decades now. His best known album and hit song remains *Vendredi sen* [Good Friday] from the 1990s, which was awarded an African Music Prize.[46] His most recent album is *Bon bon bon*, recorded in collaboration with a young woman singer, Wendy Duval.[47] His other former collaborators, such as Jenny Létourdie[48] and Brian Matombé[49] are also local exponents of a similar style, with perhaps more emphasis on the dance rhythms than the lyrics. Another recently successful figure has been Philippe Toussaint, with his meditation on "Gravité Lanmour" [The Gravity of Love].[50] In general, however, the popular music of the Seychelles is less ambitious than that of Reunion or Madagascar, and it is not very widely known outside of the islands. Even the authoritative Rough Guide to World Music has little of interest to say about the rich local musical heritage of the islands.[51]

Postcolonial vulnerability

The lesson of the contrasting postcolonial situations of the island micro-states of the Comoros and the Seychelles appears to be that it is increasingly difficult to assert cultural autonomy from such a such a limited economic base. Even though the Seychelles seem to have been more successful in this respect than the Comoros, it is clear that without the protection of the former colonial super-powers it is difficult to maintain political, economic and cultural independence. It is hardly surprising, then, that the population of Mayotte should have voted so consistently to remain, like Reunion, within the folds of the French republic, however paradoxical that may seem. It seems clear that with the onward march towards globalization this vulnerability can only become exacerbated, and that the margin of manoeuvre for successfully multi-ethnic micro-states such as the Seychelles will become ever more restricted, becoming progressively more dependent on the large trading power-bases of the European Union, North America and China. It may well be, however, that the solution will be to occupy a specialised "niche" in the way that the Seychelles have successfully done over the last two decades or more. This comes at a price, however, as this means that adaptability will be essential in order to survive, and the effects of the 2004 tsunami on island states such as the Maldives or even Sri Lanka show just how fragile these states can be. The post-independence history of the Comorian federation shows how important coherence and astute management of resources can be for the survival of a small island state, and that the price of disunity and quarrelling, admittedly a perennial Comorian weakness, can be very high in terms of depleted resources and standard of living. Yet there is no denying the success of the Seychelles in human and ecological terms, with a well-integrated population and a reasonable standard of living, and an enviable reputation as one of the last unspoilt havens of an organic, balanced and humane lifestyle.

Notes

1. For the main dates in the political development of the Comoros, see Joubert (1991) *Littératures de l'Océan indien*, 276-78.
2. Mohamed A. Toihiri, *La République des imberbes* (Paris: L'Harmattan, 1985).
3. Mohamed A. Toihiri, *Le Kafir du Karthala* (Paris: L'Harmattan. 1992).
4. See the entry "Comores" in *Atlaséco: atlas économique et politique mondial*, ed. Bertrand Clare (Paris: Médiaobs / *Le Nouvel Observateur*, 2005), 56.
5. See the entry "Mayotte" in Clare, *Atlaséco*, 143.
6. See Dominique Auzias and Jean-Paul Labourdette, eds. *Mayotte Comores* (Paris: Nouvelles Editions de l'Université, "Petit Futé" guide series, 2004), 8.
7. Carole Beckett, *Anthologie d'introduction à la poésie comorienne d'expression française* (Paris: L'Harmattan, 1995).
8. Moussa Said Ahmed, *Guerriers, princes et poètes aux Comores* (Paris: L'Harmattan, 2000).
9. Sony Lab'ou Tansi, *La Vie et demie* (Paris: Seuil, 1979).
10. Salim Hatubou, *Le Sang de l'obéissance* (Paris: L'Harmattan, 1996).
11. Danielle Nivo Galibert, "Note de lecture: Salim Hatubou, *Le Sang de l'obéissance*," *Notre Librairie*, 135 (Sept.-Dec. 1998), 141-42.
12. Nassur Attoumani, *Nerf de boeuf* (Paris: L'Harmattan, 2001).
13. Nassur Attoumani, *Le Calvaire des baobabs* (Paris: L'Harmattan, 2001).
14. Nassur Attoumani, *Contes traditionnels de nos ancêtres . . . les menteurs: recueil de contes mahorais* (Paris: L'Harmattan, 2003).
15. See Mohamed Toihiri, "Nassur Attoumani: le violeur de tabous," *Notre Librairie*, 158 (April-June 2005), 102-5.
16. See Graeme Ewens and Werner Graebner, "The Comoros" in *World Music, Vol. 1: Africa, Europe and the Middle East*, eds. Simon Broughton, Mark Ellingham and Richard Trillo (London: Rough Guides, 1999), 505-7.
17. See Maalesh, *Wassi wassi* (Paris: Mélodie, CD, n. d.).
18. See Mikidache, *Kaul / Words* (Paris: Long Distance / Wagram, CD, n. d.).

19. See *Chamsi na mwezi—gabusi and ndzendze from Moheli, Comoros* (Germany: Dizim records, CD, n. d.).
20. See the entry "Seychelles" in Clare, *Atlaséco*, 195.
21. See website: http://www.seychelles.net/festivalkreol/.
22. Rodolphine Young, *Fables de La Fontaine traduites en Créole seychellois* (Hamburg: Buske, 1983).
23. See Joubert, *Littératures de l'Océan* Indien, 270. The reference is to Marbot, *Les Bambous* (n. p. 1826).
24. See Annegret Bollée, *Le Créole français des Seychelles: esquisse d'une grammaire, textes, vocabulaire.* (Tubingen, Germany: Max Niemayer Verlag, 1977).
25. Michel Carayol and Robert Chaudenson, *Lièvre, Grand-Diable et autres contes de l'Océan indien* (Paris: Edicef, 1979).
26. Lambert-Félix Prudent, ed., "Seychelles" in *Anthologie de la nouvelle poésie créole* (Paris: Editions Caribéennes / ACCT, 1984), 493-523.
27. Leu Mancienne, *Fler fletri* (Paris: ACCT, 1985).
28. Antoine Abel, *Montann en leokri* (Mahé: Piblikasion nasional, 1981).
29. Anon. *Leko bann ekriven* (Mahé: Seychelles National Printing, 1986).
30. Sherrell Pitt-Kennedy, *Mang lalin/Mango moon* (Mahé: Lenstiti kreol, 2004).
31. Benediste Hoareau, *En kado nwel* (Mahé: Lenstiti kreol, 1994)
32. Jeris Dogley, *Mwan Florans* (Mahé: Lensititi kreol, 1994).
33. Lise Morel, *Letranze dan mwan* (Mahé: Lensititi kreol, 2003).
34. Antoine Abel, *Paille-en-queue* (Mahé: Imprimerie Saint-Fidèle, 1969).
35. See Joubert, *Littératures de l'Océan Indien*, 271-72.
36. Antoine Abel, *Coco sec* and *Une Tortue se rappelle*, (Paris: P.-J. Oswald, 1977).
37. Antoine Abel, *Contes et poèmes des Seychelles* (Paris: P.-J. Oswald, 1977).
38. Jean-François Sam-Long, ed., *Anthologie de la poésie seychelloise* (Saint-Leu, Reunion: Presses du Développement, 1984).
39. See Joubert, *Littératures de l'Océan Indien*, 271.
40. Guy Lionnet, *Par les Chemins de la mer* (Saint-Denis: Université de la Réunion, 2001).
41. See Joubert, *Littératures de l'Océan Indien*, 271.
42. Glyn Burridge, *Voices* (Victoria, Mahé: Nighthue publications, 2000).

43. See Jean-Pierre La Selve, *Musiques traditionnelles de la Réunion* (Saint-Denis: Azalées, 1995), 203-24.

44. *Forgotten music of the islands: dances and romances* (Paris: Ocora / Radio France, 2002), CD No. C582005.

45. *Mizik séselwa* (London: BBC Radio 3, n.d.).

46. Jean-Marc Volcy, *Vendredi sen* (Mahé: Youth Enterprise Services, n. d.), audio cassette; re-issued on CD.

47. Jean-Marc Volcy, *Bon bon bon* (Mauritius: Geda Music, 2005), CD No GD020.

48. Jenny Letourdie can be heard on the title track of Volcy's *Vendredi sen*.

49. Brian Matombe, *Lanbyans tropic* (Mahé: Segavibes Records, 2005).

50. Philippe Toussaint, *Gravite lanmour* (Victoria, Mahé: Sound on Sound Studio, 2004), CD.

51. See Broughton, Ellingham and Trillo, eds., *World Music, Vol. 1: Africa, Europe and the Middle East* (London: Rough Guides, 1999), 507.

Chapter 8

Trouble in Paradise

A test-bed for a hybrid world civilization?

One of the pressing reasons for an interest in the cultures of the islands of the Francophone Indian Ocean lies in their multi-cultural, multi-ethnic and multi-religious societies. In may ways they represent a successful example of a situation which is likely to be a common one world-wide in the years to come. Migration, economic mobility, faster communications, cheaper transport all mean that whole populations are on the move between continents and formerly autonomous nation states. Are there lessons to be learned from the experiences of these Indian Ocean islands, and if there are, can we find them expressed and embodied in their literary and cultural output?

There are several reasons to be cautious before making exaggerated claims for the relevance of these areas, after all more often considered as marginal and peripheral to the mainstream of the all-powerful Western democracies grouped around an Atlantic network of inter-relations. Most of these states make claims for their multi-cultural and multi-ethnic status, for their religious and political tolerance. Yet most of the nations of the European Union are still rooted in their sense of an ethnically-based national identity, and their pretensions to multi-cultural open-ness are showing signs of strain, as in the Autumn 2005 riots in France's city suburbs and the dramatic alienation of Britain's young home-grown Islamist suicide bombers of July 2005. Some North American cities can make a more convincing case as models for multi-ethnic, multi-cultural integration: Toronto in Canada, for instance, is home to a wide variety of diasporic communities who seem to live together in relative tolerance and harmony; and so is its Quebec rival Montreal. The cities of the United States are also multi-ethnic and multi-cultural in composition, but the tensions between ethnic communities in cities such as New York and Los Angeles regularly erupt into well-publicized violent confrontation: the latest dramatic example in 2005 is that of New Orleans in the wake of hurricane Katrina. A criticism often made in French intellectual circles of these situations is to blame it on what is called "communalism," in which the various ethnic and cultural communities are allowed to cultivate their relative autonomy and difference, thereby fomenting rivalry and conflict. As recent events have shown all too dramatically, the egalitarianism of French republican principles has not been enough to prevent similar conflicts occurring in metropolitan France. Even the more positive examples of Toronto and Montreal seem to depend on the subservience of immigrant and even native American communities to an Anglophone or Francophone hegemony which has been predetermined by the country's history of colonial rivalry.

The first point to make about the Indian Ocean islands in this respect is that little in their own history would have allowed us to foresee such a claim to exemplary status. All the islands were marked by the most brutal forms of slavery as recently as 150 years ago, and in the case of the plantation economies of Mauritius, Reunion and the Seychelles this was then replaced by the only slightly more humane conditions imposed on immigrant indentured labour forces. This dramatic history is reflected, remarkably discreetly, all things considered, in novels such as Daniel Vaxelaire's *Chasseur de Noirs*, Jean-François Samlong's Madame Desbassayns, Nassur Attoumani's *Nerf de Boeuf* and Abhimayu Unnuth's *Sueur de Sang*.[1] What is remarkable, however, is that this well-documented and cruel history seems not to have generated a climate of calls for bloodthirsty revenge. Novels such as Marcel Cabon's *Namasté*, as well as the examples already cited, bear witness to a spirit of reconciliation and humanism, whilst not shying away from depicting the realities of extreme poverty and colonial exploitation. In the light of their history, it is remarkable that these islands have not seen more confrontation than they have. As has often been observed in these pages, such conflicts as there have been in the post-independence years can usually be attributed to situations of economic exploitation or perceived injustice, rather than racial hatred or religious intolerance.

The dynamics of these moments of social tension and latent violence have been depicted and explored by many of the works referred to in previous chapters: for Madagascar, Charlotte Rafenomanjato's novel *Le Cinquième Sceau* and Raharimanana's essay *L'Arbre anthropophage*; for Mauritius, Carl de Souza's novels *La Maison qui marchait vers large* and *Les Jours Kaya*; for Reunion, Anne Cheynet's novel *Les Muselés* and Jean-Louis Rivière's play *Emeutes*. All of them also express a hope for the future of their respective societies whilst not flinching from an uncompromising indictment of their weaknesses. Many more works celebrate in an optimistic and symbolic vein a belief in the multicultural richness of the islands' cultures. Some of the most striking examples are as follows: from Réunion, Philippe Pelen's multi-lingual drama *Mâ*; from Madagascar, Charlotte Rafenomanjato's pamphlet *La Marche de la liberté*; and from Mauritius, Jean-Georges Prosper's essays,[2] articles[3] and poems such as his *Chants planétaires*. Prosper's theme of *La Créolie indianocéaniste* in particular is drawing on a tradition of literary multiculturalism in Mauritius which can be traced back to the poetry of Robert-Edward Hart, written and published during the colonial period, as well as the theories of "Indianoceanism" as formulated by Camille de Rauville.[4] All of these writers can be seen as attempting to establish what Edouard Glissant calls "la Relation" or relatedness,[5] in trying to situate the limited cultural perspective of their island culture in relation to a broader, global vision.

Marginality, its strengths and weaknesses

The geographical distance of the islands from both the mainland of the African continent as well as from the colonial decision-making centres of the West is one of the factors that affect the status of the island's cultures. In spite of the speedier communications of modern air travel and the internet, which have transformed the islands' access to the mainstream cultures of Europe and North America, their relative isolation remains a determining factor in their own self-image and their role in postcolonial development. There have been several moves towards the creation of a regional identity, notably the creation of the Commission de l'Océan Indien, an association of states from the Indian Ocean rim, which includes Australia, India and South Africa, the major political and economic powers of the region. On the one hand this relative isolation has encouraged their autonomy and a sense of self-sufficiency, even if in many respects their economies remain dependent on the patterns of trade with the former colonial powers of France and the European Union, notably in relation to the traditional export crops of spices, perfume essences and sugar-cane products. On the other, the strong sense of island identity sometimes verges on introversion and parochialism, however, so that the literary and cultural field of each island tends to be self-referential in the first instance. There are considerable differences even so between the islands in this respect, which can tentatively be situated in a comparative ranking order. The most proudly independent is no doubt Madagascar, authorized by its very strong sense of an ancestral national culture, as expressed, for instance, by Jacques Rabémananjara in poetic texts such as *Lamba* and *Antsa*; yet it is increasingly unable to sustain this without international aid and co-operation. Reunion too has a strong sense of its cultural specificity, but it is even so very closely bound up with its ambivalent relations with mainland France, ironically described as the "mother hen" in an ironic word-play between "métropole" and "mère-poule" in Emmanuel Genvrin's satirical play *Votez Ubu colonial*, as performed by the Théâtre Vollard. The Seychelles have made the promotion of their Creole identity and the Creole language one of the main features of their national culture, yet they too remain chronically dependent for their economic prosperity on the vagaries of the international tourist market, mostly oriented towards the European Union. The Comoros, despite their strong Islamic identity and the keen internal rivalry of the individual islands which led to the crisis of the secession of Anjouan in 1997, remain dependent on their neo-colonial ties with France, especially in the case of Mayotte, as reflected in the satirical novels of Mohamed Toihiri, such as *Le Kafir du Karthala* and the plays of Nassur Attoumani, such as the

Faustian *Interview d'un macchabé*. Mauritius, finally, with its patchwork of disparate cultures and languages, is probably the most outward-looking of the islands, maintaining strong cultural links with France, the United Kingdom and European Union as well as Australia, Singapore and South Africa, and with its considerable world-wide diaspora which includes several of its best-known writers, such as Edouard Maunick, Ananda Devi, Jean-Marie Le Clézio and Khal Torabully.

Nationalism, introversion and communalism

The twilight of European colonialism in the years following the Second World War gave rise to nationalist movements in most of the colonized territories, and the gravitation of the newly independent countries towards nationalism continued well after decolonization. Most emergent states embarked on a process of nation-building, all the more urgently needed when their frontiers were artificially delineated and their definition did not correspond to traditional ethnic or linguistic divisions. The islands of the Indian Ocean did not suffer from the arbitrariness of their borders, however, but rather from the diversity in the ethnic and cultural make-up of their populations. Thus even Madagascar, unified under a central monarchy in the early years of the nineteenth century, and possessing a common written and spoken language, still experiences the underlying tensions between its constituent peoples, as witnessed by Raharimanana in his essay *L'Arbre anthropophage* of 2004: his father was subjected to a politically-motivated trial simply because he publicly argued in favour of regional autonomy in his local radio broadcasts. This unfortunate episode took place in the aftermath of the disputed presidential election of 2001-2002 and this illustrates only too well the fragility of postcolonial politics, even in a country as apparently unified as Madagascar. In the wake of a virtual civil war, the new government presumably felt the need to assert its political control over the whole country in the face of any movements that might threaten national cohesion. It is interesting to compare this exacerbated nationalism with that of an earlier writer, Jean-Josph Rabéarivelo, in his novels *L'Aube rouge* and *L'Interférence*, both written during height of the French colonization of Madagascar in the

1920s, although published much later. Rabéarivelo presents the violent French take-over of Madagascar in 1896 as a tragic loss of independence, from a nationalist standpoint; yet his real allegiance is to the dominance of the Merina monarchy and aristocracy, for whom he feels a partially hereditary loyalty.

This illustrates all too well the underlying tension between communalism and nationalism that is echoed in other islands of the region. The inter-island rivalry of the Comoros islands would be the most extreme example, which has led to the fragility of the Comorian federation and its history of chronic political instability. The theme of rivalry between the islands surfaces even in the depiction of the most brutally authoritarian socialist and nationalist régime in Mohamed Toihiri's *La République des imberbes*. Such tensions are also a feature of Mauritian politics, although mercifully not enough to create a situation of political instability. The various ethnic and religious communities of Mauritius do not live in separate areas and are not identified with separate territories, with perhaps the notable exception of Rodrigues, a far-flung island dependency of Mauritius that has a more homogeneous Creole and Catholic population than the mainland. For all the undercurrents of rivalry between the diverse communities of the island, they are obliged to find a way of co-existing and this has paradoxically favoured the stable parliamentary regime of the country. Tensions do flare up from time to time, however, and these have been depicted in many novels, notably those of Carl de Souza. *Le Sang de l'Anglais* recounts the tragic allegiance of an anglophile, marginalized in relation to the Franco-Mauritian oligarchy of the plantation managers; *La Maison qui marchait vers le large* the hostility between a proud but impoverished Franco-Mauritian landlord and his Muslim tenants in a run-down suburb of Port-Louis; and *Les Jours Kaya* the tragedy of a young couple caught up in the riots of 1999, provoked by the death in police custody of the Creole singer Kaya. Communal rivalry is thus a recurrent theme in the work of this contemporary novelist. In a similar way the novels of Ananda Devi often depict the oppressive introversion and conformism of the Indo-Mauritian community of Hindu beliefs, in novels such as *Pagli*, which highlights the breaking of a taboo against sexual relations between Hindus and Creoles.

Reunion island has been refreshingly free in recent years from communalist rivalry, and many novels depict the solidarity of the different ethnic groups of the island in the face of poverty and adversity. This is an underlying theme of several picturesquely comic novels depicting community relations in the rural backwaters of the island, such as Dhavid's *Ti-krever*, Monique Agénor's *Bé-Maho* and Axel Gauvin's *L'Aimé*. These communities are not devoid of introversion, however, and their relations with the wider world are often defensive and difficult. Whilst they celebrate the humane qualities of the humblest sectors of Reunionese society, they also often express a subtle autonomist undercurrent which questions the dependence of this sometimes introverted island microcosm on its links with metropolitan France. This, for instance, is the rather bitter subtext of Axel Gauvin's tragi-comic novel *Train fou*, as well as the explicit message of his lyrics for the anthem sung by the group Ziskakan, "Bato fou."[6] In a similar vein, popular resistance to the hegemony of the French republican authorities is the theme of many polemical songs sung in Creole by Danyel Waro, such as "Adékalom."[7] All these texts give the lie to the perhaps over-optimistic celebration of the harmonious and racially integrated tropical paradises by authors mentioned earlier, such as Philippe Pelen and Jean-Georges Prosper.

Cultural forms as a vehicle for social and political tensions

Inevitably the postcolonial literatures of the islands have served to express the aspirations of their societies towards independence, defending their right to their own cultural specificity even when, as in the case of Reunion and Mayotte, they have chosen to remain in the political and social framework of the French republic. The remaining islands have now been independent states for over 30 years, and not surprisingly the nationalist-inspired literature of the 1950s and earlier has given ways to a literature more concerned with internal social problems particular to the situation of each island. One of the features of this has been a resurgence of interest in literatures written in languages other than those of the former colonial powers. The late 1970s, in the wake of the independence of Mauritius and the Seychelles, saw the emergence of a substantial literature in Creole, and not just in the recently independent islands, but in Reunion as well. The earliest plays and poetry in *morisien* by Dev Virahsawmy date from this period, as do the earliest song lyrics by Danyel Waro, Gilbert Pounia and the Ziskakan collective in Reunion. This was also the period which saw the first attempts in Reunion to write novels in Creole, by Daniel Honoré with *Louis Redona* and later Axel Gauvin, with *Kartié trwa let*, as well as Gauvin's pamphlet and manifesto *Du créole opprimé au créole libéré* of 1977. Even many Reunionese poets who chose to express themselves in French did so under the banner of "La Créolie," such as Jean Albany, Gilbert Aubry and Jean-François Samlong. This movement was clearly a reaction against the situation of excessive dependency and the cultural hegemony exercised by the centralised French authorities. The comparable period in the postcolonial history of Madagascar and the Comoros, on the other hand, was less fruitful in literary terms, even if it corresponded to the period of "malgachisation" of the education system in Madagascar and the radical revolutionary régime of Ali Soilih. These movements did not bear literary fruit until the mid 1980s, with publications in French by exiled writers such as Michèle Rakotoson, with *Dadabé* and *Le Bain des Reliques*, both fictions expressing a profound questioning of the nature of Malagasy identity; and the first major novel by Mohamed Toihiri, *La République des imberbes*, a bitter satire on the denial of Comorian traditions by the new revolutionary régime. In many ways the critical reaction of these writers to the post-independence situation in Madagascar and the Comoros marks a contrast with the flowering of a literature in Creole as a protest against the excessive domination of French language and culture in the other islands. What is common to these differing reactions is the mediation of the conflicts in the postcolonial societies of the region through literary expressions that reflect, even in their choice of linguistic and artistic form, the issues affecting their culture of origin. The relationship between a political and social situation and the literature it produces, as Bourdieu has rightly suggested, is one of relative autonomy. Even when there is an apparent correspondence of subject matter, as in the Malagasy and Comorian examples given above, the link is oblique rather than direct in terms of form and choice of language: the literary work is mediated through a complex hierarchy of literary fields, as described in chapter 3. Thus it is no surprise that the two works by Rakotoson and Toihiri cited above were both written in exile and published in France.

Advantages and limitations of the postcolonial approach

In chapter 3, I outlined the case for applying certain aspects of postcolonial theory to this body of literary and cultural production. The advantage of using this thoroughly international range of critical approaches is that it allows us to situate the writings of the Francophone Indian Ocean islands in a broader context of post-independence writing in English and other colonial languages such as Spanish and Portuguese, emanating from neighbouring territories such as southern Africa, Australia and the Indian sub-continent. This is well beyond our agenda here, however, but it does suggest ways in which the study of these literatures and cultures might be further developed. The use of concepts such as hybridity, mimicry, *Relation*, etc. has proved widely revealing and pertinent, and provides a common currency of critical notions that should facilitate further comparative exploration.

Quite apart from the individual illustrations of these themes suggested in previous chapters, it would be useful to review their wider relevance briefly here. The notion of hybridity, quite apart from its French equivalent *métissage*, can be linked to the notion of creolization, a process evoked by both Edouard Glissant and Edward Kamau Brathwaite in relation to Caribbean cultures, and further defined by Robert Young and Ashcroft et al.[8] This is clearly relevant to all the island cultures we are discussing here, all of which emerged from a process of acculturation involving both French and British colonial influences and varied cultural inputs from Africa, India and the far East. This process can be seen at work in very many of the literary works referred to here, in terms of language, literary form and content: the examples are too numerous to mention. It also applies equally well to other cultural forms emanating from the islands, such as the local musical genres of the sega[9] and the *maloya*.[10]

The notion of mimicry is similarly a useful one, inasmuch as it offers a way of conceptualising a process by which the dominant colonial influences of France and to a lesser extent Britain can be subverted and transformed by the island cultures. Quite apart from the particular examples already referred to, the concept can be applied to the ironic evocation of the influence of Western modernity, in a range of novels, such as Daniel Vaxelaire's *Bleu nuit*, Carl de Souza's *La maison qui marchait vers large*, Axel Gauvin's *Train fou* and Michèle Rakotoson's *Le Bain des reliques*. In all of these texts, the negative aspects of European influence are lampooned, such as the superficiality of the mass media, the irresponsibility of international and neo-colonial capitalist development, and the proliferation of the drugs trade.

The notion of the subaltern is also relevant to a wide range of writing from the region, particularly that which attempts to give a voice to underprivileged and destitute groups in the island societies. This applies to several contemporary authors from Madagascar, such as Raharimanana, in his collection of short stories *Lucarne*, and Michèle Rakotoson's novel *Henoy: Fragments en écorce*, both of which attempt to represent the view of the dispossessed urban poor of the Malagasy cities, in particular the capital, Antananarivo. It is also applicable in Mauritius, to Abhimanyu Unnuth's epic "peasant novel" *Sueurs de sang* and Ananada Devi's evocation of urban prostitution in *Rue la Poudrière*. In all these cases, however, as in the theorising of Spivak, the "ventriloquising" of the subaltern voice by a privileged narrator is problematic, in spite of the generous, idealistic and social motivations of the fictional creations.[11]

The notion of otherness is implicit in the title of this study, with the implication that this regional literature might usefully be compared with that of the Caribbean. As suggested in the chapter on Reunion,[12] the notion of *créolité* as propagated by Bernabé, Chamoiseau and Confiant[13] is of limited usefulness in relation to this body of writing, quite apart from the fact that the Indian Ocean writers thought of it first! The main reason for this is the persistence in the region of a large body of writing which clearly relates to other non-creolized cultures. In particular the large output of national literature written in the Malagasy language is not reducible to Caribbean notions of *créolité*; neither is the large output of novels in Hindi by the Mauritian writer Abhimanyu Unnuth, most of which have yet to be translated into French, let alone Creole. Even so, the notion of the cultural *difference* of the Indian Ocean islands gives one pause for thought: what assumptions are being made here about the status of this body of writing? This is not an Orientalist distinction, but rather an attempt to respect the cultural allegiances of the writers of the zone, however disparate, at the same time as situating them in a notional field based on the geographical region of the south-west Indian Ocean. The aim here is to create a literary and critical discourse which can be endorsed by its principal practitioners, rather than imposed from outside.

The notion of a "postcoloniality" which is not restricted to the post-independence period is useful in this area of study because it allows us to consider a certain number of works which clearly anticipate the emergence of postcolonialism, such as Bernardin de Saint-Pierre's *Voyage à l'Ile de France*, a possible candidate for the first postcolonial text in the French literary canon. One might argue that such texts belong in the field of French literature, like Bernardin's Paul et Virginie, but they also represent influential foundational texts for the islands' own literary traditions, as implicitly acknowledged by Daniel Vaxelaire in his novel about Bernardin's island odyssey, *Une si jolie naufragée*.

The themes of migration and diaspora are obviously recurrent motifs in the literature of the islands, as in novels depicting the origins of slavery, such as Nassur Attoumani's *Nerf de Boeuf*, and the literature of the indentured labour force in Reunion, such as Firmin Lacpatia's *Boadour*, and in Mauritius, with Abhimanyu Unnuth's *Sueurs de sang* and Marcel Cabon's *Namasté*. The notion of migration is relevant too in accounts of recent expatriate experiences, such as the Malagasy heroine of Michèle Rakotoson's *Elle, au printemps* or the Mauritian Khal Torabully's collection of poems *Cale d'étoiles: coolitude*.

The concept of *Relation* borrowed from the Caribbean writer Edouard Glissant takes on a particular dimension when applied to the literatures of the Indian Ocean islands. As suggested earlier it serves to highlight the extent to which the cultures of the region have been able to situate themselves in a global framework or relatedness, in spite of a tendency towards introversion and parochialism. Some writers have been more successful at this than others: the audience for the plays of Emmanuel Genvrin, written for the Reunionese theatre group *Théâtre Vollard*, has certainly not been restricted to the islands: they have achieved considerable recognition and popular success in metropolitan France and elsewhere. This is even more true of their Reunionese rivals the *Théâtre Talipot*, under the direction of Philippe Pelen, who have achieved a world-wide international success with their multimedia drama *Les Porteurs d'eau*.[14] On the other hand the Creole writing from the islands has not surprisingly found it difficult to achieve a similar level of recognition, despite the international success of the Reunionese singer-songwriter Danyel Waro in World Music circuits, and published translations of the Mauritian plays of Dev Virahsawmy, such as *Toufann*.

All these borrowings from postcolonial theory have proved themselves useful in analysing this body of literary and cultural production, but is that enough for us to conclude that postcolonialism is the best way of characterising in general terms the recent output of the islands? Some objections do arise, and one is the question asked of author at a conference in Mauritius by the Malagasy critic Liliane Ramarasoa "Jusqu' à quand sera-t-on postcolonial?" [Until when shall we remain postcolonial?] Obviously this comment was inspired by Malagasy nationalism and sense of a cultural specificity drawing on the strong pre-colonial culture of Madagascar, which the postcolonial approach appears to minimize. Even so, there have been suggestions that perhaps the "postcolonial moment" is drawing to a close, and that the world-wide influence of the former colonial powers is waning. Can one envisage a point in the future when the postcolonial influence of France and Britain will be subsumed into a new national or transnational ethos, in much the way that early Norman French influence was absorbed over centuries into British culture? It may happen sooner than one thinks, if the movement of globalisation and mobility gathers pace and a genuinely planetary civilisation replaces the former colonial zones of influence and the political divisions of the Cold War era. Already there is a noticeable regionalisation which is changing the patterns of trade of the Indian Ocean islands away from their former dependency on Europe towards a greater interaction with the closer regional economic centres of South Africa, India, Singapore, China and Australia, facilitated in the case of the two French territories of Reunion and Mayotte by moves towards the de-centralisation of the French state.

Towards a multi-faceted future

Another factor which may affect the future development of the islands is the increased mobility of the world's population. Already there have been considerable migrations within the islands of the Indian Ocean, so that there are growing diasporic communities of Malagasy and Comorian origin in the richer islands of Mayotte and Reunion, along with growing numbers of metropolitan French wishing to settle there. The pressures leading to economic migration have created the phenomenon of "people trafficking" and cargoes of "boat people" such as those evoked in a recent novel by Carl de Souza, *Ceux qu'on jette à la mer*. We are witnessing mass economically-motivated movements of population comparable to those of the periods of slavery and the recruitment of indentured labour forces, even if in a climate more humane and less violent: such trends could radically transform the cultures of the Indian Ocean islands.

Already the wealthier islands of Reunion and Mauritius have not been slow to take advantage of the improvements in telecommunications and the proliferation of the internet. The islands now have their own cyber-cultures, which has the effect of drastically reducing the marginalization of the islands' cultural output, and bringing them into the mainstream. They are now affected by the same trends and fashions as the industrialised West, with the corresponding threat, but also the corresponding opportunities, for the promotion of their local cultures. Another element which is working in the same direction is the development and reduction in cost of long-distance air-travel: it is no longer an unaffordable luxury for the islanders to travel to Europe, to Australia, to South Africa, to India or Singapore, and the islands themselves are becoming less exotic as destinations for tourists and travellers.

This is likely to have the effect of blurring the distinctiveness of the islands' cultural production, but at the same time opening up new possibilities for publishing, for musical and theatrical performance. Already the world-wide tour of the Théâtre Talipot's show *Les Porteurs d'eau* [The Water-Carriers] has shown the way. The publication of literary works in France has always been common for the authors of the region, but one can look forward to syndicated international publishing arrangements involving translations and televison and video production rights. It has to be said that few Indian Ocean authors have yet achieved such world-wide notoriety, but it is not inconceivable that some may do so in the not too distant future. Already Lindsay Collen, a Mauritian novelist of South African origin, has twice been winner of the Commonwealth Literary Prize for Africa, with her novels in English *The Rape of Sita* and *Boy*. The original version of the latter was a novel in Creole, *Mision Garson*, published in Mauritius by the left-wing publishing house LPT; it is now, if not yet a best-seller with rights courted by Hollywood, at the very least an internationally successful title for the London-based Bloomsbury Press.

Whatever the future may hold for the Indian Ocean islands, their cultures should at least be respected as offering an interesting case-study in multiculturalism and ethnic integration, and probably more successful in this respect than the societies of the self-confident Western democracies. Their literatures and analogous forms of expression provide a stimulating and rewarding body of material through which the mainstream cultures of the world can reflect on the problems and perspectives of their multi-cultural future.

Notes

1. For full details, see General Bibliography. In the light of the large number of general references in this chapter to works already cited, it seems unnecessary in most cases to reproduce the full publication details given there.

2. See below: Jean-Georges Prosper, La Créolie indianocéaniste (Vacoas, Mauritius: Editions Le Printemps, 1996).

3. See Jean-Georges Prosper, "La créolie indianocéaniste: un humanisme planétaire" in L'océan Indien dans les littératures francophones, ed. Kumari R. Issur and Vinesh Y. Hookoomsing (Paris and Mauritius: Karthala / Presses de l'Université de Maurice, 2001), 107-12.

4. Camille de Rauville, Indianocéanisme, Humanisme et Négritude (Mauritius: Regent Press and Stationery, 1968). See also Michel Beniamino, "Camille de Rauville et l'"indianocéanisme" in Issur and Hookoomsing, eds., L'océan Indien , 87-105.

5. See chapter 3, "Relation and relatedness."

6. "Bato fou," as recorded by Ziskakan, on Ziskakan, *Bato fou* (Saint-André: Piros / Sonodisc, 1991) CD; and on Ziskakan, *Soley glasé* (Paris: Sankara / Mercury, 1996), CD 532 410-2 (lyric included). The lyric was originally published in Axel Gauvin, *Romans po detak la lang demay le ker* (Saint-Leu, Reunion: Presses du Développement, 1983).

7. "Adekalom" recorded on Danyel Waro, *Batarsité* (Saint-André, Reunion: Piros, 1994), CD CDP5198. Lyrics also published in Danyel Waro, *Demavouz la vi* (Saint-Denis: Grand Océan, 1996).

8. See "Creolization" in Bill Ashcroft, Gareth Griffiths and Helen Tiffin, *Key Concepts in Post-Colonial Studies* (London and New York: Routledge, 1998), 58-59.

9. See chapter 5, "Creole poetry and music" and Jacques K. Lee, *Sega: the Mauritian folk-dance* (London: Nautilus Publishing, 1990).

10. See chapter 6, "A cross-fertilized musical field" and Jean-Pierre La Selve, *Musiques traditionnelles de La Réunion*, 2nd ed., (Saint-Denis: Azalées, 1995), 185-99.

11. See "Subaltern" in Ashcroft, Griffiths and Tiffin, Key Concepts, 215-19.

12. See chapter 6, "Créolie and Créolité."

13. Jean Bernabé, Patrick Chamoiseau and Raphaël Confiant, *Eloge de la Créolité / In Praise of Creoleness* (Paris: Gallimard, 1989).

14. See Discography rather than General Bibliography: *Théâtre Talipot,* Les Porteurs d'eau / The water carriers *(Saint-Pierre, Reunion: Théâtre Talipot, 1998), CD No MP9901.*

General Bibliography

Abel, Antoine. *Paille-en-queue*. Mahé: Imprimerie Saint-Fidèle, 1969.
———. *Coco sec*. Paris: P.-J. Oswald, 1977.
———. *Contes et poèmes des Seychelles*. Paris: P.-J. Oswald, 1977.
———. *Une Tortue se rappelle*. Paris: P.-J. Oswald, 1977.
———. *Montann en leokri*. Mahé: Piblikasion nasional, 1981.
Agénor, Monique. *L'Aïeule de l'Isle Bourbon*. Paris: L Harmattan, 1993.
———. *Bé-Maho*. Paris: Le Serpent à Plumes, 1996.
———. *Comme un vol de papang'*. Paris: Le Serpent à Plumes, 1998.
Albany, Jean. *Zamal*. Paris: author's publication/Editions Bellenand, 1951. Reprinted Paris: author's publication, 1980.
———. *Bleu mascarin*. Paris: author's publication, 1969.
———. *Vavangue*. Paris: author's publication, 1972.
———. Ptit'glossaire—le piment des mots créoles. Paris: author's publication, 1974.
Anderson, Ian. "Madagascar." Pp. 523-32 in *World Music, Vol. 1: Africa, Europe and the Middle East*. Edited by Simon Broughton, Mark Ellingham and Richard Trillo. London: The Rough Guides, 1999.
Andriajafy, Danielle. "Le théâtre: une aubaine . . . pour une élite." In "La Littérature malgache d'expression française," edited by Siméon Rajaona. *Notre Librairie*, 110, (1992), 69-75.
Armand, Alain. *Zordi*. Saint-Denis: Les Chemins de la Liberté, 1978.
Asgarally, Renée. *Quand montagne prend difé*. Mauritius: Mascarena University Publications, 1977.
Ashcroft, Bill, Gareth Griffiths and Helen Tiffin. *The Empire writes back: theory and practice in post-colonial literatures*. London and New York: Routledge, 1989.

Ashcroft, Bill, Gareth Griffiths and Helen Tiffin, eds. *The post-colonial studies reader*. London and New York: Routledge, 1995.
Ashcroft, Bill, Gareth Griffiths and Helen Tiffin. *Key concepts in post-colonial studies*. London and New York: Routledge, 1998.
Attoumani, Nassur. *La Fille du polygame*. Paris: L'Harmattan, 1992.
———. *Le Turban et la capote*. Saint-Denis: Grand Océan, 1997.
———. *Interview d'un macchabée*. Paris: L'Harmattan, 2000.
———. *Le Calvaire des baobabs*. Paris: L'Harmattan, 2000.
———. *Nerf de boeuf.* Paris: L'Harmattan, 2000.
———. *Contes traditionnels de nos ancêtres . . . les menteurs: recueil de contes mahorais*. Paris: L'Harmattan, 2003.
Aubry, Gilbert. *Rivages d'Alizé*. Saint-Denis de La Réunion: author's publication, 1971. New edition, Saint-Denis de La Réunion: Nouvelle Imprimerie Dionysienne, 1980.
Aubry, Gilbert and Jean-François Sam-Long. *Créolie*. Saint-Denis de La Réunion: UDIR, 1978.
Auzias, Dominique and Jean-Paul Labourdette. *Mayotte Comores*. Paris: Nouvelles Editions de l'Université, "Petit Futé" guide series, 2004.
Azéma, Jean-Henri. *Olographe*. Madrid: Editions des Trois Salazes, 1978.
———. *D'Azur à perpétuité*. Madrid: Editions des Trois Salazes, 1979.
———. *Le Pétrolier couleur antaque*. Saint-Denis: Trois Salazes, 1982.
———. *Le Dodo vavangueur*. Saint-Denis: Trois Salazes, 1986.
Bacou, Abdou S. *Brûlante est ma terre*. Paris: L'Harmattan, 1997.
Banham, Martin, James Gibbs and Femi Osofisan, eds. *African Theatre: Playwrights and politics*. Oxford, Bloomington and Johannesburg: James Currey / Indiana University Press / Witwatersrand University Press, 2001.
Beckett, Carole. *Anthologie d'introduction à la poésie comorienne d'expression française*. Paris: L'Harmattan, 1995.
Beniamino, Michel. *Lecture de "Vali pour une reine morte" de Boris Gamaleya*. Sainte Clotilde, Reunion: Institut de Linguistique et d'Anthropologie de la Réunion, 1985.
———. *L'Imaginaire réunionnais. Recherches sur les déterminations constitutives du rapport entre le sujet et l'île*. Saint-Denis: Editions du Tramail, 1992.
Bernabé, Jean, Patrick Chamoiseau and Raphaël Confiant. *Eloge de la créolité/In praise of creoleness*. Paris: Gallimard, 1989.
Bhabha, Homi K. *The location of culture*. London and New York: Routledge, 1994.
Bibique [Joseph Tipveau]. *Sur la piste des frères de la côte*. Saint-Denis: Editions de la Réunion insolite, 1984.

Bollée, Annegret. *Le Créole français des Seychelles: esquisse d'une grammaire, textes, vocabulaire.* Tubingen, Germany: Max Niemayer Verlag, 1977.

Bourdieu, Pierre. *Les Règles de l'art: genèse et structure du champ littéraire.* Paris: Seuil, 1992.

Bourgeacq, Jacques and Liliane Ramarasoa, eds. *Voices from Madagascar/Voix de Madagascar.* Athens: Ohio University Press, 2002.

Bradt, Hilary. *Guide to* Madagascar, 5th ed. Chalfont St. Peter, UK / Old Saybrook CO: Bradt, 1997.

———. *Guide to Madagascar,* 8th ed. Chalfont St. Peter, UK / Old Saybrook CO: Bradt, 2005.

Bragard, Véronique. "Cris de femmes maudites, brûlures du silence: La symbolique des éléments fondamentaux dans l'oeuvre d'Ananda Devi." *Notre Librairie*: No. 142, (2000), 66-73.

———. "Eaux obscures du souvenir: Femme et mémoire dans l'oeuvre d'Ananda Devi." Pp. 187-99 in *Convergences and interferences: newness in intercultural practices / Ecritures d'une nouvelle ère / aire.* Edited by Kathleen Gyssels, Isabel Hoving and Maggie Ann Bowers. Amsterdam: Rodopi, 2001.

———. "Transoceanic Echoes: Coolitude and the work of the Mauritian Poet Khal Torabully." *International Journal of Francophone Studies,* 8:2, 2005, 219-33.

Broughton, Simon; Mark Ellingham and Richard Trillo, eds. *World Music. Volume I: Africa, Europe and the Middle East.* London: The Rough Guides, 1999.

Burridge, Glyn. *Voices.* Victoria, Seychelles: Nighthue Publications, 2000.

Butlin, Ron, ed. *Mauritian Voices—new writing in English.* Newcastle, UK: Flambard, 1997.

Cabon, Marcel. *Namasté.* Port Louis, Mauritius: Le Cabestan, Royal Printing Co., 1965. Reprinted Rose Hill, Mauritius: Editions de l'Océan Indien, 1981.

Canova, Pascale. *La littérature seychelloise—production, promotion, réception.* Paris: L'Harmattan / Organisation internationale de la Francophonie, 2006.

Carayol, Michel and Robert Chaudenson. *Lièvre, Grand-Diable et autres contes de l'Océan indien.* Paris: Edicef, 1979.

Carpooran, Arnaud. *L'Ile Maurice: des langues et des lois.* Paris: L'Harmattan / Agence intergouvernementale de la Francophonie, 2003.

Chane-Kune, Sonia. *Aux Origines de l'identité réunionnaise.* Paris: L'Harmattan, 1993.

Cheynet, Anne. *Matanans et langoutis*. Saint-Denis de La Réunion: R.E.I. 1972.
———. *Les Muselés*. Paris: L'Harmattan, 1977.
Clare, Bertrand, ed. *Atlaséco: atlas économique et politique mondial*. Paris: Médiaobs / Le Nouvel Observateur, 2005.
Collen, Lindsey. *There is a tide*. Port Louis, Mauritius: LPT, 1990.
———. *The Rape of Sita*. Port Louis, Mauritius: LPT, 1993. Reprinted London: Bloomsbury, 2004.
———. *Vizit labalenn*. Port Louis, Mauritius, Mauritius: LPT, 1995.
———. *Mision garson*. Port Louis, Mauritius: LPT, 1996.
———. *Getting rid of it*. London: Granta, 1997.
———. *Mutiny*. London: Bloomsbury, 2001.
———. *Boy*. London: Bloomsbury, 2005.
Combeau, Yvan, Prosper Eve, Sudel Fuma, Edmond Maestri. *Histoire de La Réunion. De la colonie à la région*. Paris and Saint-Denis: SEDES / Université de La Réunion, 2001.
Dayot, Eugène. *Bourbon pittoresque*. 1848. Reprinted in *Oeuvres choisies*. Paris: Challamel, 1878. Reprinted, Saint-Denis de La Réunion: Imprimerie Croix-Sud, 1967. Reprinted in *Oeuvres choisies*. Saint-Denis de La Réunion: Nouvelle Imprimerie Dionysienne, 1977.
De Chazal, Malcolm. *Sens plastique*. Paris: Gallimard, 1948.
———. *Petrusmok*. Curepipe, Mauritius: Eds. de la Table Ovale, 1951.
De Parny, Evariste de Forges. *Chansons madécasses*. London: n. p., 1787. Reprinted pp. 73-80 in *Océan indien—Madagascar, La Réunion, Maurice*, edited by Serge Meitinger and J.-C. Carpanin Marimoutou. Paris: Omnibus, 1998.
De Rauville, Camille. *Indianocéanisme, humanisme et négritude*. Mauritius: Regent Press and Stationery, 1968.
———. *Littératures francophones de l'Océan indien*. Saint-Denis: Editions du Tramail, 1990.
De Rossi, José. "Dox, la tradition rénovée" In "Madagascar 1: la littérature d'expression malgache." Edited by Siméon Rajaona. *Notre Librairie*, 109, (1992), 100-1.
Desai, Gaurav and Supriya Nair, eds. *Postcolonialisms*. Oxford: Berg, 2005.
Deschamps, Hubert. *Histoire de Madagascar*. Paris: Berger-Levrault, 1972.
De Souza, Carl. *Le Sang de l'Anglais*. Paris: Hatier, 1993.
———. *La Maison qui marchait vers le large*. Paris: Le Serpent à plumes, 1996.
———.*Les jours Kaya*. Paris: Editions de l'Olivier, 2000.

———. *Ceux qu'on jette à la mer*. Paris: Editions de l'Olivier, 2001.
Devi, Ananda. *Solstices*. Mauritius: Regent Press, 1977. Reprinted, Mauritius: Editions de l'Océan Indien, 1997.
———. *Le Poids des êtres*. Mauritius: Editions de l'Océan Indien, 1987.
———. *Rue la Poudrière*. Dakar and Abidjan: Nouvelles Editions Africaines, 1989. Reprinted, Mauritius: Editions de l'Océan Indien, 1997.
———. *Le Voile de Draupadi*. Paris: L'Harmattan, 1993.
———. *L'Arbre fouet*. Paris: L'Harmattan, 1997.
———. *Pagli*. Paris: Gallimard, "Continents noirs" series, 2001.
Dhavid [David Huet]. *Ti Kréver—l'enfant bâtard*. Saint-André, Reunion: Océan Editions, 1990.
———. *Tienbo l'kèr*. Saint-André, Reunion: Océan Editions, 1993.
———. *Doboute tanbi*. Saint-André, Reunion: Océan Editions, 1994.
Dirlik, Arif. "The postcolonial aura: Third World Criticism in the Age of Global Capitalism." *Critical Enquiry,* 20 (Winter 1994): 328-56. Reprinted pp. 561-588 in *Postcolonialisms*. Edited by Gaurav Desai and Supriya Nair. Oxford: Berg, 2005.
Dodd, Jan. *Mauritius, Réunion and Seychelles*, 5th ed. Footscray, Australia: Lonely Planet, 2004.
Dox. *Chants capricorniens*. Antananarivo, Madagascar: Editions du Centre Albert Camus, 1995.
Ewens, Graeme and Werner Graebner. "The Comoros." Pp. 505-7 in *World Music, Vol. 1: Africa, Europe and the Middle East*. Edited by Simon Broughton, Mark Ellingham and Richard Trillo. London: Rough Guides, 1999.
Fanchette, Régis. *A private journey . . . itinéraire privé*. Mauritius: Editions de l'Océan Indien, 1996.
Faure, Michel and Daniel Vaxelaire. *La Buse*. Reunion: Editions AGM, 1978-1979.
Fievez, Josiane. "La littérature chinoise. Entretien avec Joseph Tsang Mang Kin" in "La Littérature mauricienne," *Notre Librairie*, No 114 (1993).
Fonkoua, Romuald and Pierre Halen, eds. *Les Champs littéraires africains*. Paris: Karthala, 2001.
Forsdick, Charles and David Murphy, eds. *Francophone postcolonial studies: a critical introduction*. London: Arnold, 2003.
Galibert, Danielle Nivolisoa. "Note de lecture: Salim Hatubou, *Le Sang de l'obéissance*." *Notre Librairie*, 135 (Sept.-Dec. 1998), 141-42.
Gamaleya, Boris. *Vali pour une reine morte*. Saint-Denis de La Réunion: Réunion Edition Impression, 1973. Reprinted, Saint-André, Reunion: Imprimerie Graphica, 1986.

———. *Le Volcan à l'envers ou Mme Desbassyns, le Diable et le Bondieu.* Saint-Leu, Reunion: Presses du Développement, 1983.

———. *Ombline ou le volcan à l'envers.* Saint-André, Reunion: Océan Editions, 1998.

Gauvin, Axel. *Du créole opprimé au créole libéré.* Paris: L'Harmattan, 1977.

———. *Quartier trois-lettres.* Paris: L'Harmattan, 1980.

———. *Romans po detak la lang demay le ker.* Saint-Leu, Reunion: Presses du Développement, 1983.

———. *Kartyé trwa lèt.* Saint-Denis: Editions Ziskakan, 1984.

———. *Faims d'enfance.* Paris: Seuil, 1987.

———. *L'Aimé.* Paris: Seuil, 1990.

———. *Bayalina.* Saint-Denis: Grand Océan, 1995.

———. *Cravate et fils.* Paris: Seuil, 1996.

———. *Train fou.* Paris: Seuil, 2000.

Genvrin, Emmanuel. *Nina Ségamour.* Saint-Denis: Eds. Théâtre Vollard, 1986.

———. *Marie Dessembre.* Saint-Denis: Eds. Théâtre Vollard, 1987.

———. *Etuves.* Saint-Denis: Eds. Théâtre Vollard, 1988.

———. *Lepervenche chemin de fer.* Saint-Denis: Grand Océan, 1991.

———. *Votez Ubu colonial.* Saint-Denis: Grand Océan, 1994.

———. *Baudelaire au paradis.* Paris: L'Harmattan, 1998.

Glissant, Edouard. *Le Discours antillais.* Paris: Seuil, 1981. Reprinted, Paris: Gallimard, 1990.

———. *Poétique de la Relation.* Paris: Gallimard, 1990.

———. *Tout-monde.* Paris: Gallimard, 1993.

———. *Traité du Tout-monde.* Paris: Gallimard, 1997.

Guébourg, Jean-Louis. *Les Seychelles.* Paris: Karthala, 2004.

Guha, Ranajit, ed. *Subaltern studies I and II: Writings on South Asian history and society.* Delhi: Oxford University Press, 1982/1983.

Hallward, Peter. *Absolutely postcolonial.* Manchester and New York: Manchester University Press, 2001.

Hart, Robert-Edward. *Sensations de route.* Port Louis, Mauritius, Mauritius: General Printing and Stationery, 1918.

———. *Poèmes anglais.* Port Louis, Mauritius: La Typographie moderne, 1929.

———. *Le Cycle de Pierre Flandre.* Port Louis, Mauritius: la Typographie Moderne, 1928-1934. Comprising 4 novels: *Mémorial de Pierre Flandre*, 1928; *Respiration de la vie,* 1932; *La Joie du monde,* vols. I and II, 1934.

———. *Bhagavad-Gita.* Port Louis, Mauritius: Standard Printing, 1936.

———. *Poèmes védiques*. Port Louis, Mauritius: Standard Printing, 1941.
Hatubou, Salim. *Le Sang de l'obéissance*. Paris: L'Harmattan, 1996.
Hausser, Michel and Martine Mathieu. *Littératures francophones. III.Afrique noire Océan Indien*. Paris: Belin, 1998.
Hawaldar, Shakuntala. *I have seen strange things*. Port Louis, Mauritius: Mauritius Printing Co., 1971.
———. *Moods, moments and memories*. Beau Bassin, Mauritius: the Triveni, 1972.
———. *You*. Port Louis, Mauritius: Lem Wee Graphics, 1981.
———. *Hymns from Beau Bois*. Mauritius: publisher unknown, 1994.
Hawkins, Peter. "*Homo authénegrafricanitus?* Applying Bourdieu to Francophone African Literature." *ASCALF Yearbook*, No. 2 (1996), 28-35.
———. "Two contrasting strategies for a postcolonial theatre in Réunion." *International Journal of Francophone Studies*, Vol. 2, No. 1 (2000), 45-50.
———. "Ubu in the tropics: the rise and fall of the Théâtre Vollard." In *African theatre; playwrights and politics*. Edited by Martin Banham, James Gibbs and Femi Osofisan. Oxford, Bloomington and Johannesburg: James Currey / Indiana University Press / Witwatersrand University Press, 2001.
———. "Y a-t-il un champ littéraire mauricien?" In *Les Champs littéraires africains*. Edited by R. Fonkoua and P. Halen. Paris: Karthala, 2001.
———. "*Libertalia*: le métissage utopique de Daniel Vaxelaire." Pp. 455-62 in *L'Océan Indien dans les littératures francophones*. Edited by Kumari R. Issur and Vinesh Y. Hookoomsing. Paris and Mauritius: Karthala / Presses de l'Université de Maurice, 2001.
———. "How appropriate is the term 'post-colonial' to the cultural production of Reunion?" Pp. 311-20 in *Francophone post-colonial cultures*. Edited by Kamal Salhi. Lanham, MD: Lexington, 2003.
Honoré, Daniel. *Louis Redona*. Saint-Denis: Les Chemins de la Liberté, 1980.
———. *Cemin Bracanot'*. Saint-Leu: Presses de l'ILR, 1984.
———. *Marceline doub'kèr*. Saint-Denis: UDIR, 1988.
Houat, Louis-Timagène. *Les Marrons*. Paris: Ebrard, 1844. Reprinted, Sainte Clotilde and Sainte-Rose, Reunion: CRI, 1988 / Editions AIPDS, 1998.
Hugon, Monique. "Entre deux langues. Entretien avec Michèle Rakotoson," *Notre Librairie*, No. 110 (1992).

Hugon, Monique and Jean-Louis Joubert, eds. "Littérature mauricienne." Special issue of *Notre Librairie*, No. 114 (1993).
Humbert, Marie-Thérèse. *A l'autre bout de moi*. Paris: Stock, 1979.
Issur, Kumari R. and Vinesh Y. Hookoomsing, eds. *L'Océan Indien dans les littératures francophones*. Paris and Mauritius: Karthala / Presses de l'Université de Maurice, 2001.
Jack, Belinda. *Francophone literatures: an introductory survey*. Oxford: Oxford University Press, 1996.
Joubert, Jean-Louis. *Littératures de l'Océan Indien*. Vanves, France: EDICEF / AUPELF, 1991.
Khal [Khal Torabully]. *Cale d'étoiles—coolitude*. Reunion: Azalées / Editions du Flamboyant, 1992.
Lacpatia, Firmin. *Boadour—Du Gange . . . à la Rivière des Roches*. Saint-Denis: A.G.M. 1978.
La Selve, Jean-Pierre. *Musiques traditionnelles de La Réunion*, (2nd ed.). Saint-Denis: Azalées. 1995.
Lazarus, Neil, ed. *The Cambridge companion to postcolonial literary studies*. Cambridge: Cambridge University Press, 2004.
Le Clézio, Jean-Marie Gustave. *Le Procès*. Paris: Gallimard, 1963.
———. *Le Chercheur d'or*. Paris: Gallimard, 1985.
———. "Préface" in Abhimanyu Unnuth, *Sueurs de sang*. Paris: Stock, 2001.
Lee, Jacques K. *Sega: the Mauritian folk-dance*. London: Nautilus Publishing, 1990.
Lionnet, Françoise. *Autobiographical voices: race, gender, self-portraiture*. Ithaca, NY: Cornell University Press, 1989.
———. "Créolité in the Indian Ocean: two models of cultural diversity." *Yale French Studies*, 82 (1993), 101-112.
———. *Postcolonial representations: women, literature, identity*. Ithaca, NY: Cornell University Press, 1995.
———. "Creole vernacular theatre: transcolonial translations in Mauritius." *MLN*, 118, No. 4 (Sept. 2003), 911-932.
Lionnet, Guy. *Par les Chemins de la mer*. Saint-Denis: Université de la Réunion, 2001.
Lorraine, Alain. *Tienbo le rein, Beaux visages cafrines sous la lampe*. Paris: L'Harmattan, 1976.
Magdelaine-Andrianjafitrimo, Valérie. "'Ethnotexte' et intertextualité: la mise en scène des représentations culturelles dans les 'romans ethnographiques.'" Chapter 5, pp. 93-145 in *Contes et romans: univers créoles 4*. Edited by Valérie Magdelaine-Andrianjafitrimo and Carpanin Marimoutou. Paris: Anthropos, 2004.

Magdelaine-Andrianjafitrimo, Valérie and Carpanin Marimoutou, eds. *Contes et romans: univers créoles 4*. Paris: Anthropos, 2004.

———. *Un état des savoirs à la Réunion. Tome II: Littératures*. Saint-Denis: LCF-UMR 8143 CNRS / Université de la Réunion, 2004.

Mair, Lyn and Lynnath Beckley. *Seychelles*. Chalfont St. Peter, UK: Bradt, 2001.

Mancienne, Leu. *Fler fletri*. Paris: ACCT, 1985.

Marbot. *Les Bambous* [Adaptation of La Fontaine's Fables into Creole]. N. p. 1826.

Marimoutou, Carpanin. *Fazèle*. Saint-Denis: Les Chemins de la Liberté, 1979.

———. *Arracher cinquante mille signes*. Saint-Denis: Editions Goutte d'eau dans l'océan, 1980.

———. *Romans pou la tèr ek la mèr*. Saint-Denis: Grand Océan, 1995.

Marimoutou, Carpanin and Françoise Vergès. *Amarres: créolisations india-océanes*. Paris: l'Harmattan, 2005.

Martial, David. *Identité et politique culturelle à l'île Maurice*. Paris: L'Harmattan, 2002.

Masson, Loys. *L'Etoile et la clef*. Paris: Gallimard, 1945.

———. *Le Notaire des noirs*. Paris: Robert Laffont, 1961. Reprinted, Mauritius: Eds. de l'Océan Indien, 1985.

———. *Les Noces de la vanille*. Paris: Robert Laffont, 1962. Reprinted, Mauritius: Editions de l'Océan Indien, 1981.

Mathieu, Martine, "Océan indien." Pp.152-255 in Hausser, Michel and Martine Mathieu. *Littératures francophones. III. Afrique noire Océan indien*. Paris: Belin, 1998.

Maunick, Edouard. *Les Manèges de la mer*. Paris: Présence africaine, 1964.

———. *Fusillez-moi*. Paris: Présence africaine, 1970.

———. *Toi laminaire*. Mauritius and Réunion: Editions de l'Océan Indien / CRI, 1990.

Maurin, Henri, Jacques Lentge and Daniel Vaxelaire, eds. *Mémorial de La Réunion*, in 7 parts and 8 volumes. Saint-Denis: Australe Editions, 1980.

Meitinger, Serge and J.-C. Carpanin Marimoutou, eds. *Océan indien — Madagascar, La Réunion, Maurice*. Paris: Omnibus, 1998.

Nelson, Cary and Lawrence Grossberg, eds. *Marxism and the interpretation of culture*. London: Macmillan, 1988.

Nirina, Esther. *Lente Spirale*. Antananarivo, Madagascar: Madprint / Editions Revue de l'Océan indien, 1990.

———. *Rien que lune*. Saint-Denis de la Réunion: Grand Océan, 1998.

———. *Mirolana an-tsoatra / Dire par écrit / Le dire par écrit.* Saint-Denis de la Réunion: Grand Océan, 2004.
Parry, Benita "Problems in current theories of colonial discourse." *Oxford Literary Review*, 9, 1 and 2 (1987). Reprinted pp. 36-44 in *The postcolonial studies reader*. Edited by Bill Ashcroft, Gareth Griffiths and Helen Tiffin. London and New York: Routledge, 1995.
Paulhan, Jean. *Les Hain-tenys merina.* Paris: Geuthner, 1913. Reprinted as *Hain-teny merina: poesies populaires malgaches.* Antananarivo, Madagascar: Foi et Justice, 1991.
Pelen, Philippe. *Mâ.* Saint-Denis: Grand Océan, 1996.
Pounia, Gilbert. *Somin Granbwa.* Saint-Denis: Grand Océan, 1997.
Prabhu, Anjali. *Hybridity: limits, transformations, prospects.* Albany: State University of New York Press, 2007.
Prosper, Jean-Georges. *Chants planétaires: pour un nouveau siècle et millénaire.* Port Louis, Mauritius: Proag printing, 1990.
———. *Histoire de la littérature mauricienne de langue française* (nouvelle édition). Mauritius: Eds. de l'Océan Indien, 1994.
———. *La Créolie indianocéaniste.* Vacoas, Mauritius: Editions Le Printemps, 1996.
Prudent, Lambert-Félix, ed. "Seychelles." Pp. 493-523 in *Anthologie de la nouvelle poésie créole.* Paris: Editions Caribéennes / ACCT, 1984.
Rabéarivelo, Jean-Joseph. *Presque-songes.* Tananarive, Madagascar: Henri Vidalie, 1934. Reprinted in *Poèmes*. Paris: Hatier, 1990.
———. *Traduit de la nuit.* Tunis: Editions du Mirage, 1935. Reprinted in *Poèmes*. Paris: Hatier, 1990.
———. *Vieilles Chansons des pays de l'Imerina.* Tananarive, Madagascar: Imprimerie officielle, 1939.
———. *L'Interférence.* Paris: Hatier, 1987.
———. "L'Aube rouge." Pp.101-96 in *Océan indien—Madagascar, La Réunion, Maurice.* Edited by Serge Meitinger and J.-C. Carpanin Marimoutou. Paris: Omnibus, 1998
Rabéarizafy Nestor. "Les Gasy font des bulles." In *Madagascar 2. La littérature d'expression française.* Edited by Siméon Rajaona, in *Notre Librairie*, 110 (1992), 83-92.
Rabémananjara, Jacques. *Les Dieux malgaches.* Gap, France: Ophrys, 1947.
———. *Antsa.* Paris: R. Drivon, 1948. Reprinted, Paris: Présence africaine, 1956.
———. *Lamba.* Paris: Présence africaine, 1956.
———. *Les Boutriers de l'aurore.* Paris: Présence africaine, 1957.
———. *Les Agapes des dieux.* Paris: Présence africaine, 1962.

Rafenomanjato, Charlotte-Arrisoa. *Le Pétale écarlate*. Antananarivo, Madagascar: Société malgache d'édition, 1990.

———. *La Marche de la liberté*. Saint-Denis de la Réunion and Paris: Azalées / L'Harmattan, 1992.

———. *Le Cinquième Sceau*. Paris: L'Harmattan, 1993.

Raharimanana, Jean-Luc. "Jacques Rabémananjara, poète et dramaturge," *Notre Librairie*, 110 (1992).

———. *Lucarne*. Paris: Le Serpent à plumes, 1996.

———. *Nour, 1947*. Paris: Le Serpent à plumes, 2001.

———. *L'Arbre anthropophage*. Paris: Editions Joëlle Losfeld, 2004.

Rajaona, Siméon, ed. *Madagascar. 1. La literature d'expression malgache*. In *Notre Librairie*, 109 (1992).

———. *Madagascar. 2. La literature d'expression française*. In Notre Librairie, 110 (1992).

Rakotoandrianoela, H. "1820-1915: naissance des arts littéraires." *Notre Librairie*, 109 (1992), 40-41.

Rakotoson, Michèle. *Dadabé*. Paris: Karthala, 1984.

———. *Le Bain des reliques*. Paris: Karthala, 1988.

———. *Elle, au printemps*. Saint-Maur, France: Sepia, 1996.

———. *Henoy. Fragments en écorce*. Avin and Hannut, Belgium: Editions Luce Wilkin, 1999.

———. *Lalana*. La Tour d'Aigues, France: Editions de l'Aube, 2002.

Ramarasoa, Liliane, ed. *Anthologie de la literature malgache d'expression française des années 80*. Paris: L'Harmattan, 1994.

Ramarasoa, Liliane. "Les (en)jeux des noms de lieux dans la poésie malgache d'expression française. Cas de Jean-Joseph Rabéarivelo." Pp. 21-32 in "La littérature malgache." Lecce: Argo, *Interculturel / Francophonies*, 1 (2001).

Ramharai, Vicram. *La literature mauricienne d'expression créole. Essai d'analyse socio-culturelle*. Port Louis, Mauritius: Editions Les Mascareignes, 1990.

Ramiandrasoa, Jean-Irénée. "Le théâtre malgache classique: 1922-1945." *Notre Librairie,* 109 (1992), 71-79.

Ratrimoarivony-Rakotoanosy, M. "Evolution de la culture écrite." *Notre Librairie*, No 109 (1992), 15-16.

Rivière, Jean-Louis. *Carousel*. Saint-Denis: Eds. Théâtre Vollard, 1992.

———. *Emeutes*. Saint-Denis: Grand Océan, 1997.

Said, Edward W. *Orientalism*. New York: Random House, 1978.

———. *Culture and imperialism*. London: Chatto and Windus, 1993.

Said Ahmed, Moussa. *Guerriers, princes et poètes aux Comores*. Paris: L'Harmattan, 2000.

Sam-Long, Jean-François. *Terre arrachée*. Saint-Denis: Nouvelle Imprimerie Dionysienne, 1982.
Sam-Long, Jean-François, ed. *Anthologie de la poésie seychelloise*. Collection Anchaing. Saint-Leu, Reunion: Presses du Développement. 1984.
———. *Madame Desbassayns*. Le Tampon: Editions Jacaranda, 1985.
———. *Pour les bravos de l'Empire*. Le Tampon: Editions Jacaranda, 1987.
Scarr, Deryck. *Seychelles since 1770: History of a slave and post-slavery society*. London: Hurst, 2000.
Selvon, Sydney. *A comprehensive history of Mauritius*. Port Louis, Mauritius: MDS, 2001.
———. *L'Histoire de Maurice—des origines à nos jours*. Port Louis, Mauritius, Mauritius: Editions MDS, 2003.
Senghor, Léopold Sedar, ed. *Anthologie de la nouvelle poésie nègre et malgache*. Paris: Presses Universitaires de France, 1948.
Senghor, Léopold Sedar, "De la liberté de l'âme ou éloge du métissage." Pp. 98-103 in *Liberté 1. Négritude et Humanisme*. Paris: Seuil, 1964.
Skerrett, Judith and Adrian. *Seychelles*. London and Singapore: Insight Pocket Guides / APA publications, 2004.
Sony Lab'ou Tansi. *La Vie et demie*. Paris: Seuil, 1979.
Spivak, Gayatri Chakravorty. "Can the Subaltern speak." In *Marxism and the interpretation of culture*. Edited by Cary Nelson and Lawrence Grossberg. London: Macmillan, 1988. Reprinted in Ashcroft et al. (1995) pp. 24-28.
Swaney, Deanna and Robert Willox. *Madagascar and Comoros*, 2nd ed. Hawthorn, Australia: Lonely Planet, 1994.
Théâtre Vollard. *Vingtième: 20 ans d'un théâtre réunionnais*. Saint-Denis: Band' décidée, l'Autre Hémisphère, 1999.
Toihiri, Mohamed A. *La République des imberbes*. Paris: L'Harmattan, 1985.
———. *Le Kafir du Karthala*. Paris: L'Harmattan, 1992.
———. "Nassur Attoumani: le violeur de tabous." *Notre Librairie*, 158 (April-June 2005), 102-5.
Tranquille, Danielle: "Inscriptions of Dev/fiance: Métissage in Mauritian Literature." *International Journal of Francophone Studies*, 8:2 (2005), 199-218.
Treudhardt, Patrice. *20 désanm et d'entre tous les Zanzibar*. Saint-Denis: Les Chemins de la Liberté, 1979.

Unnuth, Abhimanyu. *Les Empereurs de la nuit.* Translated into French by Aslakha Callikan-Proag. Moka, Mauritius: Editions de l'Océan Indien / Mahatma Gandhi Institute, 1983.

———. *Le Culte du sol.* Translated into French by Kessen Budhoo and Shakuntala Boolell. Vacoas, Mauritius: Editions Le Printemps, 1997.

———. *Sueurs de sang.* Translated from the original Hindi by Kessen Budhoo and Isabelle Jarry. Paris: Stock, 2001. Original title in Hindi, *Lal Pasina*, 1993.

Vaxelaire, Daniel. *Chasseur de noirs.* Paris: Lieu commun, 1982. Reprinted, Saint-Denis: Orphie, 2000.

———. *L'Affranchi.* Paris: Lieu Commun, 1984. Reprinted, Paris: Phébus, 1996.

———. *Les Mutins de la liberté.* Paris: Lieu commun, 1986. Reprinted, Paris: Phébus, 1995.

———. *Les Chasseurs d'épices.* Paris; J.-C. Lattès, 1990. Reprinted, Saint-Denis: Orphie, 2001.

———. *Vingt-et-un jours d'histoire. Ile de La Réunion.* Saint-Denis: Azalées, 1992.

———. *Grand Port.* Paris: Phébus, 1993.

———. *Cap Malheureux.* Paris: Phébus, 1994.

———. *Bleu nuit.* Paris: Flammarion, 1996.

———. *Une si jolie naufragée ou Le roman vrai de Paul et Virginie.* Paris: Flammarion, 2001.

———. *Supplique pour ne pas être pendu avec les autres pirates.* Saint-Denis: Orphie, 2003.

Vérin, P., ed. *L'Invention de l'écriture à Madagascar et aux Comores.* Etudes Océan indien, 22. Paris: INALCO, 1997.

Vergès, Françoise. *Monsters and revolutionaries: colonial family romance and métissage.* Durham NC and London: Duke University Press, 1999. See also Marimoutou and Vergès.

Virahsawmy, Dev. *Disik sale.* Port Louis, Mauritius: MMMSP / Olympic Printing, 1974.

———. *Lafumé dâ lizié.* Port Louis, Mauritius: MMMSP / Olympic Printing, 1977.

———. *Li.* Port Louis, Mauritius: MMMSP / Olympic Printing, 1979. Trilingual version in Mauritian Creole, Reunionese Creole and French. Saint-Denis: Les Chemins de la Liberté, 1979

———. *Mo rapel.* Port Louis, Mauritius, Mauritius: MMMSP / Olympic Printing, 1980.

———. *Zeneral Makbef.* Port Louis, Mauritius: Bukié Banané, 1981.

———. *Dropadi.* Terre Rouge, Mauritius: Bukié Banané, 1982.

———. *Dokter Nipat*. Rose Hill, Mauritius: Bukié Banané, 1983.

———. *Toufann*. Port Louis, Mauritius: La Sentinelle, 1991. Translation into English by Nisha and Michael Walling in *African theatre: playwrights and politics*. Edited by Martin Banham, James Gibbs and Femi Osofisan. Oxford, Bloomington and Johannesburg: James Currey / Indiana University Press / Witwatersrand University Press, 2001.

———. "Quand le theatre nourrit sa langue." *Notre Librairie*, No. 114 (1993), 116-18.

———. *Enn ta senn dan vid*. Port Louis, Mauritius: LPT, 1995.

———. *Trazedji Makbess*. Port Louis, Mauritius: LPT, 1997.

Waro, Danyel. *Romans ekri dans la zol en Frans*. Saint-Denis de La Réunion: Les Chemins de la Liberté, 1978.

———. *Gafourn*. Saint-Denis: Editions Ziskakan, 1987.

———. *Demavouz la vi*. Saint-Denis: Grand Océan, 1996.

Young, Robert. *White Mythologies: writing, history and the West*. London and New York: Routledge, 1990.

Young, Rodolphine. *Fables de La Fontaine traduites en Créole seychellois*. Hamburg: Buske, 1983.

Discography

Albany, Jean, Hervé Imare, Alain Peters, Jean-Michel Salmacis and Pierre Vidot. *Chante Albany*. Saint-Denis: ADER, 1978, cassette. Reissued on CD, Saint-Denis and Saint-André, Réunion: Ader / Piros, 2004.
Chamsi na mwezi—gabusi and ndzendze from Moheli, Comoros. Germany: Dizim records, CD, n. d.
D'Gary. *Mbo loza*. Amiens, France: Label bleu / Indigo, CD, n. d.
Fenoamby. *Fanajana (Respect)*. Réunion: Discorama, 1993, CD 93.05.
Forgotten music of the islands: dances and romances / Musiques oubliées des îles: danses et romances. Paris: Ocora / Radio France, 2002, CD No. C582005.
Gizavo, Régis. *Mikea*. Amiens, France: Label bleu / Indigo, CD, n. d.
Gramoune Lélé. *Namouniman*. Amiens, France: Label bleu / Indigo, 1993, CD LBLC 2508.
———. *Soleye*. Amiens, France: Label bleu / Indigo, 1995, CD LBLC 2528
———. *Dan kèr Lélé*. Amiens, France: Label bleu / Indigo, 1998, CD LBLC 2558.
Jaojoby. *e tiako*. Amiens, France: Label bleu / Indigo, 1997, CD LBLC2533.
Kaya. *Zistoir Revoltan*. Saint-Denis: Discorama, 1996, CD 96.16.
Lo Rwa kaf. *Somin galisé*. Saint-Denis: Discorama, 1992, CD 9209.
Maalesh. *Wassi wassi*. Paris: Mélodie, CD, n. d.
Matombe, Brian. *Lanbyans tropic*. Mahé, Seychelles: Segavibes Records, 2005, CD.
Marimoutou, Carpanin. *Koz langaz*. Marseille: DCC, poet la Rénion, No.1, 1999, CD.
Mikidache. *Kaul/Words*. Paris: Long Distance / Wagram, CD, n. d.

Mizik séselwa. London: BBC Radio 3, n. d. 2 x 30 minute radio programs.
Rossy. *One eye on the future, one eye on the past*. USA: Shanachie records, 1993, CD No. 64046.
Tarika. *Soul Makassar*. London: Sakay, 2001, CD No. SAKD7037.
Théâtre Talipot, *Les Porteurs d'eau / The water carriers*. Saint-Pierre, Reunion: Théâtre Talipot, 1998, CD No MP9901.
Tiana. *Miharina (Renaissance)*. Réunion: JBE Musik, 2005, CD JBE008.
Ti-frère. *Hommage à Ti-Frère*. Paris: Radio France / Ocora, 1991, CD C560019.
Toussaint, Philippe. *Gravite lanmour*. Victoria, Mahé: Sound on Sound Studio, 2004, CD.
Vali, Justin. *The truth*. Box, UK: Real World, 1995, CD No. CDRW 51.
Viry, Firmin. *Ti mardé*. Amiens, France: Label bleu / Indigo, 1998, CD LBLC 2548.
Volcy, Jean-Marc. *Vendredi sen*. Mahé, Seychelles: Youth Enterprise Services, n. d., audio cassette, re-issued on CD.
Volcy, Jean-Marc. *Bon bon bon*. Mauritius: Geda Music, 2005, CD No GD020.
Waro, Danyel. *Gafourn*. Saint-Denis and Saint-André, Reunion: Editions Ziskakan / Piros, 1987, audio cassette/CD.
———. *Batarsité*. Saint-André, Reunion: Piros, 1994, CD CDP5198.
———. *Foutan fonnker*. Paris: Cobalt, 1999, CD 09293-2.
———. *Bwarouz*. Paris: Cobalt, 2001, CD 09351-2.
Ziskakan. *Bato fou*. Saint-André: Piros / Sonodisc, 1991, CD.
———. *Kaskasnikola*. Paris: Mango / Island, 1993, CD 514 974-2.
———. *Soley glasé*. Paris: Sankara / Mercury, 1996, CD 532 410-2.
———. *Ziskakan 20 tan.* Saint-Denis: Discorama, 1999, CD.
———. *Rimayer*. Saint-Denis: Discorama, 2001, CD 2001.09.
———. *Ziskakan live*. Saint-Denis: Discorama, 2004, DVD 2004.12 and CD.

Index

Abdallah, Ahmed, 11, 146-47
Abel, Antoine, 154, 155-56
Académie française, 102
Académie malgache, 66
Africa, 1, 4, 12, 18, 84, 109, 133, 145, 148, 165, 171
African population, 31, 37, 94, 121, 148, 150
African Union, 145, 153
Agénor, Monique, 130-31, 169
AIDS, 80, 152
Air Austral, 42
Air Mauritius, 42
Air Seychelles, 42
Albany, Jean, 124-25, 155, 170
alcoholism, 128
Algeria, 10
Ally, Daniel, 156
ancestor worship, 13, 17, 35, 121, 135
Ancien Régime, 9
Andrianampoinimerina, King, 34
Andriantsuli, 147
Anglicanism, 9, 17
Anjouan, 6, 11, 22, 145, 147, 148, 166
Antananarivo, 18, 80, 81, 82, 85, 147, 172
Antandroy, 18, 37, 129

Antillanité, 53
Antongil, 69
apartheid, 7, 146, 150
Arabic, 6, 149
Arabic script, 9, 149
Arab traders, 6, 19, 22, 27, 29, 30, 79, 148
Armand, Alain, 127, 136
Asgarally, Renée, 95
Ashcroft, Bill, 52, 122, 171
Attoumani, Nassur, 150-52, 164, 167, 173
Aubry, Gilbert, 125, 170
Augagneur, Victor, 67
Australia, 93, 106, 155, 166, 167, 171, 174, 175
avant-garde drama, 85
Azema, Jean-Henri, 125-26

Bachelard, Gaston, 58
Bacou, Abdou S., 150
Baudelaire, Charles, 68, 69, 74, 75, 133
Beckett, Carole, 149
Beckett, Samuel, 85
Begag, Azouz, 150
Beniamino, Michel, 58, 126
Benin, 32
Ben Jelloun, Tahar, 150

Bérenger, Paul, 12
Bernabé, Jean, 20, 126, 127, 172
Bernardin de Saint-Pierre, 94, 130, 173
Betsimileo, 37
Betsimisaraka, 149
Bhabha, Homi K., 21, 38, 48, 49, 50, 68, 69, 109
Bhagat, S. M. and B. K., 110
Bhojpuri, 15, 94, 95
Bible, 35, 66
binary oppositions, 50
Bissoondoyal, Basdeo, 110
Bollée, Annegret, 154
Bollywood, 13
Boudry, Robert, 67
Bourbon. *See* Reunion
Bourdieu, Pierre, 55, 112, 170
Brathwaite, Edward Kamau, 20, 171
Brazil, 135
British: British Council, 111; colonial rivalry, 9, 147, 164, 171; colonization, 89; influence, 9, 10, 35, 37, 164, 171; monarchy, 2; society, 23, 93
Buddhism, 6, 17, 37, 95, 121
Burridge, Glyn, 156
Butlin, Ron, 111

Cabon, Marcel, 106, 164, 173
Cambodia, 150
Camo, Pierre, 67, 99
Canada, 164
Canova, Pascale, 155
Cape colony, 28
Carayol, Michel, 154
Caribbean x, 10, 19-20, 49, 53, 172; Francophone, 48, 59; islands, 2, 101, 119; population, 19

Carraccioli, Angelo, 31, 129
cartoons, xiii
Catholicism, 6, 8, 15, 17, 19, 35, 37, 83, 87, 95, 96, 121, 125, 168
Le Centre du Monde, xiii
Centre hospitalier universitaire de Saint-Denis, 41-42
Césaire, Aimé, x, 10, 36, 69, 102, 104, 127, 131
Chamoiseau, Patrick, 20, 126, 127, 172
Charef, Mehdi, 150
Chaudenson, Robert, 154
Cheynet, Anne, 126, 128, 165
China, 150, 158, 174
Chinese population, 5, 13, 17, 19, 34, 37, 93, 95, 121
Chirac, Jacques, 14
Chraïbi, Driss, 150
classical theater, 84-86
Claudel, Paul, 76
Club de la Chaumière, 94
CNRS, 57
coffee, 28
Collen, Lindsey, 97, 111-12, 113, 176
Commission de l'Océan Indien, 41, 166
Commonwealth, xi, 16, 37, 47, 97, 111, 176
communalism. *See* cultural separatism
Comoros, 6-7, 11, 16, 27, 31, 36, 42, 119, 145-53, 158, 166, 168; 1960 referendum, 146; 1974 referendum, 146, 147; education, 16, 145, 148; Federal Islamic Republic, 36; music, 152-53; oral literature, 149, 151; popula-

tion, 19, 148, 173; Shirazian sultanates, 148-49; Union des Comores, 7, 11, 36, 145, 147
Compagnie des Indes orientales, 3, 6, 8, 28, 29
Confiant, Raphaël, 20, 126, 127, 172
coprah, 34
Corbière, Tristan, 68, 74
Corneille, Pierre, 85
cosmopolitanism, 99, 112
Creole: culture, ix, 21, 97-98, 153-54; in the Caribbean, 20; language, xii, 14, 21, 32-33, 40, 41, 42, 50, 93, 94, 95, 104, 120, 121, 124, 125, 126, 127, 128, 129, 130, 131, 132, 134, 136, 137, 153-56, 166; literature, 57, 93, 95, 98, 107-9, 111, 124, 125, 126, 127, 128, 130, 135, 136-37, 153-55, 157-58, 166, 164, 169-70, 172; in Mauritius, 5, 14, 40, 57, 93, 94, 95, 98, 107, 108, 109, 111, 113, 174; in Reunion, 6, 14, 40, 120, 121, 124-26, 127, 128, 129, 130, 132, 134, 135-37; in Seychelles, 8, 15, 40, 57, 153-55, 156, 157-58, 170
Créolie, 124-26, 135, 164
Créolité, 20, 124-26, 172
cultural identity, 37-38, 41, 93, 102, 122, 127, 129-31, 133-34, 166-67, 167-69
cultural separatism, 93, 96-97, 101, 106, 164, 166, 167-68

Damas, Léon-Gontran, 69

dance, 41, 157
Dayot, Eugène, 123
debt, 42
De Chazal, Malcolm, 98, 99-101, 124
De Gaulle, General, 2, 4, 146
De Lapervanche, Léon, 10, 36, 132
Deleuze, Gilles, 47
Denard, Bob, 11, 146, 150
De Parny, Evariste, 122-23
Département d'Outre-Mer (DOM), x, 2, 10, 20, 36, 53, 119, 132, 145
De Rauville, Camille, 52, 165
Derrida, Jacques, 47, 49, 51
De Souza, Carl, 97, 106-7, 165, 168, 172, 175
Devi, Ananda, 58, 59, 98, 105, 167, 168, 172
D'Gary, 87
Dhavid, 130, 169
diaspora, 42, 49, 53, 93, 104, 146, 175
diglossia, 40, 57
Diop, Alioune, 69
Dirlik, Arif, 54, 55
Divali, 13
diversity, 47, 88, 107, 121-22
Dodille, Norbert, 56
dodo, 28, 29
Dogley, Jeris, 155
Dominica, 20
Dox, 67, 76, 85
Dutch East India Company, 28, 29, 94
Duval, Wendy, 157
Dzaoudzi, 147

Edinburgh Fringe festival, 134
Editions de l'Océan Indien, 98

education systems, 15-17
Eluard, Paul, 75
The Empire writes back, 48, 52
English language, 15, 16, 39; in Mauritius, 5, 15, 16, 39, 93, 97, 111-12; in Seychelles, 15, 39, 154
ethnicity, 18-19, 21-22, 37-38, 88, 112, 121-22, 163-64, 167, 169, 176
ethnographic studies, 58, 105, 149
European Charter for Minority Languages, 14, 120
European population, 19, 37
European Union, 5, 10, 20, 22, 36, 93, 119, 148, 163, 166, 167, 174
expatriate writers, 77, 79-80, 82-83, 101-5, 122-25

Fanchette, Régis, 112
Fanon, Frantz, x, 47
Fenoamby, 87
Festival international des Francophonies in Limoges, 85, 132
Filet, Jean-Onésime, 30-31
First World War, 129
folk-tales. *See* oral literature
Fort Dauphin, 3, 6, 28, 30
Franco-Mauritians, 8, 93, 95, 96, 97, 99, 103, 104, 106, 168
Francophone studies, 59
Francophonie, xi, 36, 37, 39, 70, 85, 88, 97, 102, 106, 113
French colonialism, 3, 4, 6, 7, 8-9, 28-30, 35, 36, 37, 39, 48, 65, 66-67, 69-70, 83, 94, 119-21, 123, 124, 129-31, 145-46, 147, 164, 165, 169, 171, 174
French Communist party, 36
French co-operation, 15, 167
French education system, 15, 67, 148
French language, 1, 2, 14, 39, 40-41, 66, 67; in Comoros, 6, 145-46; in Madagascar, 4, 15, 40, 66, 67, 84, 85; in Mauritius, 5, 8, 16, 93, 94, 95, 97, 98, 112, 113; in Reunion, 5, 15, 126, 127, 128, 131, 132; in Seychelles, 8, 153, 154
French legal system, 151
French Ministry of Culture, 133
French National Assembly, 69, 119
French Republic, 5, 36, 119, 122, 145, 146, 147, 152, 158, 164, 169; 2nd, 32; 3rd, 3, 36; 4th, 4, 10, 36

Galibert, Danielle Nivo, 150
Gallieni, 3, 35, 66
Gallimard, 100, 105
Gamaleya, Boris, 126-27, 135
Garden of Eden, 22, 30, 155
Garriga, Sarda, 32
Gaullism, 131
Gauvin, Axel, 20, 127, 128-29, 136, 137, 169, 170, 172
Genêt, Jean, 85
Genvrin, Emmanuel, 131-33, 166, 173
German occupation of France, 10, 131
Gide, André, 68
Giono, Jean, 106
Gisavo, Régis, 87

Index

Glissant, Edouard, x, 20, 47, 49, 53-54, 165, 171, 173
globalization, 55
global warming, 42
Gooyer, Cornelius Simonz, 29
Gordon, General, 30, 155
Gorée island, 32
Grande Comore, 6, 145
Gramoune Lélé, 33, 135
graphic novels, xiii
Grenadines, 20
Griffiths, Gareth, 52, 122
Guadeloupe, x, 10, 20, 119
Guattari, Félix, 47
Guénard, Marie, 156
guidebooks, xi
Gujerat, 95
Guyane, 10, 20, 119

hain-teny, 65, 66-67, 72-75,
Haïti, 20, 53, 107
Hart, Robert-Edward, 98-99, 105-6, 124, 165
Hatubou, Salim, 150
Hawaldar, Sakuntala, 112
Hermann, Jules, 100, 124
Hindi, 15, 16, 40, 93, 95, 97, 107, 110, 113, 134
Hinduism, 5, 6, 9, 13, 16, 34, 37, 57, 95, 96, 97, 98, 99, 105, 106, 108, 110, 112, 121, 128, 168
hira-gasy, 84, 86
historical novel, 129-31
Hoareau, Benediste, 155
Honoré, Daniel, 128, 170
Hookoomsing, Vinesh Y., 56,
Houat, Louis-Timagène, 123
Huet, David. *See* Dhavid
Hugo, Victor, 69, 75, 123
Hugon, Monique, 80

Hugues, Modeste. *See* Modeste Hugues.
Humbert, Marie-Thérèse, 59, 104
hybridity, 21, 37, 38-39, 48, 49-50, 53, 68, 101, 134, 136, 163, 171

Ile Bourbon, 28. *See also* Reunion
Ile de France, 4, 7, 28, 94. *See also* Mauritius
Ile Sainte-Marie, 3, 30, 31
immigration, 7, 22, 107, 119, 130, 133, 148, 163
indentured labor, 5, 9, 20, 34, 94-95, 97, 104, 110, 129, 164, 173, 175
independence, 2, 4, 5, 120, 146, 147, 153, 158, 165, 166, 167, 169, 170
India, 9, 13, 166, 171, 174, 175; Indian culture, 13, 49, 95, 96, 99, 105, 110, 134; Indian population 20, 34, 37, 95, 96, 99, 103, 104, 105, 106, 110, 121, 168
Indianoceanity, 51, 165
Indian Ocean Rim association, 166
Indonesia, 28
inter-marriage, 18
International Francophone Organisation. See *Francophonie*
Internet, 42, 165, 175
Ionesco, Eugène, 85
Islam, 5, 6, 8, 13, 17, 37, 93, 95, 96, 106, 121, 146, 148, 151, 152, 163, 166
Issur, Kumari, 56

Jack, Belinda, ix
Jaojoby, 87
Jaomanoro, David, 71
Japan, 17, 135
Jarry, Alfred, 131, 133
Jonson, Ben, 108
Joubert, Jean-Louis, xi, 56, 100, 103
Jugnauth, Anerood, 12

Kabary, 65, 75, 84
Kabosy, 86
"Karana," 19, 22
Kaya, 5, 97, 106, 107, 109, 168
Keita, Salif, 86
Kenya, 31
Key Concepts in Post-Colonial Studies, 52
Khal, 104, 167, 173
Koranic schools, 16
Kourouma, Ahmadou, 86

Laborde, Jean, 3, 35
Lacaussade, Auguste, 123-24
Lacpatia, Firmin, 58, 129, 173
La Fontaine, 154
Lamartine, Alphonse de, 69, 75
LCF, 57
Leblond, Marius et Ary, 124
Le Clézio, Jean-Marie Gustave, 103-4, 110, 113, 167
Leconte de Lisle, 124
Ledikasyon pu travayer (LPT), 111, 176
Lekritir 1977, 14, 40
Lémurie, 100, 124
Lenstiti kreol, 14, 153
Le Tampon, 120, 131
Létourdie, Jenny, 157
L'Homme, Léoville, 97

Libertalia, 31, 129
linguistics, 57
Lionnet, Françoise, 58
Lionnet, Guy, 156
literary history, 56-57
Littératures de l'Océan indien, 56
London Missionary Society, 3, 9, 34, 65
Lorraine, Alain, 126
Lo Rwa Kaf, 33, 135
Lutheran church, 17

Maalesh, 152
Madagascar: 3-4, 11, 13-14, 18-19, 21, 22, 27, 28, 29, 30, 31, 32, 34-35, 36, 37, 40, 42, 53, 65-91, 99, 121, 123, 126, 129, 130, 131, 147, 148, 149, 165, 166, 167, 168, 170; 1947 revolt, 4, 10, 69, 83; 1991 uprising, 4, 71, 81, 82; British influence, 9, 35; education system, 15-16, 40; independence, 2, 4, 36, 70-72, 166; literature, 56, 65-91; "malgachisation," 4, 15, 40, 71, 170; monarchy, 19, 34-35, 37, 65-66, 131, 167-68; population, 3, 13, 19, 21, 22, 174; primary schools, 16; republican institutions, 11, 36; traditional religion, 17, 33, 35, 75, 79; universities, 42
Magdelaine-Andrianjafitrimo, Valérie, 58
Mahé de la Bourdonnais, 29
Mahé island, 7, 30
Malagasy language, 3, 6, 9, 10, 14, 15, 21, 27, 35, 40, 41,

Index

65-66, 67, 84, 85, 87, 123, 126, 134, 135, 167
Malays, 19, 37
Maldives, 158
maloya, xii, 13, 33, 135-37, 157, 171
Mancham, James, 11
Mancienne, Leu, 154
Mandarin Chinese, 15, 16, 94, 95, 96, 113
marginality, 48, 163, 165-67, 175
Le Margouillat, xiii
Marimoutou, Jean-Claude Carpanin, 52, 57, 127, 136
Martinique, x, 10, 20, 119, 126
Marxism, 146
Marxist criticism, 54-55
Mascarene islands, 33-34, 124. See also Mauritius, Reunion, Rodrigues
Masson, Loys, 98, 103, 104
Mathiot, Patrick, 156
Matombé, Brian, 157
Maunick, Edouard, 101-2, 167
Maurice of Nassau, Crown-Prince, 4, 29
Mauritianity, 93, 99, 104
Mauritius, 4-5, 18, 28, 29, 31, 32, 33, 34, 36-37, 39, 40, 42, 53, 93-118, 120, 121, 122, 154, 157, 164, 165, 167, 168, 170, 173, 174, 176; British invasion of 1810, 4-5, 7, 94, 129; education system, 9, 16; independence in 1968, 5, 95, 96, 107, 110, 111, 169; minority groups, 18, 21, 93, 96-97, 167; music, 13, 109, 157;

monarchy, 36, 96; republic, 36, 96, 102, 168
Mayotte, 2, 7, 11, 16, 17, 19, 22, 36, 119, 145-52, 158, 166, 175
Médor, Marie-Cécile, 156
mercenaries, 146
Merina peoples, 3, 13, 18-19, 37; monarchy, 19, 34, 35, 65-66, 167, 168
métissage. See hybridity
migration, 21, 22, 53, 80, 104, 107, 163, 173, 175
Michel, James, 12, 153
Mikidache, 152
mimicry, 50, 68, 106, 108, 171-72
minor literature, 54
missionaries, 27, 35, 65-66, 83
mission schools, 16, 41
Misson, Olivier, 31, 129
M'Kakamba, Théâtre, 151
mobility, 41, 175
Modeste Hugues, 87
Moheli, 7, 145, 152
Molière, 108, 151
Mongo Beti, 150
Monnerville, Gaston, 10
Morel, Lise, 155
Morisien. See under Creole, in Mauritius
Moroni, 147, 150
moutia, 157
Mozambique, 32
multiculturalism, xiv, 21, 107, 113, 121-22, 134, 163-64, 165, 176
multi-party democracy, 8
Muslims. *See* Islam
Mythocritique, 58

Napoleon, 32, 129
nationalism, 167-69, 174
Neumann, Ingrid, 154
Ngazidja. *See* Grande Comore
Ngugi Wa Thiongo, 70
Nirina, Esther, 67, 71, 76-78
Notre Librairie, xiii, 56, 113
Nosy Bé, 3
Nosy Boraha. *See* Ile Sainte-Marie
Nosy Lava, 70
Nouvelle Calédonie, 119

octroi de mer, 120
oral literature, 65, 149, 151, 153, 154
otherness, 51-52, 172-73
Ouidah, 32

painting, xiii
Pakistan, 13, 22, 95, 121
Parry, Benita, 54, 55
patois, 32, 107
Paulhan, Jean, 66, 73, 100
Pelen, Philippe, 134, 165, 174, 175
perfume essences, 42, 166
Persian traders, 6, 27
Peters, Alain, 125
Phoenicians, 29
pirates, 31, 126, 129
Pitt-Kennedy, Sherrell, 154-5, 156
Poivre, Pierre, 28, 30, 129
polygamy, 151
Pool, Elva, 156
popular music, 12, 41, 86-87, 109, 134-37, 152-53, 157-58
popular theater, xiii, 41, 83-86, 107-9, 131-34
Port Louis, 101, 105, 168

Portuguese, 29, 30
postcolonialism, ix, x, 52, 59, 119, 131, 134, 137, 171-75
postcolonial studies, ix, x
The post-colonial studies reader, 52
postcolonial theory, ix, x, 47-49, 59, 87-88, 99, 101, 104, 106, 107, 108, 113, 171-75; self-referentiality, 47
Pounia, Gilbert, 136, 170
Praslin, 7, 30
Présence africaine, 65, 66, 97
Prosper, Jean-Georges, 52, 56, 165, 169
Protestantism, 3, 6, 8, 9, 16, 17, 35, 37, 65-66, 88, 95, 121
Prudent, Lambert-Félix, 154
publishing, 67, 68, 69, 71, 98, 111, 120, 146, 175
Puerto Rico, 20

Quebec, 164

Rabearivelo, Jean-Joseph, 67-69, 72-75, 77, 78, 84, 99, 167-68
Rabemananjara, Jacques, 4, 67, 69-70, 74-76, 85, 166
Racine, Jean, 85
racism, xiv
Radama I, King, 3, 32, 35, 65
Radama II, King, 35, 66
Radio France Internationale, 71, 78, 79, 81, 82, 84, 156
Rafenomanjato, Charlotte Arrisoa, 58, 79, 80-82, 85, 165
Raharimanana, Jean-Luc, 71-2, 76, 79, 82-83, 85, 165, 167, 172
Rakotoson, Michèle, 58, 71, 79-80, 81, 82, 85, 170, 172, 173

Index

Ramantsoa, General, 70
Ramarasoa, Liliane, 56, 174
Ramgoolam, Navinchandra, 12
Ramharai, Vicram, 56, 113
Ranaivo, Flavien, 67, 72
Ranavalona I, Queen, 35, 66
Ranavalona II, Queen, 35, 66
Ranavalona III, Queen, 35, 131
Randimbiarison, Ricky, 134
Ratsiraka, Admiral Didier, 4, 11, 19, 36, 70, 71, 81
Ravalomanana, Marc, 4, 11, 19, 71, 79, 83, 88
Ravel, Maurice, 123
reflexiveness, 47
reggae, 109, 152, 157
Relation, relatedness, 53-54, 165, 171, 173
René, France-Albert, 7, 12, 153
Renel, Charles, 78
Reunion, 5-6, 22, 28, 31, 34, 42, 52, 53, 100, 119-43, 153, 154, 155, 157, 158, 164, 165, 166, 169, 170, 172, 173, 175; British occupation, 6, 119; Communist Party of Reunion, 127, 135; Conseil général, 137; Conseil régional, 10; French constitution, 20, 119-20; history, 129-31, 132; music, 12-13, 109, 132, 134-37, 153, 158; religion, 17, 121; riots of 1991, 22, 133
Rimbaud, Arthur, 68
Rivière, Jean-Louis, 133, 165
Rodrigues, 29, 103, 157, 168
Rossy, xiii, 86

Said, Edward W., 49, 51, 52
Saïd Ahmed, Moussa, 149
Saïd, Mohamed Cheikh, 147
Saint-Denis, 120, 129, 132, 133
Saint-Leu, 128
Salegy, 13, 87
Sakalava, 18, 37, 79
Sam-Long, Jean-François, 20, 125, 129, 156, 164, 170
Schoelcher, Victor, 32
Sculpture, xiii
Séchelles, Vicomte de, 7
Second World War, 3, 69, 98, 102, 110, 122, 131, 132, 147, 167
sega, 12, 32-33, 109, 133, 135, 157, 171
Senegal, 32
Senghor, Léopold Sedar, 1, 38, 67, 69, 76, 104
Seychelles, 7-8, 11-12, 28-34, 53, 109, 153-59, 164, 166; Creole official language, 14, 153-54, 166; music, 157-58; population, 18, 21, 53; republic, 7, 37, 153
Shakespeare, 108, 131
Singapore, 16, 167, 174, 175
slavery, 5, 7, 12, 14, 29, 30, 31-33, 34, 94, 109, 122, 123-24, 126, 129, 132, 164, 175; abolition, 5, 6, 9, 32, 34 94, 132; trading, 4, 7, 9, 27, 28, 31-33, 83, 94, 126, 150
Soilih, Ali, 146, 149
Somalia, 31
Sony Lab'ou Tansi, 149
soukous, 13
South Africa, 7, 17, 102, 111, 146, 150, 166, 167, 171, 174, 175
spice trade, 27, 28, 42, 129, 166

Spivak, Gayatri Chakravorty, 49, 51, 53, 83, 172
Sri Lanka, 158
St. Lucia, 20, 101
subaltern, 49, 50-51, 83, 172
sugar cane, 5, 6, 28, 33, 42, 100, 166
surrealism, 99, 100
symbolism, French, 68, 72, 99
Swahili, 6, 148

La Table ovale, 94
Tahiti, 119
Talipot, Théâtre, xiii, 133-34, 174, 175
Tamil language and culture, 13, 94, 136
Tananarive. *See* Antananarivo
Tanzania, 31
Tarika, xiii, 87
Tehem, xiii
Territoire d'Outre-Mer, "TOM," 119, 145, 147
"third space," 39, 50
Tiana, 87
Tiffin, Helen, 52, 122
Ti-Frere, 109
Toalagnara. *See* Fort Dauphin
Toihiri, Mohamed, 146, 149-50, 166-67, 168, 170
Torabully, Khal. *See* Khal
tourism, 5, 8
Toussaint, Philippe, 158
Tout-Monde, 54
translation, 66, 67, 68, 77, 85, 95, 110, 136
Treuthardt, Patrice, 127, 136
Trinidad, 20
Trulès, Jean-Luc, 131
tsipika, 86
Tsiranana, Philibert, 70

TV5, 8
twarab, 146

UNESCO, 102, 134
United States, 17, 86, 87, 93, 111, 158, 164
Université de la Réunion, 16, 42, 55, 59, 120
Université de l'Océan Indien, 41
University of Mauritius, 56, 59
Unnuth, Abhimanyu, 40, 95, 110, 164, 172, 173
Urdu, 15, 16, 95, 96
Uteem, Cassam, 12

Valentin, Bernard, 156
Valéry, Paul, 68
Vali, Justin, xiii, 86
valiha, 86, 87, 126
Varigault de Valenfort, Daniel, 156
Vaxelaire, Daniel, 129-30, 164, 172, 173
Vell, June, 156
Vergès, Françoise, 58
Vergès, Paul, 135
Vergès, Raymond, 10, 36, 132
Verlaine, Paul, 68, 74
Vichy régime, 4, 10, 125, 131, 147
Vietnam, 10
Virahsawmy, Dev, xiii, 14, 95, 108-9, 170, 174
Viry, Firmin, 33, 135
visual arts, xiii
Volcy, Jean-Marc, 157
Vollard, Ambroise, 131, 133
Vollard, Théâtre, xiii, 84, 131-33, 134, 166, 173
VVS, 67

Waro, Danyel, 125, 135-36, 169, 174
wildlife, 1, 28
world literature, 55
world music, xii, xiii, 135, 152, 157-58

xenophobia, 19, 21, 22, 42

Young, Robert, 49, 171
Young, Rodolphine, 154
Youssou N'Dour, 86

Zafy, Albert, 71
Zanzibar, 27, 148
Ziskakan, 125, 127, 136-37, 163

About the Author

Peter Hawkins is senior lecturer in French at the University of Bristol, UK. He has taught courses on postcolonial literatures in French for many years and held temporary visiting posts at the University of Benin, Nigeria, from 1977-1979 and at the Université de la Réunion from 1994-1997. He was the first president of ASCALF (Association for the Study of Caribbean and African Literature in French), founded in 1989, and organised many internationally-supported annual conferences in this context at the French Institute in London between 1988-1993 and 1997-2000. He published the papers of the first pioneering conference of 1998 as *Protée noir* in 1992, with L'Harmattan, in collaboration with Annette Lavers, and has since published widely on Francophone literatures from Sub-Saharan Africa, the Caribbean and the Indian Ocean. ASCALF was relaunched as SFPS, the Society for Francophone Postcolonial Studies, in 2002. He has collaborated extensively with colleagues at the Universities of Mauritius and Reunion and has recently concentrated his attention on the Francophone literatures of the Indian Ocean region: an international conference was organised in July 2006 in Bristol, in collaboration with SFPS and AIEFCOI (Association Internationale des Etudes Francophones et Comparées sur l'Océan Indien), based at the University of Mauritius. He has also taught courses and published on French popular *chanson* and French cinema. He received the French academic award of *Chevalier des palmes académiques* in 1998.